UI Animations with Lottie and After Effects

Create, render, and ship stunning animations natively on mobile with React Native

Mireia Alegre Ruiz

Emilio Rodriguez Martinez

Packt

BIRMINGHAM—MUMBAI

UI Animations with Lottie and After Effects

Group Product Manager: Rohit Rajkumar

Publishing Product Manager: Vaideeshwari Muralikrishnan

Senior Editor: Keagan Carneiro

Content Development Editor: Abhishek Jadhav

Technical Editor: Shubham Sharma

Copy Editor: Safis Editing

Project Coordinator: Rashika Ba

Proofreader: Safis Editing

Indexer: Pratik Shirodkar

Production Designer: Alishon Mendonca

Marketing Coordinator: Teny Thomas and Elizabeth Varghese

First published: June 2022

Production reference: 1310522

Published by Packt Publishing Ltd.

Livery Place

35 Livery Street

Birmingham

B3 2PB, UK.

ISBN 978-1-80324-380-1

www.packt.com

To Max, my family, my partner and my wonderful friends – you all know who you are.

Oh well, and to Grammarly too, without its suggestions this book couldn't have been possible.

– Mireia

To Eugenia and my family who supported me through thick and thin.

– Emilio

Contributors

About the authors

Mireia Alegre Ruiz as a head of UX/UI and is proficient as a UX product designer and Illustration - Visual designer with motion graphics and video editing skills. Mireia has more than 20 years of professional experience sketching, illustrating, and creating micro animations from scratch since the old Macromedia Flash days. With a graphic design background, she made a move and specialized in digital design back in the early 2000s. Over the past few years, she has worked as a product designer for both international advertising agencies and Barcelona-based start-ups as a product designer. Always with the user in the center of the picture, and based on design thinking and Agile methodologies, her principles are very clear: make people's lives easier through the fair use of technology.

Emilio Rodriguez Martinez is a senior software engineer who has been working on highly demanding JavaScript projects since 2010. He transitioned from web development positions into mobile development, and has released dozens of successful apps for iOS and Android. Emilio has helped the React Native community through contributions to React Native's core codebase but also by maintaining the lottie-react-native library which is one of the most popular libraries in the React Native ecosystem.

About the reviewers

Joseph Khan is an engineering manager working with Seera Group based out of Dubai, UAE. He leads the development efforts for their Lumi brand, which is a car rental application. He is an AWS certified engineer and is also a former Packt author. He is enthusiastic about web standards, JavaScript, JAMStack, and architecting cloud applications

He has a B.Tech in Computer Science from NIT Silchar, India. Besides his regular work, he likes to design cars and motorbikes, spend time with his family, and play cricket.

Igor Mandrigin is an experienced software architect and engineering leader who has launched products from zero-in startups and big internet corporations. His core experience is in mobile, distributed systems, and product security, and has other experience in blockchain and smart contracts, DevOps and high availability, and technical product management.

Marina Oorthuis is a skilled product designer based in Barcelona. She has been working in the ed-tech market for many years and loves creating experiences that facilitate the user's learning in an intuitive and meaningful way. She is an advocate of the use of animations to achieve such goals.

Table of Contents

3

Learning the Tools: Getting Familiar With After Effects

Part 2 - Cracking Lottie Animations

4

Move It! Animating Our First Lottie With After Effects

5

Share It With the World: Working With LottieFiles

6

Don't Stop! Exploring Plugins and Resources That Will Keep You Going

Part 3 - Adding Your Lottie Animations Into Mobile Apps

7

An Introduction to lottie-react-native

8

Installing lottie-react-native

9
Let's Do Some Magic: Integrating Your First Lottie Animation

10
How To Nail It: Controlling Your Animation

11
Any Questions? lottie-react-native FAQs

Preface

Lottie is a small and scalable JSON-based animation file. LottieFiles is the platform where Lottie animations can be uploaded, tested, and shared. By combining the LottieFiles plugin and the LottieFiles platform, you'll be able to create stunning animations that are easy to integrate with any device. You'll also see how to use the Bodymovin plugin in Adobe **After Effects** (**AE**) to export your animation to a JSON file.

The book starts by giving you an overview of Lottie and LottieFiles. As you keep reading, you'll understand the entire Lottie ecosystem and get hands-on with classic 2D animation principles. You'll also get a step-by-step guided tour to ideate, sketch for storytelling, design an icon that will fulfill the needs and expectations of users based on UX, and finally, animate it in AE. This will help you get familiar with the AE environment, work with vector shape layers, create and modify keyframes using layer properties, explore path, Parent & Link features, and adjust timing easily to create professional-looking animations.

By the end of this animation book, you'll be able to create and export your own Lottie animations using AE and implement them in mobile apps using React Native. You'll also have an understanding of 2D animation best practices and principles that you can apply to your own projects.

Who this book is for

This book is for developers and engineers who are already familiar with React Native, as well as UX and UI designers who want to create their own animations and integrate them with their platforms through React Native. Basic knowledge of JavaScript programming is assumed. Beginner-level illustration skills are also preferred, though not necessary.

What this book covers

Chapter 1, Get Started With Lottie, explores the world of Lottie and LottieFiles and why it is so valuable for both designers and developers. Learn what Lottie is, who created it, and how LottieFiles works. You will also discover the tools you need to make Lottie animations.

Chapter 2, Creating the Illusion: Get Rolling With the Basic Principles of 2D Classic Animation, begins with a brief overview of animation's history before focusing on the 12 principles of classic 2D animation that will help us create more realistic animations. As you become more familiar with Storytelling, Ease, and Timing, you will feel more confident about the animation ecosystem.

Chapter 3, Learning the Tools: Getting Familiar With After Effects, teaches you the basics of animation with After Effects. Terms such as composition, timeline, and keyframes will start to sound familiar and will give you the foundation to get started.

Chapter 4, Move It! Animating Our First Lottie With After Effects, is an easy to follow, step-by-step guide for creating your very first animation. By using a real-world example, you will learn to set up a composition, import files, animate, tweak and learn basic tricks and animation techniques for special effects.

Chapter 5, Share It With the World: Working With LottieFiles, is a walkthrough on how to export animations to JSON Lottie files for developers to work with. It also describes how to use the LottieFiles platform in its entirety and have some fun creating animated stickers and icon sets for Telegram.

Chapter 6, Don't Stop! Exploring Plugins and Resources That Will Keep You Going, is the chapter to find all the resources that will keep you moving forward. A detailed table of Adobe After Effects best practices and dos and don'ts for exporting animations without trouble is included. This chapter will also provide step-by-step instructions for installing all the plugins and tools for creating animations.

Chapter 7, An Introduction to lottie-react-native, provides a brief explanation of what lottie-react-native is, which platforms are supported and how to navigate through the different parts of the project such as the code repository, the npm repository and its documentation.

Chapter 8, Installing lottie-react-native, provides the first step to get our animation up and running in our mobile app. We will go through the required steps to have lottie-react-native properly installed in both iOS and Android apps. It covers common pitfalls, platform and alternatives, and everything needed to get our apps ready for our first Lottie Animation to be rendered.

Chapter 9, Let's Do Some Magic: Integrating Your First Lottie Animation, explains how to integrate a Lottie file in our app and render them through lottie-react-native. By the end of this chapter, we will have a functional animation running in both iOS and Android apps.

Chapter 10, How To Nail It: Controlling Your Animation, teaches you how to play Lottie animations forward, backward, pause it, accelerate it or decelerate it. In this chapter we will learn how to perform all these actions and many others which will give us full control on how the animation is used inside our React Native app.

Chapter 11, Any Questions? lottie-react-native FAQs, is a compilation of the most frequently asked questions when working with the lottie-react-native library. This list provides concrete answers from the library maintainer to the most common issues and challenges when using the library. The list is order by popularity and should serve as a quick reference guide not only for new developers but also for experienced engineers who got stuck in complex problems using this library.

To get the most out of this book

Software/hardware covered in the book	Operating system requirements
React 17.0.2+	Windows, macOS, or Linux
React Native 0.66.4+	
lottie-react-native 4.0.0+	

If you are using the digital version of this book, we advise you to type the code yourself or access the code from the book's GitHub repository (a link is available in the next section). Doing so will help you avoid any potential errors related to the copying and pasting of code.

Download the example code files

You can download the example code files for this book from GitHub at `https://github.com/PacktPublishing/UI-Animations-with-Lottie-and-After-Effects`. If there's an update to the code, it will be updated in the GitHub repository.

We also have other code bundles from our rich catalog of books and videos available at `https://github.com/PacktPublishing/`. Check them out!

Download the color images

We also provide a PDF file that has color images of the screenshots and diagrams used in this book. You can download it here: `https://static.packt-cdn.com/downloads/9781803243801_ColorImages.pdf`.

Conventions used

There are a number of text conventions used throughout this book.

`Code in text`: Indicates code words in text, database table names, folder names, filenames, file extensions, pathnames, dummy URLs, user input, and Twitter handles. Here is an example: "We will do so by going into the `ios` folder inside our React Native project."

A block of code is set as follows:

```
"peerDependencies": {
    "lottie-ios": "^3.2.3",
    "react": "*",
    "react-native": "|=0.46"
  },
  "dependencies": {
    "invariant": "^2.2.2",
    "prop-types": "^15.5.10",
    "react-native-safe-modules": "^1.0.3"
  }
```

When we wish to draw your attention to a particular part of a code block, the relevant lines or items are set in bold:

```
include ':lottie-react-native'

project(':lottie-react-native').projectDir = new
File(rootProject.projectDir, '../node_modules/lottie-react-
native/src/android')
```

Any command-line input or output is written as follows:

```
npm i --save lottie-react-native
```

Bold: Indicates a new term, an important word, or words that you see onscreen. For instance, words in menus or dialog boxes appear in **bold**. Here is an example: "Let's open up AE and click on the **Create a New Project** button."

> **Tips or Important Notes**
> Appear like this.

Get in touch

Feedback from our readers is always welcome.

General feedback: If you have questions about any aspect of this book, email us at `customercare@packtpub.com` and mention the book title in the subject of your message.

Errata: Although we have taken every care to ensure the accuracy of our content, mistakes do happen. If you have found a mistake in this book, we would be grateful if you would report this to us. Please visit `www.packtpub.com/support/errata` and fill in the form.

Piracy: If you come across any illegal copies of our works in any form on the internet, we would be grateful if you would provide us with the location address or website name. Please contact us at `copyright@packt.com` with a link to the material.

If you are interested in becoming an author: If there is a topic that you have expertise in and you are interested in either writing or contributing to a book, please visit `authors.packtpub.com`.

Share Your Thoughts

Once you've read *UI Animations with Lottie and After Effects*, we'd love to hear your thoughts! Scan the QR code below to go straight to the Amazon review page for this book and share your feedback.

`https://www.amazon.ae/review/create-review/error?asin=1803243805`

Your review is important to us and the tech community and will help us make sure we're delivering excellent quality content.

Part 1- Building a Foundation With After Effects and LottieFiles

In this first part, we will get familiar with After Effects and Lottie. We will learn about creating 2D animations from scratch.

We will cover the following chapters in this section:

- *Chapter 1, Get Started With Lottie*
- *Chapter 2, Creating the Illusion: Get Rolling With the Basic Principles of 2D Classic Animation*
- *Chapter 3, Learning the Tools: Getting Familiar With After Effects*

1
Get Started With Lottie

Nowadays, vector animation is used in almost every single mobile app and website. It enriches a good UX design, helps designers guide users through interactions, and brings any screen to life.

However, adding animations to our web, iOS, Android, or React Native applications wasn't always as easy as you would think. Back then, implementing animations used to be very time-consuming and would greatly increase the size of files. But then one day, Lottie was finally released, and light and color came into the world of animations, especially for mobile apps and websites.

In this chapter, we will show you how to use this book so that you can make the most of it. Also, you will learn what Lottie is, why it was created, and the great value that it provides to both designers and developers.

You will be introduced to the LottieFiles platform, what it is used for, and the difference between Lottie animations and LottieFiles.

Additionally, you will get to know the tools you are going to need to create Lottie animations and where to get them from.

By the end of this chapter, you will have complete knowledge of what a Lottie animation is and how it makes life easier for designers and developers. Also, you will gain an understanding of what the LottieFiles platform is used for and where to get all the essential tools so that you can be ready to start thinking about your first animation.

In this chapter, we are going to cover the following main topics:

- How to use this book
- Introduction to Lottie
- What are LottieFiles?
- Understanding the tools to create Lottie animations

Technical requirements

As mentioned earlier, in this chapter, we are going to talk about the essential tools we will need during the process of creating a Lottie animation. Most of these tools are free for you to use. Note that Adobe After Effects is not available for free; however, you can download a 7-day free trial version.

Additionally, you will require a browser of your choice, for example, Chrome or Safari.

How to use this book

In this section, we will guide you through the main aspects of this book and why we thought this would be the best way for you to learn how to create animations with Lottie. We don't want this book to be just another After Effects manual that teaches you how to animate an icon (of course, we will cover that too), but we think it is just as important to have the basics and be able to sketch your own ideas and bring them to life before opening any kind of software. You can jump straight to the chapter that matches your interests best, but we highly recommend going through the book from start to finish.

We want you to be conscious that creating an animation does not simply involve adding some movement to a drawing by using some computer tools. It is the whole process that creates the magic, from ideation, the first sketches, to creating the illusion of movement through different animation techniques such as ease, tempo, and timeline keyframes. At some point, you might have thought why is this book talking about all this old-school stuff such as classic 2D animation?

Well, we could just have covered the process of downloading an animation, importing it into After Effects, and converting it into Lottie so that you could implement it in your app using React Native in a very short period of time... Yes, that would have been the easiest and shortest part (and we will do that too, don't worry).

However, we want to give you some more background, tips, and techniques about animation, so when you finish reading this book, you will be able to think big and create your own unique animations from scratch. Whatever it is you want to animate, we will teach you the basics and give you enough resources and tools so that you can keep on learning in your own time and at your own pace.

That's why we decided to split the book into three main parts:

- *Part 1, Building a Foundation With After Effects and LottieFiles*
- *Part 2, Cracking Lottie Animations*
- *Part 3, Adding Your Lottie Animations Into Mobile Apps*

In the first part of this book, you are going to learn about the basics. As a first approach, we will go through Lottie; you will become familiar with the **Lottie** and **LottieFiles** keywords. While you keep reading, we will go into more depth about the entire Lottie ecosystem and will take a quick look at classic animation history.

We will get hands-on with the principles of classic 2D animation to understand the importance of ease and keyframes, two popular techniques that will help us to create the illusion of movement. We will go through the Adobe After Effects environment, getting to know the most relevant features so that, by the end of *Part 1, Building a Foundation With After Effects and LottieFiles*, we will be all set to start our first animation.

Once we have understood the basics of Lottie, 2D animations, and the Adobe After Effects environment, we will start creating our animated icon. In the second part of this book, we will guide you through a step-by-step tour of a real project to create our first unique animation. We are going to put into practice everything we have learned in the first three chapters. How? Well, we will start with a simple project in which we will be animating our first icon.

By sketching and drawing it, we will create a storyboard that will help us to understand what we want our icon to do. Once that's done, we are going to import this icon into Adobe After Effects and bring it to life by applying some of the 2D animation techniques learned earlier in the book. By the end of *Part 2, Cracking Lottie Animations*, we will know the best way to export our animations and get them ready to hand off to developers.

So, think about that; whether you are a designer or a developer, once you have finished the first two parts of this book, you will be able to ideate, sketch, illustrate, animate, and export your own unique ideas.

Let's keep moving. So, we will have finished our first animation and exported it. Everything is ready to go. We can't wait to see it implemented in our app or website. So, what next?

Now is where the third part of the book comes into play, and here is why it is so important. Let's imagine that you have spent a couple of days designing and creating your animation (yes, well done; animations are not quick things to do, at least, not the first time). You try to upload it into your app or the website of the app, but something goes wrong? Perhaps it doesn't look how it should or the animation in the app doesn't look the same as the one on the website. Maybe it is too heavy. Is it blurry? Is it responsive?

There are so many things that can ruin your fantastic animation, but let's not panic. Here's where *Part 3, Adding Your Lottie Animations Into Mobile Apps*, comes in handy. That is where you will learn everything you need to know about how to test and implement your fabulous, stunning, and well-created Lottie animation onto any platform, simply and easily. Thanks to Lottie and React Native, your animation won't look pixelated, be too heavy, or do any other weird stuff.

Once you have mastered the process of creating your own animations and uploading them onto your platforms using React Native, none of these issues will happen again, and your fantastic and unique animation will shine on the screen, just as it was meant to be.

So, now that you understand why this book has been divided into three different parts and why all of them are important, let's move on to discover what Lottie is.

Introduction to Lottie

Now that we know each other a bit better, let's see what all this Lottie fuss is about. Let's start from the beginning and talk about a bit of history.

Why is it called Lottie?

The name **Lottie** was chosen as a tribute to *Charlotte "Lotte" Reiniger*, a German film director from the 20th century who became the foremost pioneer of silhouette animation. This is a technique based on cut-out figures that are moved frame by frame and filmed with a camera.

The man behind the scenes

After Apple decided Macromedia Flash wasn't going near any iPod or iPhone, adding animations to our applications and websites became a nightmare. Animations had to be exported in low-quality formats; otherwise, developers had to recreate the code themselves. You can imagine how many of these ended up: the file sizes were too big, visualization was really poor, the process was painful, and the results were frustrating.

But then, in 2015, *Hernan Torrisi*, who had been working as an Action Script developer, came up with an idea. He started building a player and an exporter for After Effects, and this is where the **Bodymovin** plugin came to life. To be clear, the Bodymovin plugin transforms the animation into a JSON file, but we will talk about that later.

Torrisi also developed a browser-based renderer that takes the Bodymovin plugin's JSON files and plays back the animation.

Then, when Airbnb engineers *Brandon Withrow* (on iOS), *Gabriel Peal* (on Android), and *Leland Richardson* (on React Native) realized the power of these JSON-based animations, they decided to partner with animator and experienced designer *Salih Abdul-Karim* to help develop Android, iOS, and React Native renderers for the Bodymovin plugin's JSON.

Meanwhile, the LottieFiles platform was also launched, and a great community of animators, designers, and developers was born. Here, they could preview, test, and share their own animations.

In 2020, **dotLottie** was created as a way to standardize the format.

In early 2021, the same team came up with the **LottieFiles plugin**, which works just as well as Bodymovin. Both export animations in `.JSON` format; however, the LottieFiles plugin adds some extra features, which we will cover in more depth soon.

What is Lottie?

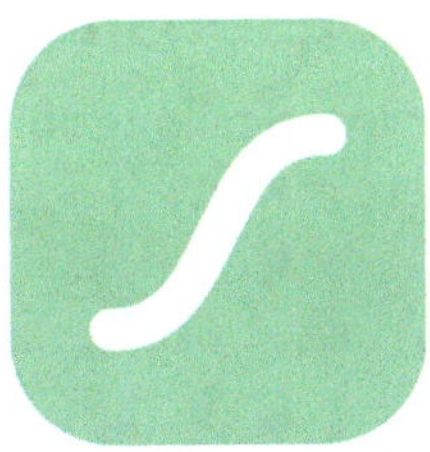

Figure 1.1 – The Lottie icon

It took me a while to understand what Lottie is exactly. There are lots of conversations going on out there about *Lottie, LottieFiles, Lottie file, Lottie animations, dotLottie*, and the *LottieFiles plugin* that can, sometimes, get a bit confusing.

Essentially, Lottie is a library for iOS, Android, and React Native that will convert the animations that we will be creating in Adobe After Effects into lines of code. It does this very easily and without the need to write any code at all; we do it by simply installing an open source plugin into After Effects and pressing a button to render our animations and then exporting them as JSON. It's like magic, right?

If you are a designer (or a developer who is willing to get creative), that means that you will be able to create your own fantastic animations using After Effects and export them in seconds, without needing a developer to code them.

If you are a developer, that means that you will no longer have to code the animations, saving you tons of time, and you will be able to implement the animations on any website or app effortlessly.

And the best of it? The animation will look as it should, the file size will be kept small, and the image will be scalable. So, it is a win-win for everyone.

Now, to clarify and summarize, initially, Lottie was used to name a library for iOS, Android, the web, and Windows. But today, it is commonly used to call the `.JSON` file that is exported from After Effects, which is also known as the animation file.

The following diagram depicts the advantages of LottieFiles:

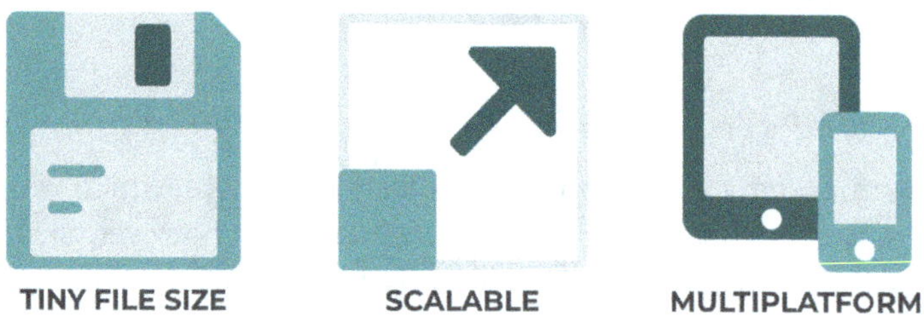

Figure 1.2 – Some of the key advantages of working with Lottie files

Do you still need more reasons to start using Lottie?

Yes, we are in love with Lottie and won't stop talking about how its appearance has made the lives of all our teams easier. And here is why.

It's very easy to use

Animating with Lottie is as easy as following a few simple steps:

1. Create your animation in **After Effects**.
2. Render and export the animation using the **LottieFiles** or **Bodymovin** plugins (we will talk about this in more depth later).

3. Test the animation in **LottieFiles Editor** to check everything is in the correct place.
4. Add the `.json` file to our web or app platform, and we are done:

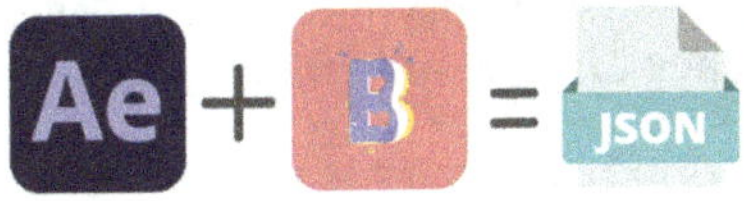

Figure 1.3 – After Effects, the Bodymovin tool's icon and the .JSON format file

It can be used everywhere

Lottie is multiplatform and open source. It can be used on any web or mobile platform. We can even create and run Lottie as stickers on messaging platforms such as **Telegram** or use them in desktop apps or watch apps:

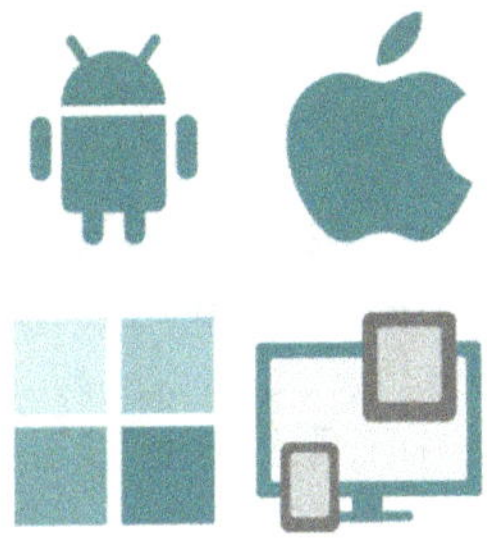

Figure 1.4 – Multiplatform

The file size won't be a problem anymore

Since Lottie is a vector-based animation, you can imagine that the file size will be very tiny. So, forget about old and heavy PNG or GIF files that can make our products look poor and low quality:

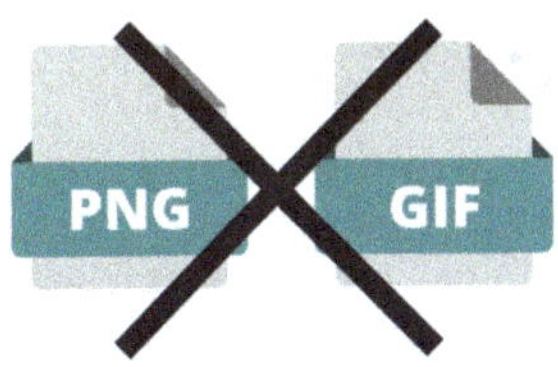

Figure 1.5 – The PNG and GIF image file formats

Interactive and dynamic

Lottie is not only made up of endless cool animated loops. It can also be used in so many ways to provide its users with some interaction. For example, we could sync our animations to the scroll of the page and see how it goes back and forth while scrolling.

Additionally, we could create a loop from one specific frame, play segments on hover, or sync the cursor position with our animation. Imagine some cute panda eyes following the user's cursor; how cool is that?

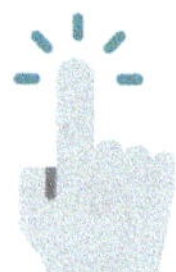

Figure 1.6 – Interactive features

Scalable

Another advantage of a vector animation file is that it can be scaled as much as you wish without becoming a pixelated image. Additionally, it is responsive, will scale up or down, and will adapt to our designs as needed. So, don't worry about pixelated images in your web or mobile applications. From now on, they will look stunning and take your UX to the next level:

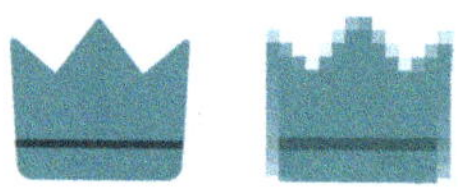

Figure 1.7 – A vector versus a rasterized image visualization

So, now that we've cleared up what Lottie is, let's move on to LottieFiles and its features.

What is LottieFiles?

LottieFiles was founded in 2018 by *Nattu Adnan* and *Shafiu Hussain*, who are based in San Francisco and Kuala Lumpur.

It first started as a community for designers and developers, but it grew very quickly and has evolved into a platform that offers tools and resources related to animation, where designers, developers, and engineers can edit, test, and display animations:

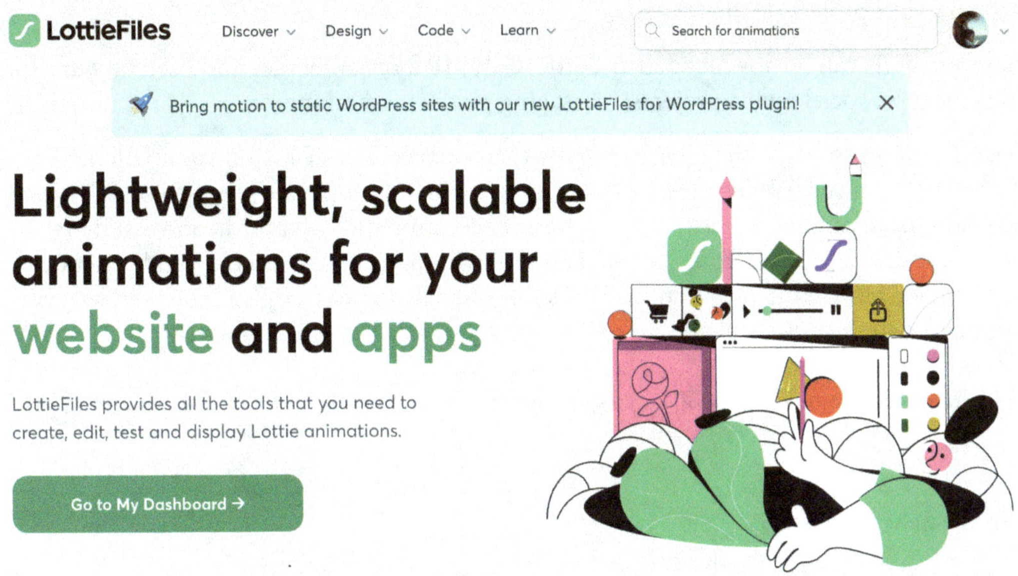

Figure 1.8 – The LottieFiles platform

The LottieFiles.com platform has made it so easy to test animations without the need to first implement them into the apps and websites. It has become so popular that it is already being used by many companies around the world such as Amazon, Disney, Google, Microsoft, Uber, Nike, and Spotify, to name a few. However, this is just one of the reasons to use it. Let's see what else we can do with LottieFiles.com.

What can I do with LottieFiles?

As mentioned earlier, LottieFiles has become very popular among designers and developers, and we could say the platform has changed the way animation is done. Thanks to LottieFiles, we can now test animations before they are implemented, edit them directly inside the platform, and much more.

Let's see, in more depth, the sort of stuff we can do on the LottieFiles platform.

The animation library

We can search from thousands of free animations made by the LottieFiles community. These animations can be used for our personal or commercial work and can be edited and adapted to our project or client needs.

The animations can be downloaded as Lottie, GIF, MP4, or JSON files and used on our websites, apps, social media projects, messaging platforms, and more.

This can save us so much time. Let's imagine that we need a basic loading animation to add between screens. We just need a spinning circle in our corporate green color. We have two options: we can either create a new After Effects animation, export it, and test it, or we can just download one from the free LottieFiles library, change its color, and generate the new code by clicking on a button. This sounds quick and easy, right? However, let's not worry about this yet. We will go into more depth about this in future chapters:

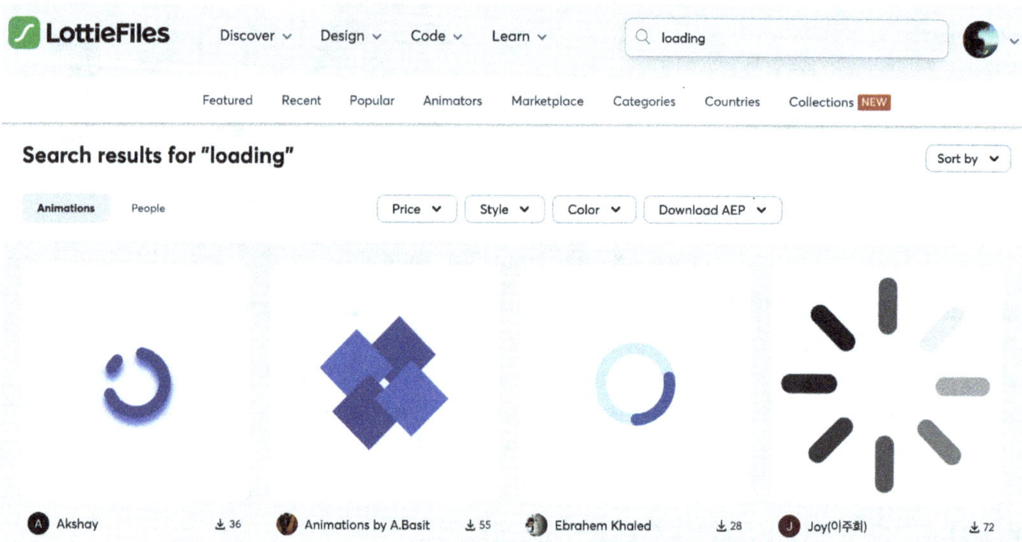

Figure 1.9 – Web view of the LottieFiles animation library

Hiring animators

LottieFiles has the largest community of brilliant designers that use Lottie. If you need a tailor-made animation and don't have the time or the skills (yet) to do it yourself, `https://lottiefiles.com/` is where you can search for lots of creative minds who can help you bring your projects to life:

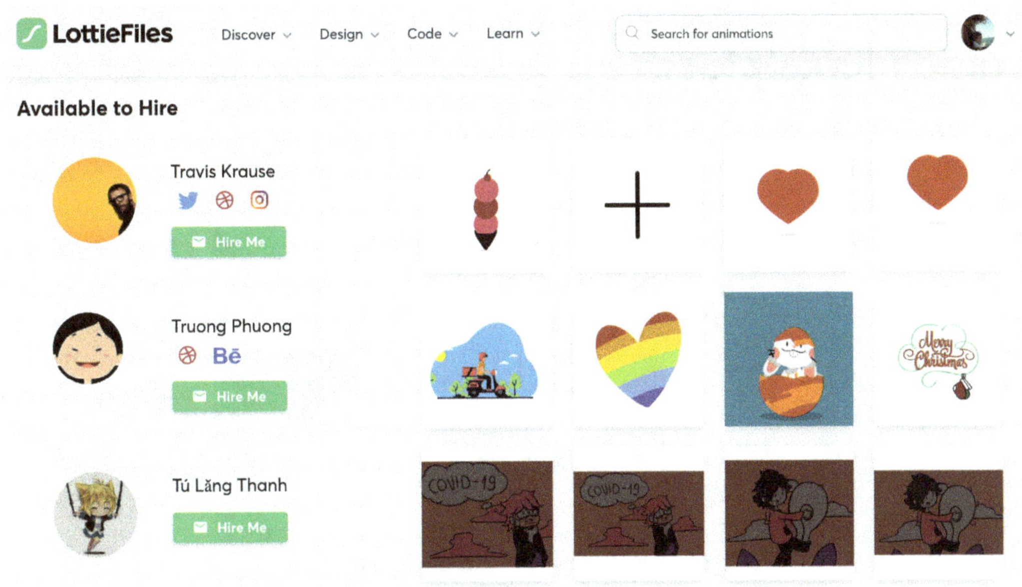

Figure 1.10 – Web view of the LottieFiles animator community

Marketplace

Launched during the COVID-19 lockdown, **LottieFiles Marketplace** offers many premium animations, both individual and in packs, made by the best motion designers in the world:

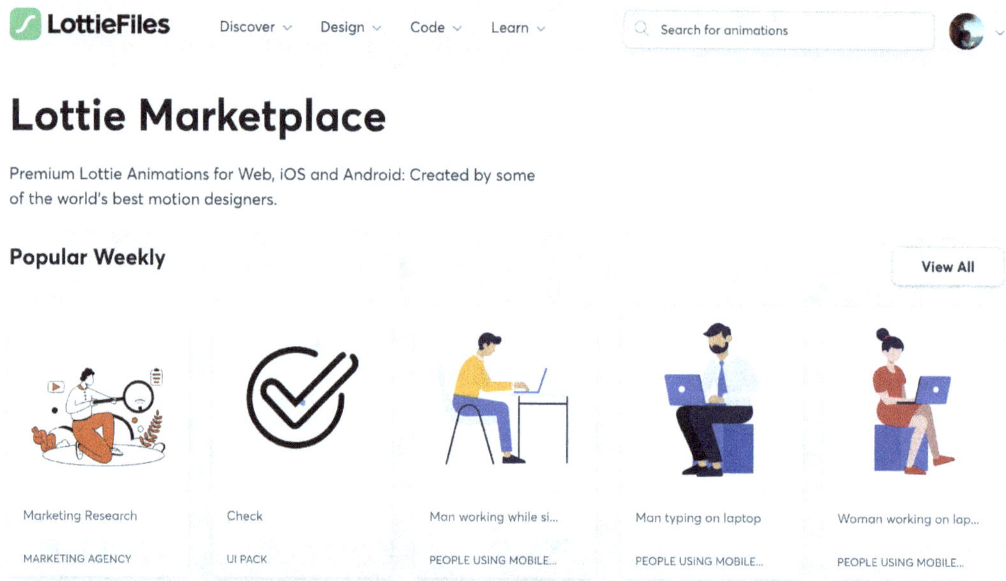

Figure 1.11 – Web view of LottieFiles Marketplace

LottieFiles preview

Within the LottieFiles platform, you can preview, test, and share your own Lottie animations before uploading them into your projects, simply by using drag and drop. Also, you can do this through the same website and in the iOS, Android, or desktop apps:

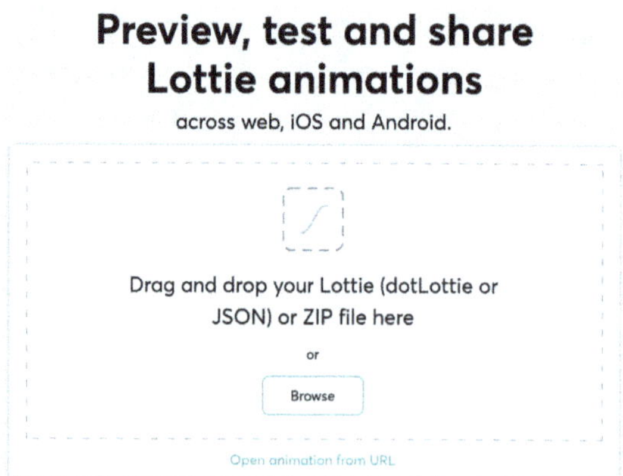

Figure 1.12 – The LottieFiles preview feature on a web browser

LottieFiles Editor

In my opinion, the editor is one of the most powerful tools that LottieFiles provides. This is where you can upload any Lottie animation (your own or the ones you've just found in the library), and tweak it very easily. You can adjust the dimensions, frame rate, duration, speed, and colors on the go. Additionally, you can export it as a Lottie `.json` file or share it back into the LottieFiles library:

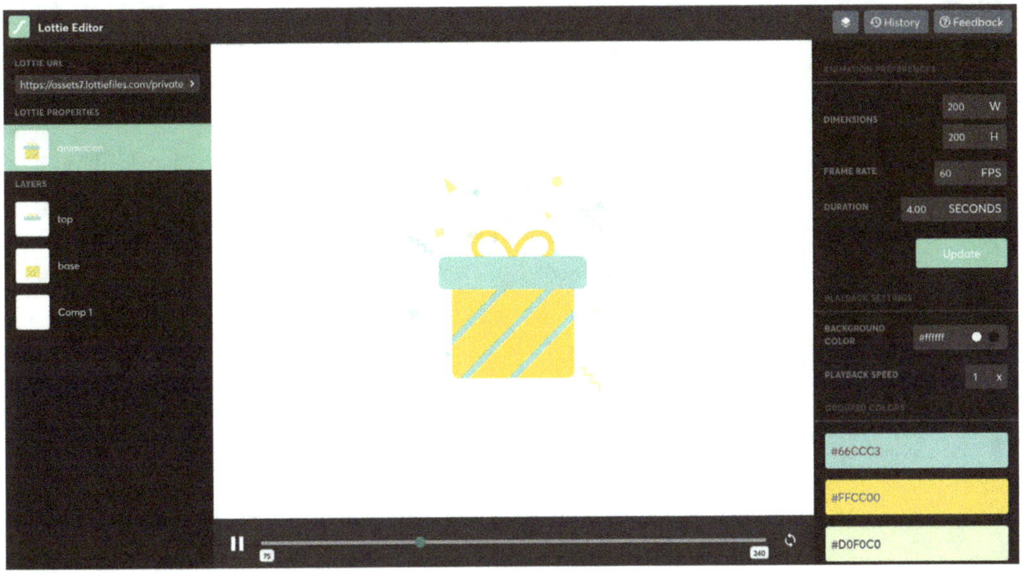

Figure 1.13 – The LottieFiles Editor feature on a web browser

From Lottie to Telegram stickers

Thanks to LottieFiles, creating stickers for Telegram is as simple as creating an animation, exporting it using the Bodymovin or LottieFiles plugin for After Effects, and having a conversation with Telegram's Sticker Bot. However, let's not worry about that yet. We will go into more depth in future chapters:

Figure 1.14 – The Telegram icon

Converting SVG into Lottie

If you want to skip Adobe After Effects to create your animations, now you can. The LottieFiles platform gives you the option to create great animations without the need to animate (I know, it sounds a bit confusing). But by just uploading an SVG file, along with the tool to convert SVG into Lottie, you can create fantastic animations within seconds:

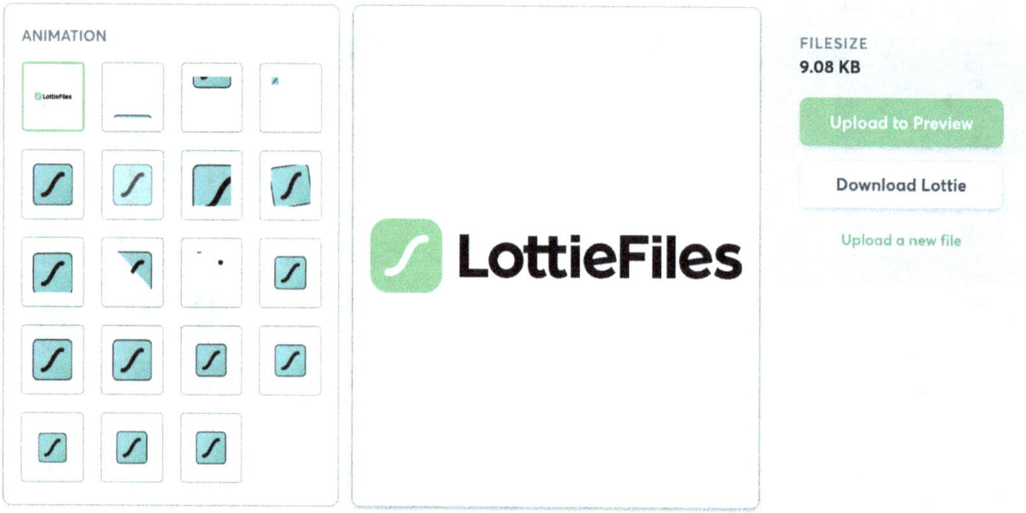

Figure 1.15 – The LottieFiles "Converting SVG into Lottie" feature on a web browser

Converting Lottie into GIF

With LottieFiles, you can also convert your Lottie aminations into GIF files very quickly, by uploading the JSON file onto the platform and managing a couple of settings. Now your animated GIF is ready to use:

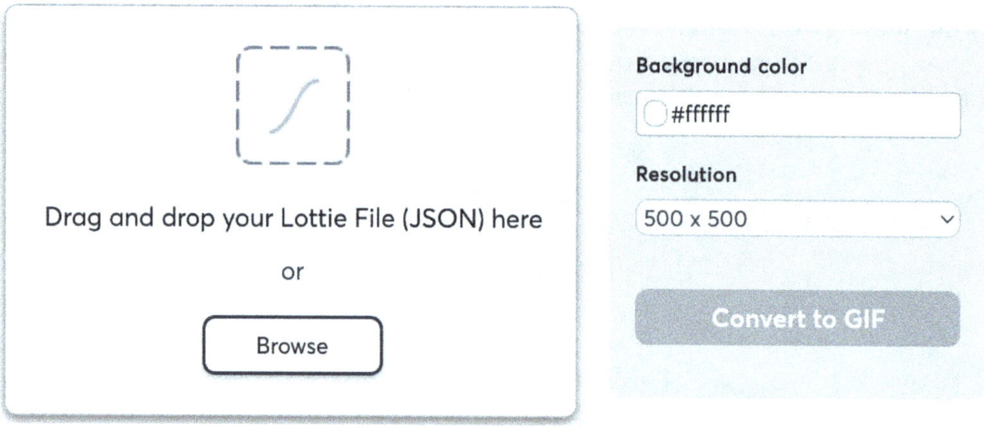

Figure 1.16 – The LottieFiles "Converting Lottie into GIF" feature on a web browser

Lottie JSON Editor

If you are a developer and don't want to go through all the After Effects parts and jump straight into code instead, with the JSON editor, you can update your animation from the inside out. Change a few parameters and check the results in real time:

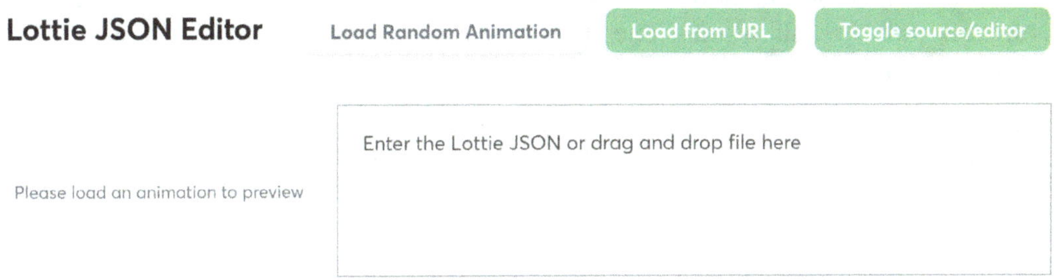

Figure 1.17 – The LottieFiles .JSON file editor feature on a web browser

Lottie Learn

The LottieFiles website also offers many resources for you to get started with Lottie. I recommend that you navigate through its video courses, blogs, FAQ pages, and forums to get more insights about what Lottie is and what you can do with it:

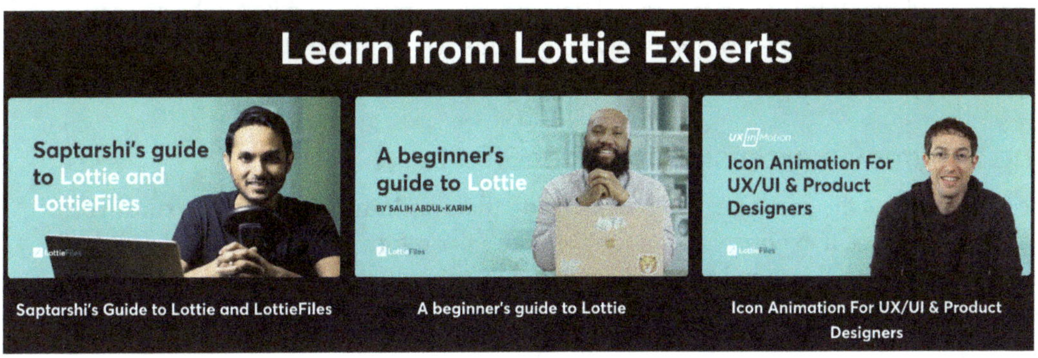

Figure 1.18 – Web view of the Lottie Learn resources for designers and developers

> **What is the Difference between Lottie and LottieFiles?**
>
> Just to be clear, Lottie is used to call the animated JSON file, while LottieFiles is the platform to upload, test, and share your Lottie animation.

So, now that we've learned what a Lottie file is and what the LottieFiles platform is used for, let's see what tools we are going to need to start creating our animations.

Tools to create Lottie animations and integrations

In this section, we'll learn about the tools and plugins we need to install before we start creating our own Lottie animations. Don't worry if you haven't heard of them before. In this section, we'll cover all the main ones such as Adobe After Effects, Adobe Animate, and the LottieFiles platform.

If you need more information about how to install these tools, plugins, and extensions, please move on to *Chapter 6, Don't Stop! Exploring Plugins and Resources That Will Keep You Going*, for a *how-to install* guide.

Adobe After Effects

Adobe After Effects is known as the industry-standard motion graphics and visual effects software. It's used to create movie titles, intros, transitions, visual effects for movies and videos, and animations.

So, if we want to create our own animations, we need to install Adobe After Effects. There's no other way, or at least there wasn't until recently (keep reading). Anyhow, bear in mind that this is not a free tool. However, before purchasing it, Adobe gives you the option to install the 7-day free trial version. This can be found at `https://www.adobe.com/products/aftereffects.html`.

The Bodymovin extension for After Effects

Bodymovin was the first After Effects extension that was initially created to export your Lottie animations. It exports your animation into `.json` format, which can later be tweaked on the go. You can download your Bodymovin plugin at `https://exchange.adobe.com/creativecloud.details.12557.bodymovin.html`:

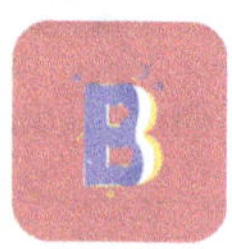

Figure 1.19 – The Bodymovin icon

The LottieFiles extension for After Effects

We've been talking a lot about the Bodymovin extension. But recently, Lottie has also released the LottieFiles plugin for After Effects, which exports your animation as a `.Lottie` file. The difference between Bodymovin and LottieFiles is the newly added features in the LottieFiles plugin. We will go into more depth on this once we talk about how to export your animations in both the Bodymovin and LottieFiles plugins.

Download the LottieFiles for After Effects extension at `https://lottiefiles.com/plugins/after-effects`:

Figure 1.20 – The Adobe After Effects icon

The Lottie extension for Adobe Animate

If you are not that familiar with After Effects and would like to try some other tools to create your animations, now you can! It seems that people at Lottie just released an early Beta version of the Lottie plugin for Adobe Animate.

We could say Adobe Animate is the evolution of what once was known as Macromedia Flash, and it is used to bring vector graphics to life.

If you want to try it, you can download the Adobe Animate plugin from `https://lottiefiles.com/plugins/animate`. However, in this book, we are going to focus on Adobe After Effects:

Figure 1.21 – The Adobe Animate icon

The LottieFiles platform

We can download and install LottieFiles on our mobiles and desktops to preview, test, and share our Lottie animation files. Here are the relevant resources for Mac and Windows:

- **LottieFiles for Desktop**: `https://lottiefiles.com/desktop`
- **LottieFiles for Android**: `https://play.google.com/store/apps/details?id=com.lottiefiles.app&hl=en&gl=US`
- **LottieFiles for iOS**: `https://apps.apple.com/us/app/lottiefiles/id1231821260`

Figure 1.22 – The LottieFiles icon

That's all we need to create our own animations. However, Lottie gives us some more integrations with other tools and software such as Figma or Sketch. You can check them out at `https://lottiefiles.com/integrations`.

Summary

So, let's just recap. In this chapter, we learned how important animations are for any UX project. We also understood the meaning behind and the origins of Lottie. We discovered who *Hernan Torrisi* is and how Lottie is making the lives of designers and programmers easier. On the other hand, we now know the difference between Lottie and LottieFiles. Additionally, we've gone through the main features of the LottieFiles platform such as Editor, Viewer, Marketplace, and the library. They have all been set up with the main tools installed, so you are ready to start creating your own animations.

Now, we can move forward and start talking about animation. Let's move on to the next chapter and learn about the basics of 2D animation.

2

Creating the Illusion: Get Rolling With the Basic Principles of 2D Classic Animation

What exactly is animation? From animated basic GIFs to large motion graphics movies, we can find animations in almost every single online piece. But, why is animation so important? Because by adding animations and micro-animations to our websites and apps, it will help us to communicate with our users in so many ways. It will attract attention, increase user engagement, communicate feedback, help us lead the user and the user behavior, and enrich the **user experience** (UX).

In this chapter, we will focus on **2D classic animation** and its **12 principles**. We will first start by briefly reviewing the history and foundations of animation and the different techniques used to create an illusion.

Once we've seen that, we will learn the **12 principles of animation, which** will help us to make our animations look more realistic. We will also learn how to set everything up with just a pencil and paper, from illustrating our first concept to creating our own storybook, to make our animations understandable.

Then, we will learn the different aspects that we will implement later on apply in **After Effects** (**AE**), such as keyframes, movement, transforms, timing, and ease.

By the end of this chapter, you will be able to differentiate between the different techniques used to create 2D animations. You will also understand the 12 principles to make your animations look real and will also know about the main features that we are going to be using in AE.

In this chapter we are going to cover the following topics:

- History and foundations of 2D animation
- The 12 principles of 2D animation
- Frames, keyframes, and inbetweens to define the main important moments of our animation
- Moving our icon from point A to point B
- Using ease, timing, and the timeline to create more realistic animations
- Sketching our first icon – from concept to storyboarding

Technical requirements

To go through this chapter, you need the following:

- Pencil
- Paper

Illustration skills are *not* mandatory! If you don't know or don't want to draw your own icon, we will give you the files to download; however, we highly recommend you get a paper and a pencil and have some fun drawing 😊.

Introduction to 2D animation

So, what is animation? Animation is the faculty to bring to life something that doesn't have it. When we talk about **classic 2D animation**, we are referring to a series of still images, drawn separately and slightly tweaked from one another; when combined, they produce the illusion of movement.

From prehistoric times, we can find references to animation that are are almost as old as humans. If we go back to 35,000 years ago when humans used to live in caves, we find figures of drawn animals with several legs, which was their way of representing the idea of movement.

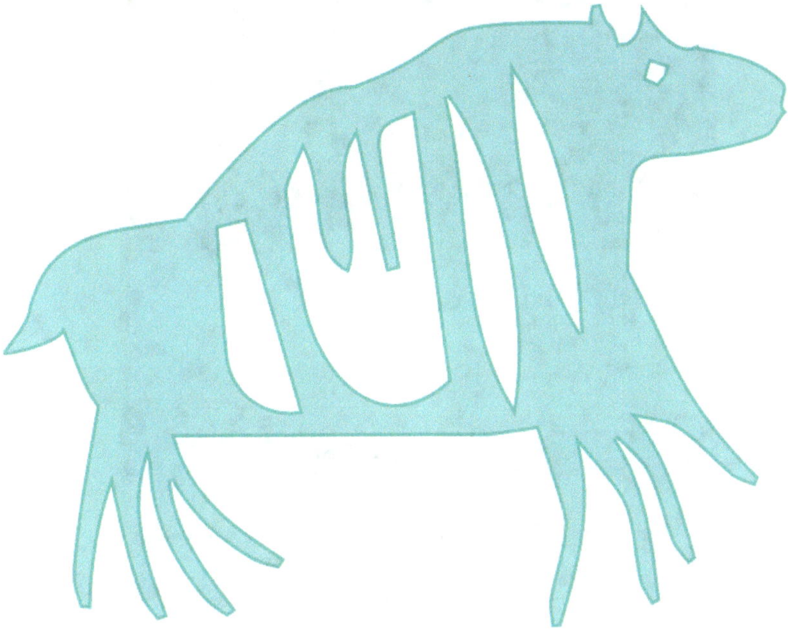

Figure 2.1 – Eight legs to show motion

Ancient Egyptians and Greeks used to draw separate images with little tweaked arms or legs to give the impression of moving figures as well. So, we can say animation has been used forever and in every culture.

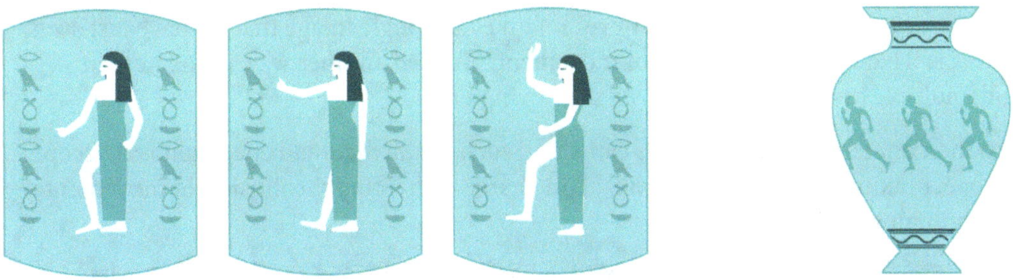

Figure 2.2 – Representation of the Ancient Egyptian goddess Isis in the columns of a temple, and Ancient Greek decorated pot with images of movement

Let's move a little bit closer in time. In 1640, *Athanasius Kircher* created the *magic lantern*, which was the first artifact that projected some *moving* images onto a wall. He did this by drawing different separate illustrations on a pane of glass and moving it at a fixed speed, giving the impression of a moving image:

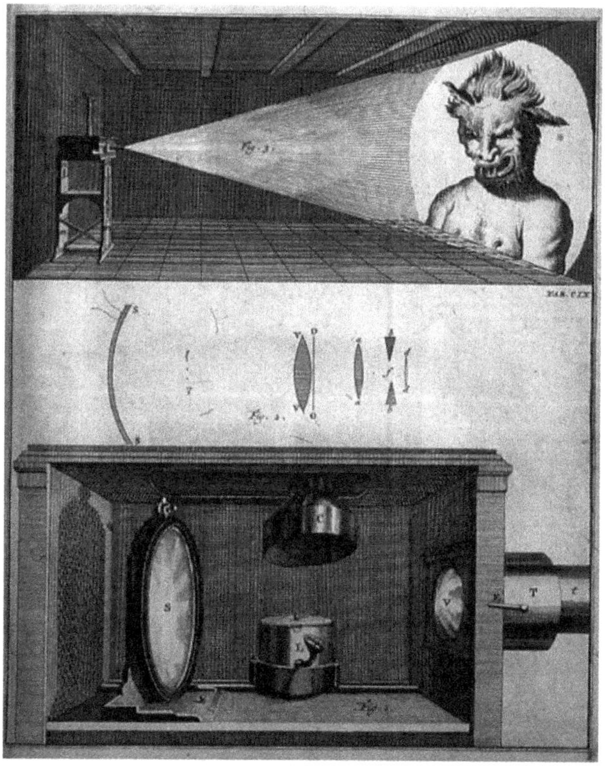

Figure 2.3 – Magic lantern by Athanasius Kircher

Besides all this, in 1824, *Peter Mark Roget* sort of discovered the **persistence of vision**, and we say *sort of* as this wasn't the first time that this topic was mentioned. Persistence of vision means that, for a while, our eyes retain every single image that we have just seen, and this is what allows the illusion of movement. Worded another way, in the human mind, multiple images blend into a single moving one.

From then on, other *optical artifacts* came out, such as the thaumatrope, phenakistoscope, zoetrope, praxinoscope, and flip book, all in charge of creating the illusion of movement to the human eye.

In 1906, *Thomas Edison* and the New York newspaper cartoonist *James Stuart Blackton* (who met back in 1896 when *James Stuart Blackton* interviewed *Thomas Edison*) released the first animated picture to the public, using stop-motion photography. It was called *Humorous Phases of Funny Faces*.

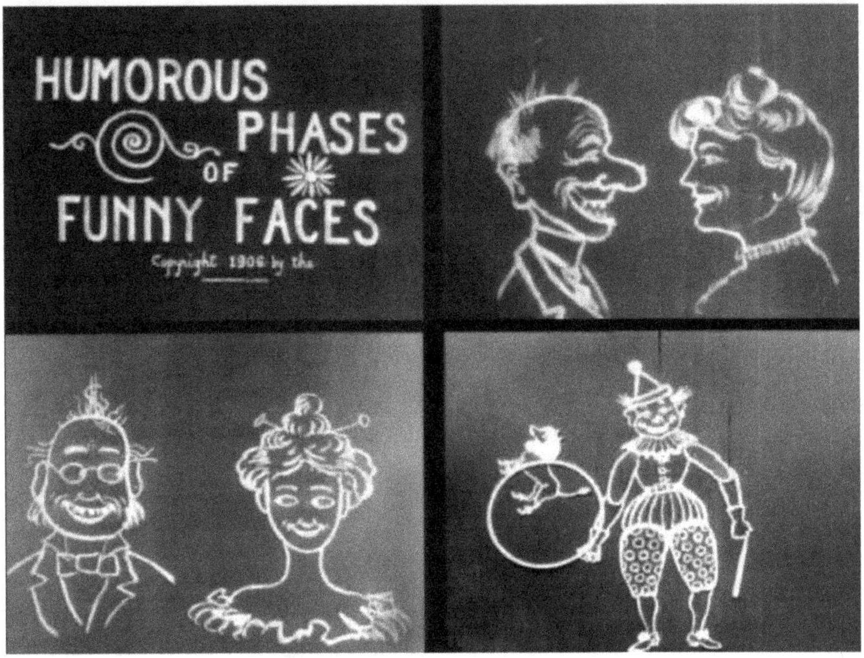

Figure 2.4 – Sequence of the first-ever animated movie, Humorous Phases of Funny Faces

But, the first hand-drawn animated film and the first considered animated cartoon film was *Fantasmagorie* by *Emile Cohl*, which premiered in Paris in 1908.

A few years went by, and in 1928, with the arrival of **Walt Disney**, *Mickey Mouse* made his first appearance in *Steamboat Willie*, the first-ever released cartoon with sound, which was created using cell animation. Every single frame was drawn onto celluloid and photographed with a multipaned camera. The background was placed in a different layer and Walt Disney managed to create a comical but realistic movement. It is also known to be the first cartoon with sync sound.

In 1937, Disney released the first-ever long animated film, *Snow White and the Seven Dwarfs*, which started the golden age of classic 2D animation.

Besides Disney, some other animation studios started to appear: *Max Fleischer* with *Popeye* shorts and *Felix the Cat* (1919), who was considered the first animated movie star and the first to be merchandised; *Warner Bros* with *Looney Tunes*, *Merrie Melodies*, and *Bugs Bunny*; and *MGM* with *Tom and Jerry*.

After the Second World War, things changed. With the arrival of TV, studios started creating TV cartoons using limited animation techniques to save time, effort, and money, of course, and to be able to produce cartoons en masse.

In 1960, the first-ever prime-time animated series appeared, *The Flintstones* by Hanna-Barbera. The same studio produced *The Yogi Bear Show* and *Scooby-Doo, Where Are You!*, among others.

Japanimation, or **anime** as we call it these days, was becoming very popular at the same time in Japan. It was based on limited animation techniques and focused on aesthetics, applying zooms and elaborate backgrounds to create ambiance.

In 1979, a young *George Lucas* founded the *Lucasfilm computer division*, the same company that *Steve Jobs* bought in 1986 and renamed *Pixar*.

By that time, **computer-generated imagery** (**CGI**) was becoming more popular, and in 1995, one of the main moments in animation history happened. Pixar's *Toy Story* was released. Other big computer animation companies emerged, including *DreamWorks* and *Illumination Entertainment*.

But, the animation scene doesn't just revolve around Disney or Pixar. There are so many artists and studios out there that deserve a whole chapter: *Studio Ghibli*, *Aardman*, and *Laika Studios*, to name just a few.

So, now that we've got a few insights about animation history, let's move on to the next section to learn the 12 principles of 2D animation that will help us make our animations look real.

The 12 principles of 2D animation

Animating an object, a character, or a type is not an easy thing to do, but with a few tips and techniques, it can become much easier and will make our animations look more realistic and trustable.

The 12 principles of animation is a concept that was introduced by Disney animators *Ollie Johnston* and *Frank Thomas*, in their 1981 book *The Illusion of Life*. They were some of the people involved in creating Disney's animation style, and the idea behind these 12 principles was to produce more realistic animations and to create the illusion that these characters acted based on the laws of physics.

We could say that *The Illusion of Life* has become the sacred book for any animator, designer, artist, or any other person interested in creating animations around the world. Of course, this book was written a long time ago but still, each principle is vital to the process and can be applied to the digital process of animation. Let's not waste any more time, and move on to see what these 12 principles are.

Squash and stretch

The principle of **squash and stretch** adds the idea of weight and flexibility to the animation. In the following example, you can see how the bouncing ball stretches and squashes while keeping the same volume in all of the stages:

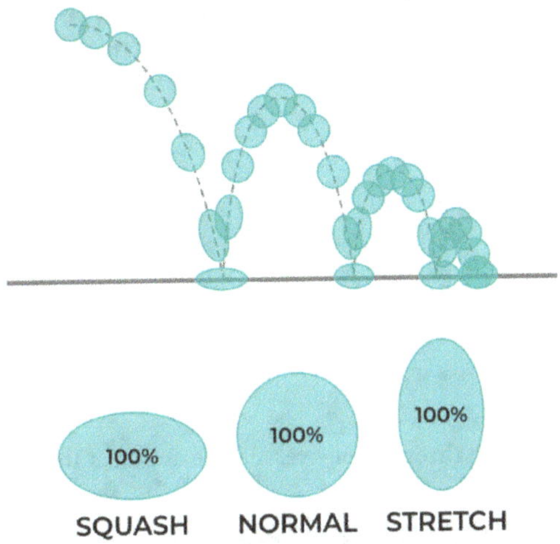

Figure 2.5 – Squash and stretch bouncing ball example

Anticipation

We use **anticipation** in order to prepare the audience for an action that is about to happen. We can use it for physical and non-physical actions. For example, imagine you are about to kick a ball; the first thing you will do before kicking it is to move your foot back. This movement is the anticipation of the action.

A non-physical action, for example, would be when a character looks to one side of the screen before another character comes in. By looking to the side, we are anticipating the action of the other character coming in as well.

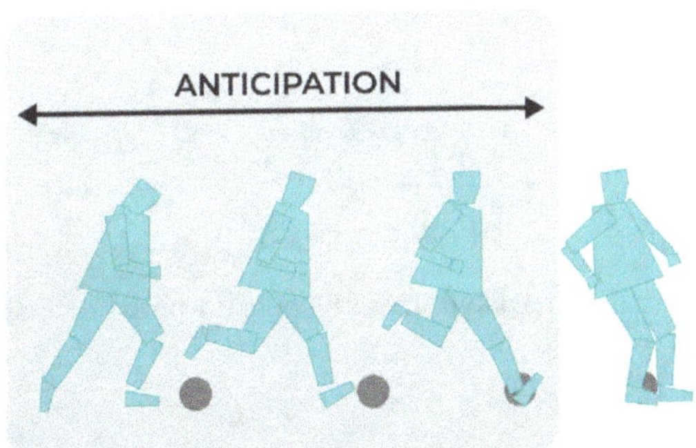

Figure 2.6 – Football player before kicking a ball anticipation action

Staging

This principle is based on what we call **staging** in cinema and theater, and it is used to drive the audience's attention to what we want on the screen, whether it is a character or an action. We can focus our viewers' attention by using light and shadow, the position of the character on the screen, and the position and angle of the camera. But, keep in mind that when staging an action or a character, it is important the audience only sees one idea at a time.

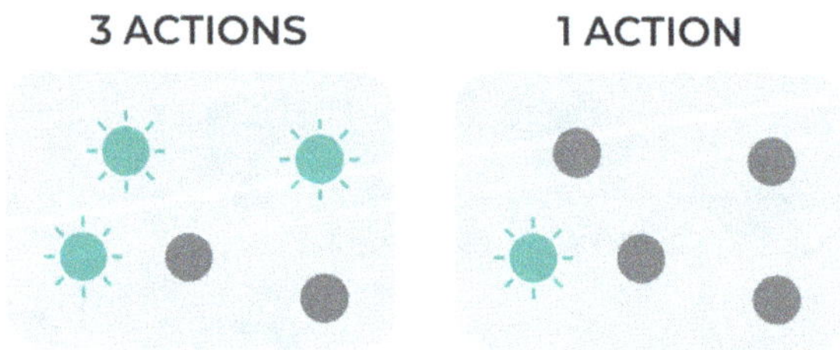

Figure 2.7 – Staging three actions versus one action at the same time

Straight-ahead action and pose-to-pose

There are two different approaches to the process of animation, **straight-ahead action** and **pose-to-pose**, and they are usually combined.

In straight-ahead action, scenes are animated frame by frame, one after the other, from beginning to end. This process is used to create more fluid and fresh-looking movements and animations.

Pose-to-pose is where we draw the main moments of the action, or what we also call the **keyframes**, and it is used when you require more control over the action.

All that said, if we talk about computing animation, pose-to-pose has more advantages as we can plan and draw the main keyframes, while the inbetween frames will be done automatically.

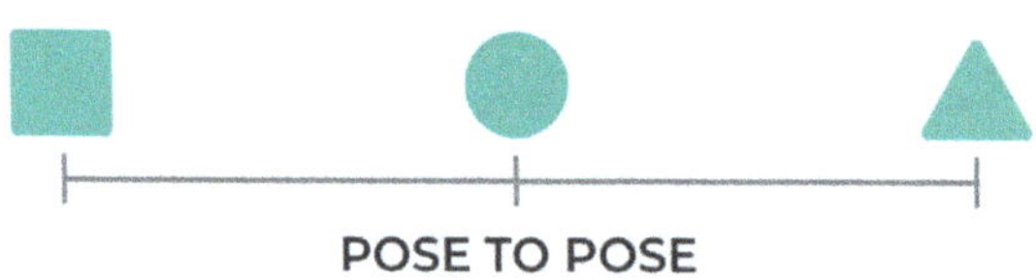

Figure 2.8 – The main three keyframes in a pose-to-pose process animation

Follow through and overlapping action

Both actions are related as they both help to give a more realistic illusion of movement. **Follow through** is when the action comes to an end. The movement stops but certain elements will still be moving. Imagine a person that stops after running; their clothes, hair, and even skin will keep moving.

Tiny variations of speed and movement of these parts are what will make our animation look even more realistic; that's what we call the **overlapping** action.

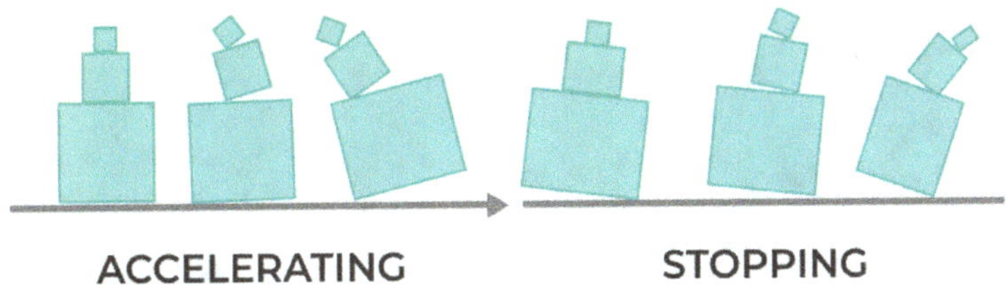

Figure 2.9 – Behavior of the squares after applying the follow through and overlapping principles

Ease in and ease out

When an object or a person moves in the real world, it accelerates at the beginning of the movement and slows down at the end of it. That effect is what we call **ease in** and **ease out** in animation, and this is what will make our animations look more believable.

Once you understand how this effect works, it will be very easy to apply in AE, so that's why we will cover it in more depth in the following sections in this chapter.

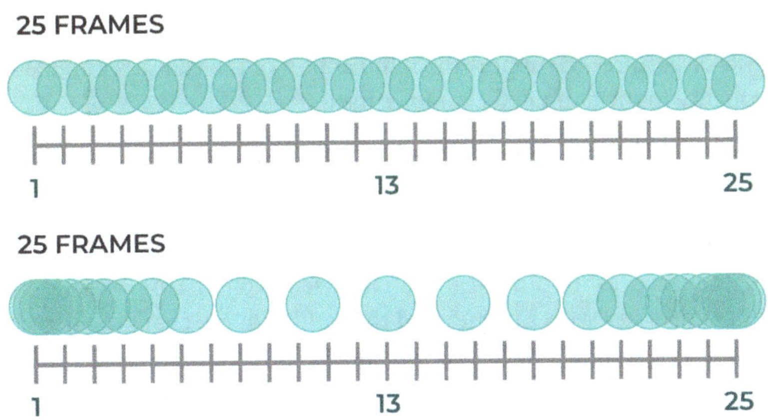

Figure 2.10 – Animation without ease versus animation with ease in and out

Arcs

Almost everything in the world moves in arched movements, for example, when we throw an object, this moves in a parabolic trajectory. If we don't take the **arc** principle into consideration, our animations will look rigid and will lack expression.

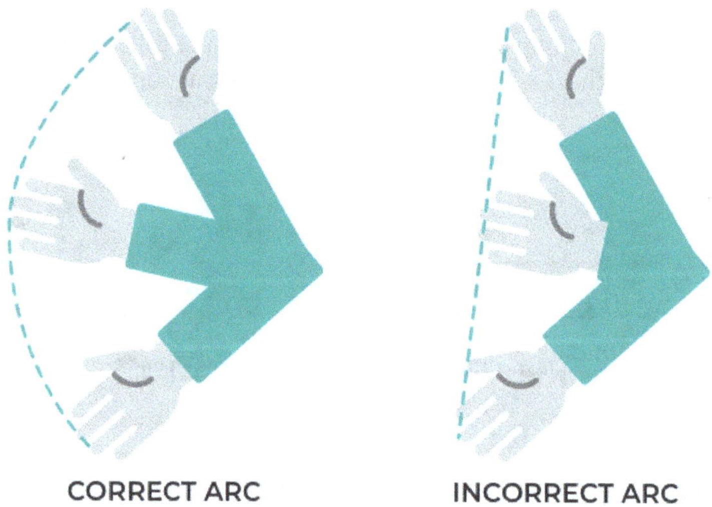

Figure 2.11 – Example of an arched and a straight keyframes animation

Secondary action

Every single movement added to the main action is called a **secondary action**, but don't get confused with follow through and overlapping actions. Secondary actions are basically small movements or gestures to support the main action of the character and are used to add more personality to the animated character itself.

Let's give you an example. Imagine our character, let's name them Max, is eating a sandwich. We could represent that in two different ways:

- **Without secondary action**: If we don't add any secondary actions to Max, he will just open and close his mouth to eat the sandwich. No blinking eyes, no eyebrow movement added, just Max's mouth and the sandwich are changing here (as seen in the following figure). That looks weird, right? Also, from looking at our storyboard, could you tell whether the sandwich tastes good or bad? Is Max enjoying it? We can't say.
- **With secondary action**: Now, let's add some secondary action here. For example, Max is going to lick his lips before eating the sandwich, will close his eyes with the first bite of the sandwich, and finally, he is going to smile.

Can you see the difference? By looking at the storyboard, we can tell Max is excited about eating the sandwich (licking his lips), is taking the time to taste it properly (closing his eyes while having a bite), and finally, is enjoying it. We could say for sure the sandwich tastes good (because he is smiling). All these small actions that help us understand the main action are called secondary actions.

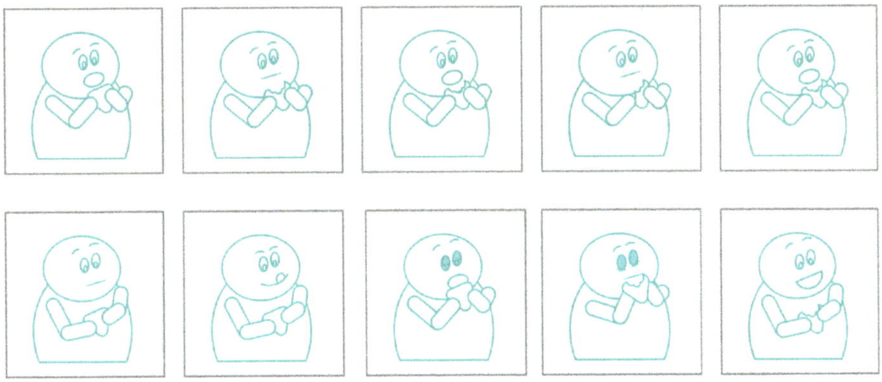

Figure 2.12 – No secondary action versus secondary action storyboards

Timing

Timing refers to the drawings or frames that we need to represent actions and it can be used to establish weight, emotions, and scale. We are going to get deeper into that in the following sections, but let's have a quick look at this simple example: imagine you have two balls, the same size but different weights.

Let's say one is made of wood and the other one of iron. Which one is going to take longer, or in other words, which one is going to take more frames, to move if we hit them? Exactly! The iron ball is heavier and takes more time to speed up, so it will move slower and travel for a shorter distance when we hit it.

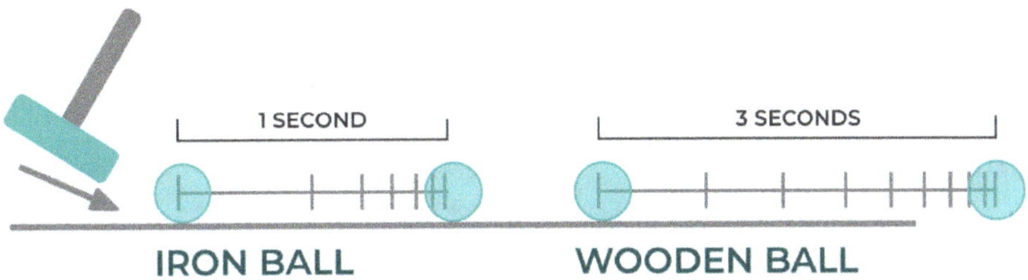

Figure 2.13 – Timing of an iron and a wooden ball

Exaggeration

In animation, sometimes more is less. **Exaggeration** can lead us to create deeper and more trustable characters. But, how do we do that? By exaggerating our characters or objects' movements and emotions; if our character is happy, let's make them happier, if they are angry, let's make them angrier, and so on. However, let's always try to keep a balance, otherwise, our animations will look surreal.

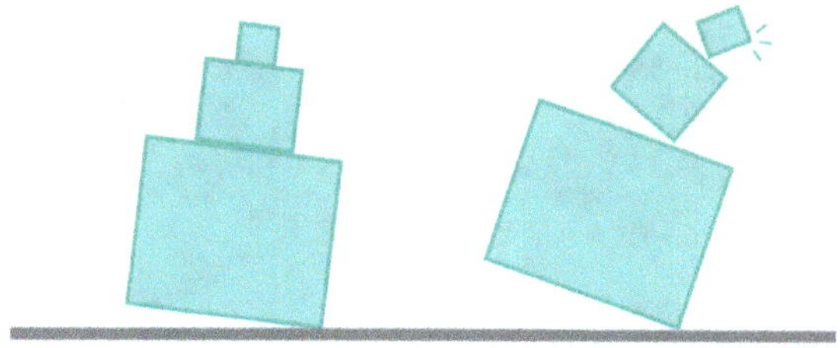

Figure 2.14 – Exaggeration principle. Example of a real versus exaggerated pile of cubes falling action

Solid drawing

Solid drawing means giving our character some sort of 3D look by giving it volume and weight through drawing, shadow, perspective, and balance. Also, we have to avoid making symmetrical characters (or mirrored), and instead, let's try to have left and right sides in different positions.

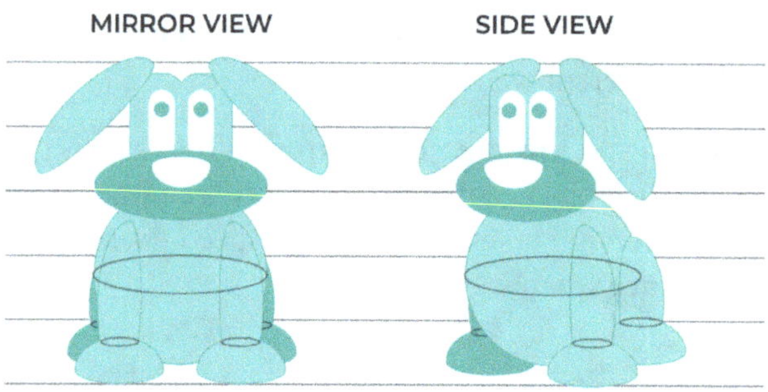

Figure 2.15 – Mirror view versus side view

Appeal

Appeal (or what is called **charisma** in real live acting) is a feature any single character needs to have in order to keep the audience interested. However, the appeal doesn't mean the character has to be good-looking; it goes far beyond that. They need to be interesting. For example, if we want our character to be more innocent, we will use rounded and big shapes for the face and eyes, or instead, if we want our character to be a villain, we are going to use sharper shapes and triangular faces.

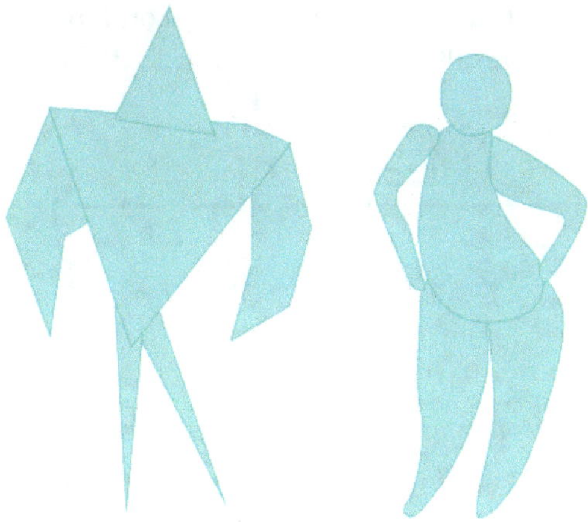

Figure 2.16 – Appeal examples

And that's our overview of the 12 animation principles. So now that you know how to make animations look more believable and engaging, we will go deeper into some of the principles we've just been through but more oriented to computer animation.

Frames, keyframes, and inbetweens

Animation comes from the Latin word *animātiō*, which means the act of giving life. It is the simulation of movement created by the sequence of several drawings, one placed after the other, that when played all together, allows us to see the magic happening. However, this movement doesn't exist, and it's based on the persistence of vision we talked about earlier in this chapter.

Frames

In computer animation, these sequential drawings are called **frames**, so every single drawing needed to create the illusion of movement is a frame itself. And not only that, but frames will also determine the duration and the quality of our animation. So, imagine we want to move an object from point A to B in 1 second. We can choose the number of frames we want to use, but let's see the difference. Let's move a ball from point A to B in 1 second using the following number of frames:

- **Option 1**: 25 frames
- **Option 2**: 5 frames

Can you figure out what the difference will be?

In option 1, our eye will see 25 frames happening in 1 second instead of the 5 frames our eyes will catch in option 2. The result will be that option 1 will be much smoother than option 2.

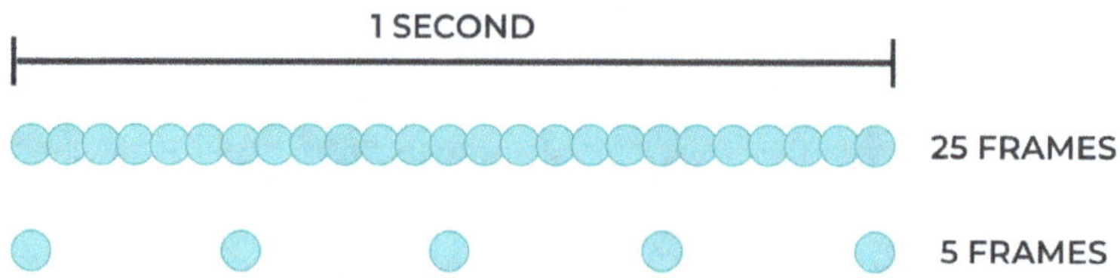

Figure 2.17 – A 1-second animation composed of 25 frames versus 5 frames

However, do we need that number of frames for this kind of animation? That depends, and here is where we would talk about **frame rate**. But, let's leave that new concept for now; we will talk about it once we get to setting up our movie in AE in *Chapter 4, Move It! Animating Our First Lottie With After Effects.*

So, back to our frames; what about keyframes?

Keyframes

Keyframes are the most important frames in the action; the simpler the animation is, the fewer keyframes we are going to need. We normally place the keyframe when there is a change in the action. For example, in *Figure 2.18*, the starting and ending positions of a movement are keyframes, and unless we want to make the ball jump in the middle, we won't need any more keyframes to set up our animation:

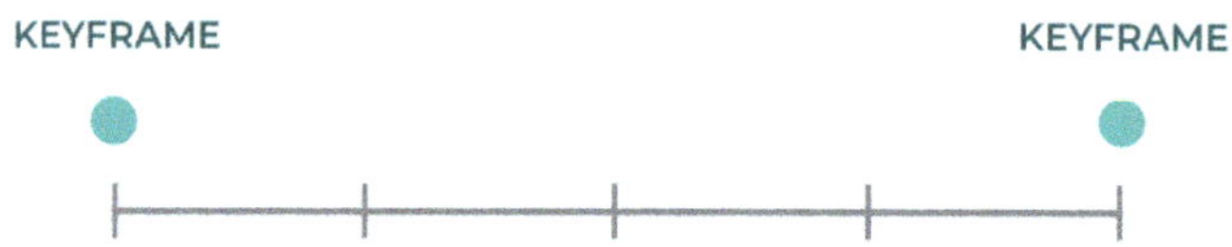

Figure 2.18 – Starting and ending keyframes of a linear movement

Instead, in *Figure 2.19*, we are going to need an extra frame in the middle, right in the place where the position of the ball is going to change, like an inflection point:

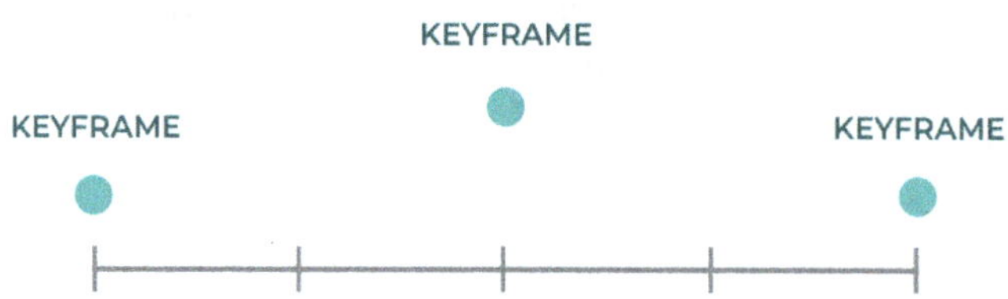

Figure 2.19 – The three keyframes of a bouncing ball

Inbetweens

But, what happens then to the other frames? We call them **inbetweens**, and these are the frames that we need in order to create the movement from keyframe 1 to keyframe 2. These inbetween frames are not defining our animation but are making it look smooth.

In classic 2D animation, someone is in charge of drawing all these inbetween frames one by one by hand; in computer animation, the tool or software we are using will probably do that for us and we call that **tweening**.

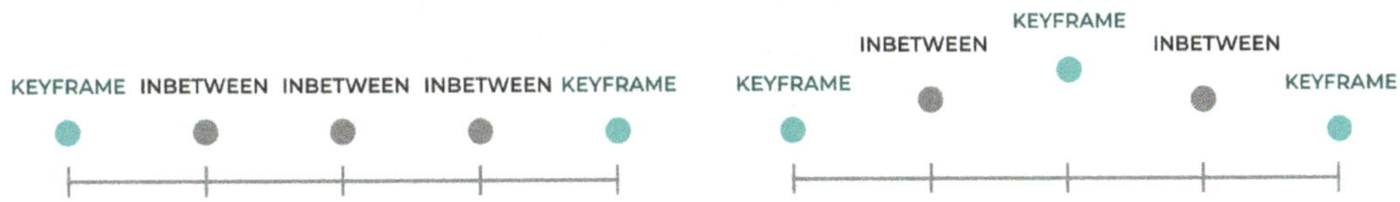

Figure 2.20 – In-between frames in a five-frame action

AE is one of these tools that will do the inbetween frames for us, so we can focus on nailing the keyframes. In AE, we can apply different parameters to these keyframes to change their aspects, such as color, position, size, rotation, zoom, or placement. These can be changed from one keyframe to another without the need for us to create them one by one between frames, which is amazing as this saves us a lot of effort and time. In *Chapter 4, Move It! Animating Our First Lottie With After Effects*, we will learn how to work with any of the mentioned parameters.

So, in these examples, we've just seen how frames, keyframes, and inbetweens work. We've learned how to represent a linear and a bouncing ball animation. Great! However, if we placed these frames in our AE document and ran it, the animation would look weird and would lack realism, and do you know why?

Sure you do! We are missing important principles we've talked about earlier in this chapter, but do you remember which ones? We are talking about timing and ease. So, let's move on to discovering these two concepts more in-depth and see how we can make our animations look more believable.

Timeline, timing, and ease

In the last section, we understood how frames work; now, let's see how we place them in time and space so our animations gain this real feeling. I'm putting these three concepts together as I think it is hard to talk about one without the others.

Timeline

So, first of all, let's talk about the **timeline**, and let's focus on linear movement. Now that we have determined our two keyframes and inbetweens, let's see how to place them in time. How do we do that? We place our frames in a timeline.

A timeline is a line divided by the number of frames we want our animation to be, so here is where **frame rate** appears again. If we decide we want a frame rate of 25, we will have 25 frames per second drawn in our timeline, so if we have a 2-second animation, we will have 50 frames in our timeline. No worries if all these concepts sound a little bit abstract; we know that if you have never been involved in animation, it can be hard to understand, and that's why we will be covering these in the next chapters as well.

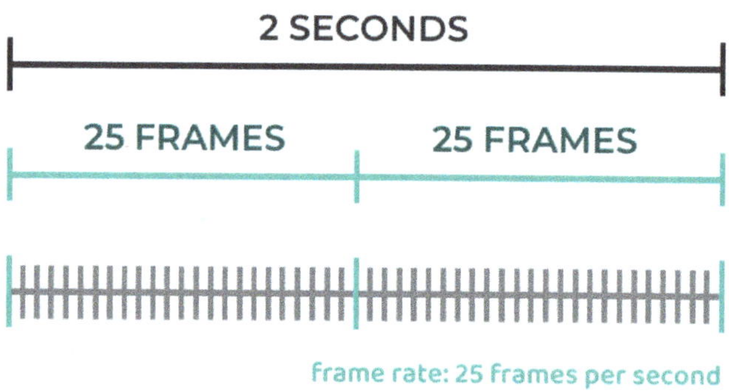

Figure 2.21 – Diagram of frame rate

Let's go back to our simple five-frame animation for now. What we've first done has been to draw the five frames, keeping the same space in between them, as in *Figure 2.22*. As we mentioned earlier, if we ran this in AE it would look awkward as the ball is missing acceleration and is not slowing down. So, what should we do? Right, we need to check the timing of each frame and add some ease.

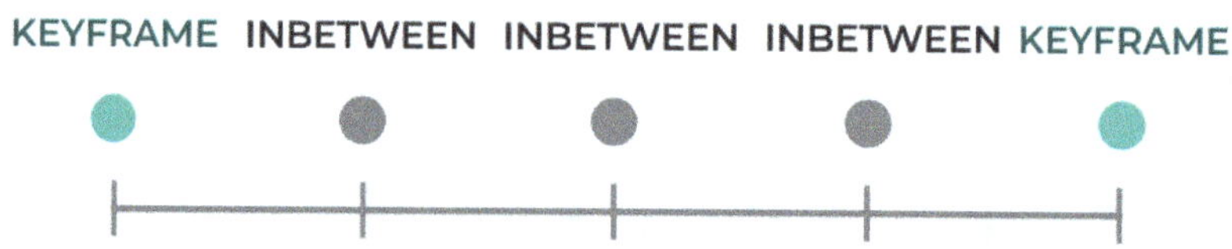

Figure 2.22 – Linear movement

Timing and ease

As we mentioned earlier, if we ran our animation in AE, it would look awkward as the ball is missing the feeling of acceleration and slowing down. In computer animation, we call that **ease**. **Ease in** for accelerating and **ease out** for slowing down. Of course, in AE we can press a button and do this automatically but we first need to understand how it works in order to know what we are doing, right?

So, if we had to represent this in our five-frame animation, we would move the second and the fourth frame closer to the extremes in order to represent acceleration and slow down the sense of motion, as in *Figure 2.23*:

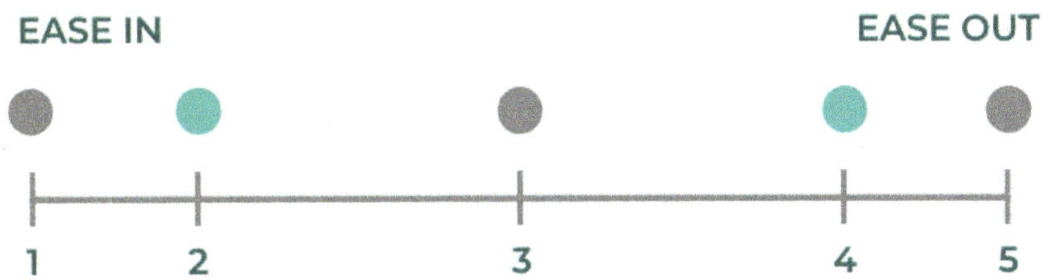

Figure 2.23 – Representation of ease in and out in our five-frame timeline

We will go back to this once we talk about AE and its features, but we think it is very important for you to understand the concepts before moving on.

So, now that you have learned the basics about the timeline, timing, and ease, let's start having some fun and move on to the next section. Let's create our first icon!

Drawing our icon

We know that in these last sections we've been going through so much history and theory. You've learned lots of new words and concepts, but it is very important to us that you first learn the foundation of classic animation before starting to jump into tools to animate. Because tools are just that... tools. Of course, they are fantastic and will save us loads of time and effort, but first, we need to plan our animation in our head to get it out! So, go grab a piece of paper and a pencil and start having some fun!

So, let's imagine we are already animators; of course, we are! And we just had a meeting with our client. Let's say our client sells T-shirts through their own app; however, when payments are done, nothing comes up on the screen, so users keep getting confused as they are not sure whether the purchase has been successfully made, and it's using up a lot of customer care resources.

So, what do you think will be the best solution for the user to understand what happens after the purchase? What do you think... something such as having a confirmation screen at the end of the purchase flow? Something simple, just an icon and a short copy?

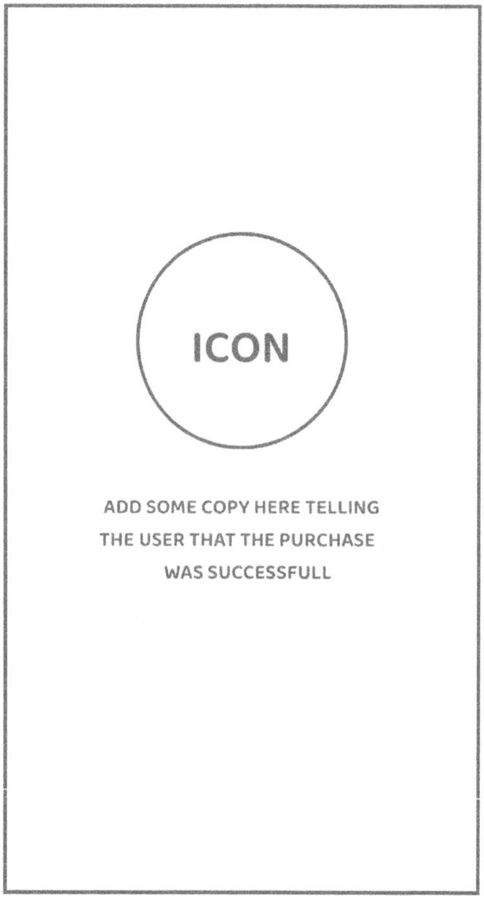

Figure 2.24 – Confirmation screen wireframe

Cool! So we've got our idea and sketched our wireframe; of course, we could leave it as it is, add a bit of color, use the right font, and *voilá*, hand it to the technical team, but come on, let's do something more fun. In the end, the customer is spending money on our client's app, so let's make them feel rewarded.

Let's think about the icon; the icon must translate to the user that the purchase has been made, so we have to communicate positiveness. A smiley face, a thumbs up, or a check would do the job, but let's keep in mind that we want to reuse this icon in some other places so it shouldn't be too specific. Something more general that can be used any time an action has been made successfully.

So, I would go with the check option. It is simple, and when we see it, we know right away the action has been accomplished. Great! We know what we want, so let's sketch it out.

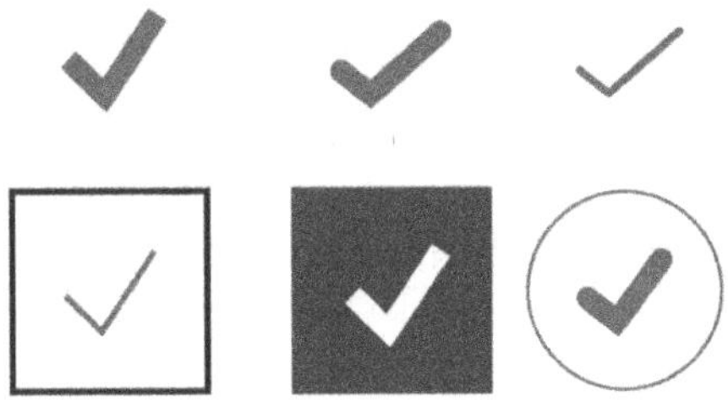

Figure 2.25 – Different styles of check

Don't worry too much about getting started on blank paper; just let yourself flow, otherwise, there are plenty of places that can give you inspiration. Just type `check icon` online, go to images, and there will be plenty of examples for you to get inspired. Also, if you don't feel like drawing it yourself, there are a few websites out there where you can download already made vector icons, such as `https://www.flaticon.com/` or `https://www.freepik.com/`.

Right, we've got our icon sketched, what should be the next step of the process? Let's get creative; let's think about movement and how we want our icon to move, so let's storyboard it.

Storyboarding

Cool! We've talked to our client, we understood the problem and the users' worries and needs, and came up with an idea. We decided to add a new screen at the end of the process with a check icon to emphasize the idea that the purchase has been made. We've sketched our icon, we know what we want, and now what? Are we going to open AE? Not yet!

It is true we've got our icon sketched and ready to illustrate so we could jump to any vector illustration tool, but do we know what we want our icon to do? For example, how is the icon going to appear on the new screen? From transparent to opaque? From small to big? From left to right? We have to make all these decisions in order to be ready to start setting everything up in AE.

Of course, you could decide this on the go, especially if we are talking about a simple animation, but we want to show you the right process to follow, so if you have a more complicated animation, you'll know how to proceed.

This is where **storyboarding** comes into the picture. A storyboard takes place in the pre-production phase and it will help us to decide/preview how our *yet-still icon* is going to come to life! So, let's think about how we want our icon to behave through actions and transitions.

Always keep in mind that the purpose of a storyboard is to present the idea, such as when we've first sketched out our icon; we know what we want and how we want it before getting into much detail, so no need for high-fidelity storyboard drawings. Let's just do it by hand or using an illustration tool and a simple vector, whatever you feel more comfortable with. You'll agree, doing it that way will save a lot of time that we can then invest into making our animation smooth in AE.

So, going back to our icon, I'm thinking out loud here:

1. I'd like that when the user accesses the screen, the icon is not there at first sight.
2. Then, the icon appears in the middle of the screen.
3. It comes up from small to big and from transparent to opaque.
4. Once the icon gets big enough, some sparks come out of it.
5. The check icon draws once the white bubble gets bigger.
6. The sparks move away from the icon.
7. The sparks go from opaque to transparent and disappear.

Cool, we've got that clear in our head, now let's try to translate it into our storyboard. But how do we do that? Let's draw it!

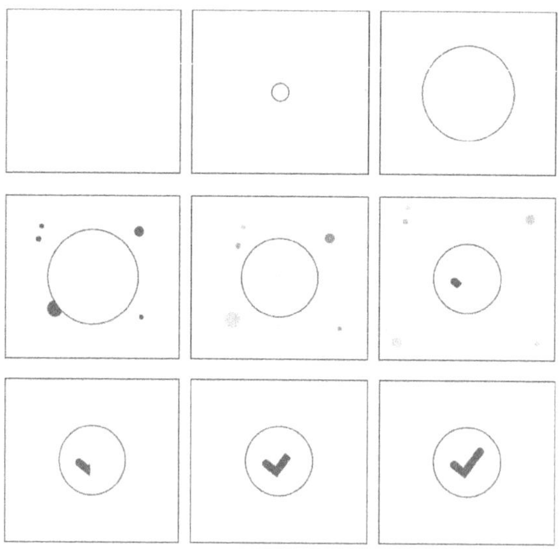

Figure 2.26 – Check icon storyboard

You will agree with me, it is one thing having the idea in our head, and another thing translating it into words, and finally, everything makes sense when we do a quick sketch and storyboard it. That is when the magic starts to happen and we are ready to move forward to start using the tools.

Summary

So, looking back in this chapter, we've been through a lot of stuff, looking back in history from ancient times to nowadays. We've learned the 12 principles of animation. We met our client, heard about their problem, and came up with a solution. We went from ideation to sketching to actually being ready to start animating our own icon, being sure that we are clear about what we want and how we want it thanks to the storyboard.

We are a step away from having our icon up and running! But, let's go step by step... I invite you to move on to the next chapter to learn about the AE environment before we jump to the second part of the book, where we will start animating our check icon. So, see you in the next chapter!

3

Learning the Tools: Getting Familiar With After Effects

Hi again! Now that we have expanded our knowledge of 2D animation, gone through classic animation history, learned about its principles, and have our sketches and storyboard ready to go, let's move on. Let's talk about Adobe After Effects (AE).

So, why Adobe **AE**? Well, as you know by now, **Bodymovin** was the first plugin ever created to export animations into `.json` files, and this plugin was made for AE. These days, more and more integrations between Lottie and animation tools are being released, which is a good sign, as it shows how popular Lottie is becoming among animators, designers, and developers. Lottie for Adobe Animate is an example; however, most of them are still at an early stage and not all features are available yet, so we will keep our focus on AE for now.

AE can be as simple or as complex as you want; from creating a small animated icon to a huge post-production cinema movie project, it is known as the industry-standard software for motion graphics and visual effects. Think of movie titles, explosions, logo animations, animated reels, and so on – a lot of these are made with AE.

However, we are not pretending to run an exhaustive course in Adobe AE; there are fantastic books out there to do that. We talk briefly about AE, focusing on the animation aspects and providing you with the fundamental features and concepts to create your own animations, giving you enough resources so that you can keep learning at your own pace.

With that said, we are going to start this chapter by getting familiar with the AE interface. By exploring some of its panels and menus, we are going to get deeper into the tools and features that are going to help us create our animations.

We will talk about compositions, how to create them, and their basic aspects. Also, we are going to learn how to move around the timeline and create frames and keyframes (which we already talked about in *Chapter 2, Creating the Illusion: Get Rolling With the Basic Principles of 2D Classic Animation*) through menus and shortcuts. We will work with layers and their main properties, such as size, color, position, and transparency.

We will look at animation techniques such as **Parent** and **Link** that will help us take our animations to the next level in the blink of an eye, and of course, we are going to get deeper into ease, learn how to work with ease in and ease out, and play around with the **Ease** panel to finally learn about the render settings to export our animation.

So, by the end of this chapter, you will be able to move around your personally customized AE interface comfortably and be ready to start your first hands-on project – our supercool, to-be-animated icon!

In this chapter, we are going to cover the following topics:

- Understanding the Adobe AE environment
- Creating our own personalized work area
- What a composition is and its main specs
- Working with the timeline
- Layers and layer properties
- Animating using two different techniques – Parent and Link
- Ease – getting into more depth
- Rendering a window and how to set it up to render your animation

Technical requirements

In this chapter, we are going to learn the basics of the Adobe AE working area, so before we start, you'll need to have installed the following tools:

- Adobe AE (if you need assistance on doing this, you can move forward to *Chapter 6, Don't Stop! Exploring Plugins and Resources That Will Keep You Going*, where you'll find more information about the installation process)
- Adobe Illustrator

Getting to know the AE workspace

Before we start, we are assuming you have already installed the Adobe AE software and the Bodymovin and LottieFile plugins, so we are ready to start. You can find a step by step installation guide ahead in *Chapter 6, Don't Stop! Exploring Plugins and Resources That Will Keep You Going*. So, if you haven't installed your plugins yet, now is the time to do it.

Cool, so are you all set and ready to go? Let's do it then:

1. Let's open up AE and click on the **Create a New Project** button. So, what we can see here, as shown in *Figure 3.1*, is AE's standard workspace organized by a variety of panels and windows.
2. For our animation projects, we are going to focus on the **Project**, **Composition**, and **Layers** and **Timeline** panels, so let's set up our workspace.

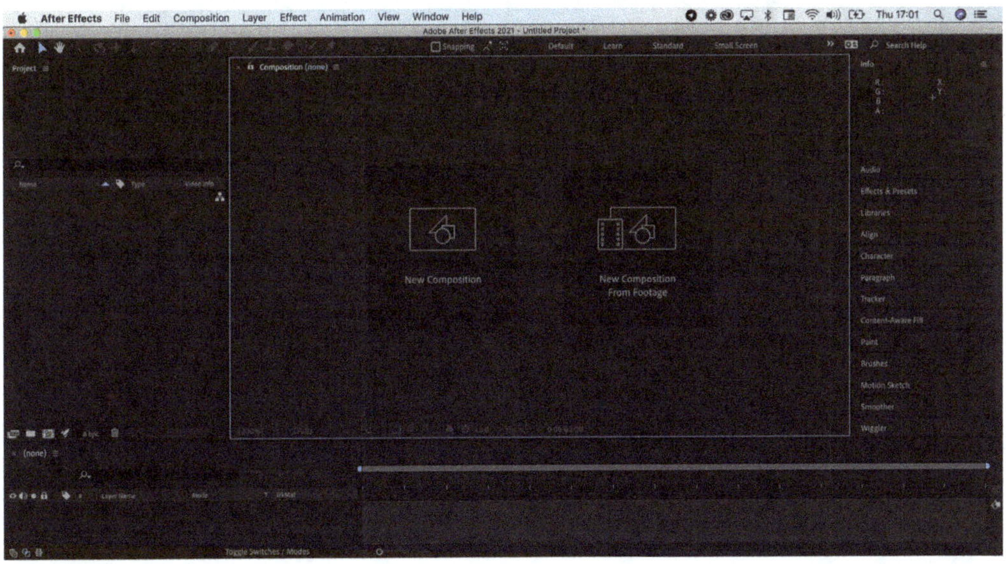

Figure 3.1 – The Adobe AE workspace

Customizing our workspace

AE offers a flexible space with tools and windows that we can manage and organize as we need. We can drag the panels by their tabs and drop them somewhere else on the screen or in and out of a group, and open new windows or close them down.

I would recommend organizing your workspace by keeping open three panels, **Project**, **Composition**, and **Layers and Timeline**, for now:

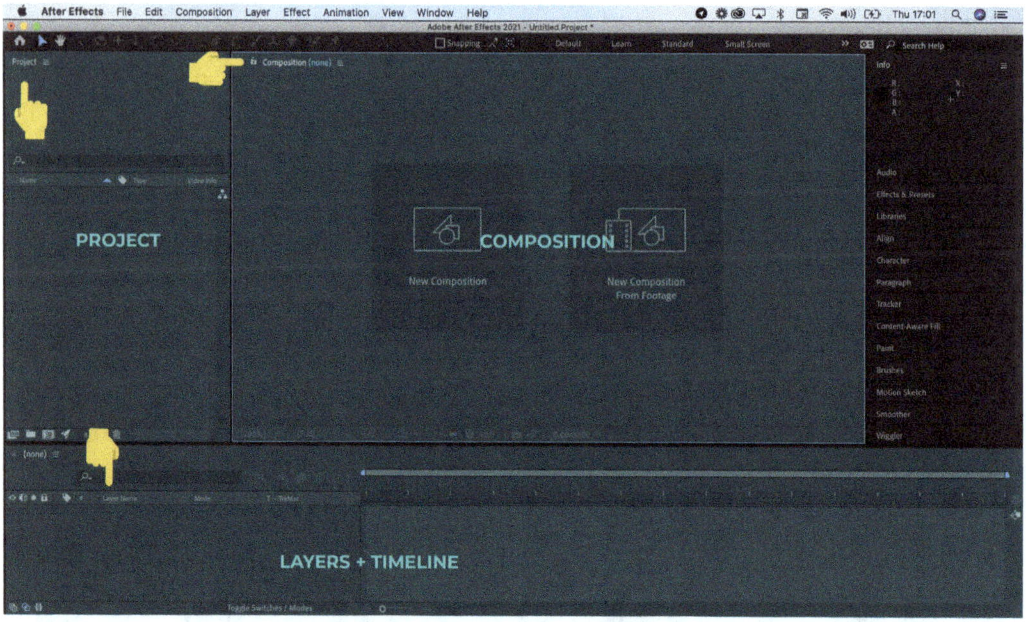

Figure 3.2 – The Project, Composition, and Layers and Timeline panels

You can always save your new panel settings by selecting the **Window | Workspace | Save as New Workspace...** option in the top bar menu:

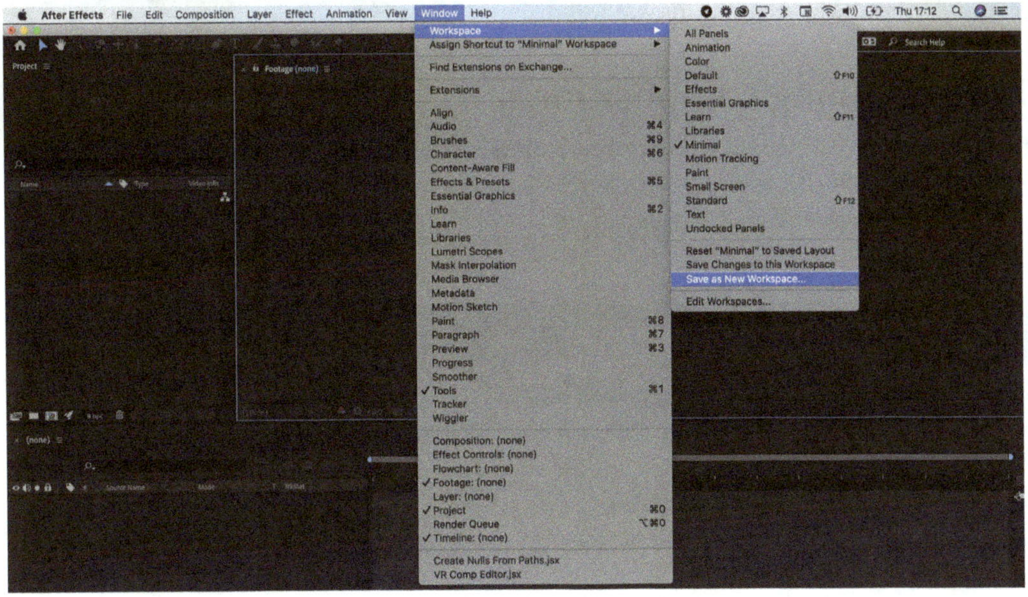

Figure 3.3 – Save as New Workspace...

Project panel

Now that our workspace is all set, let's learn more about the **Project** panel. It will be brief, but what's important to mention is that the **Project** panel is like a library where we are going to import and organize our files and where our compositions are going to be kept.

As you can see in *Figure 3.4*, the **Project** panel shows three files:

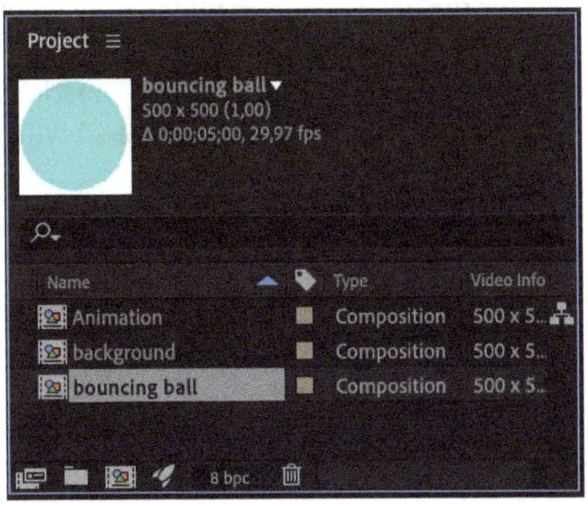

Figure 3.4 – The Project panel

In the **Project** panel, we can also see a few details about the files, such as the size, duration, and frame rate as well as the type of file – in this case, **Composition**. Don't worry if you don't understand what that means; we will discuss it next.

Understanding compositions

The first thing to learn about AE is **compositions**. Imagine them as containers of space and time, which means that anything we add to a composition, such as graphics, animations, sounds, and effects, will be kept as different layers and shown in the **Timeline** panel, as you can see in the following screenshot:

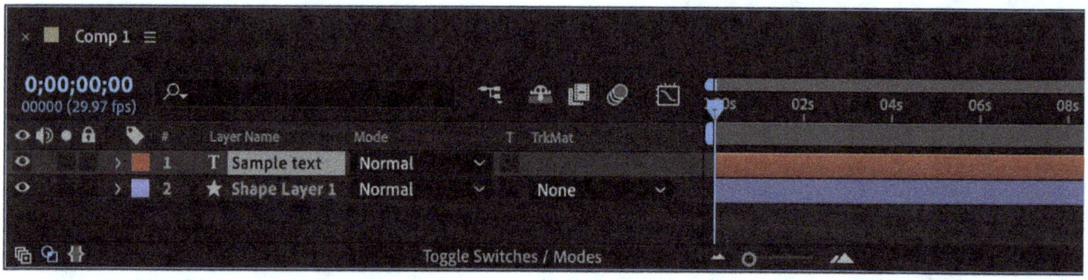

Figure 3.5 – Layers of a composition named Comp 1 in the Timeline panel

A project can have as many compositions as we need, and they can be nested as well. Does it sound a bit confusing to you? Don't worry – I'll give you an example.

Remember the files showing in our **Project** panel? Imagine that we've got to animate a bouncing ball over a background. The ball is going to move up and down in the middle of the screen, and the background is going to move from right to left to give the impression that the ball is moving forward (see the following storyboard shown in *Figure 3.6*).

We need a vertical movement for the ball and a horizontal movement for the background; also, it won't take the same amount of time for the ball to bounce as the looped background takes to move. So, the space and time of both animations are going to be different. And here's where we will create two (well, three – I will explain why in a moment) different compositions.

We create one composition for the bouncing ball and one for the background, and when we combine these two, we will have our third composition – the container that will have all the animation on it:

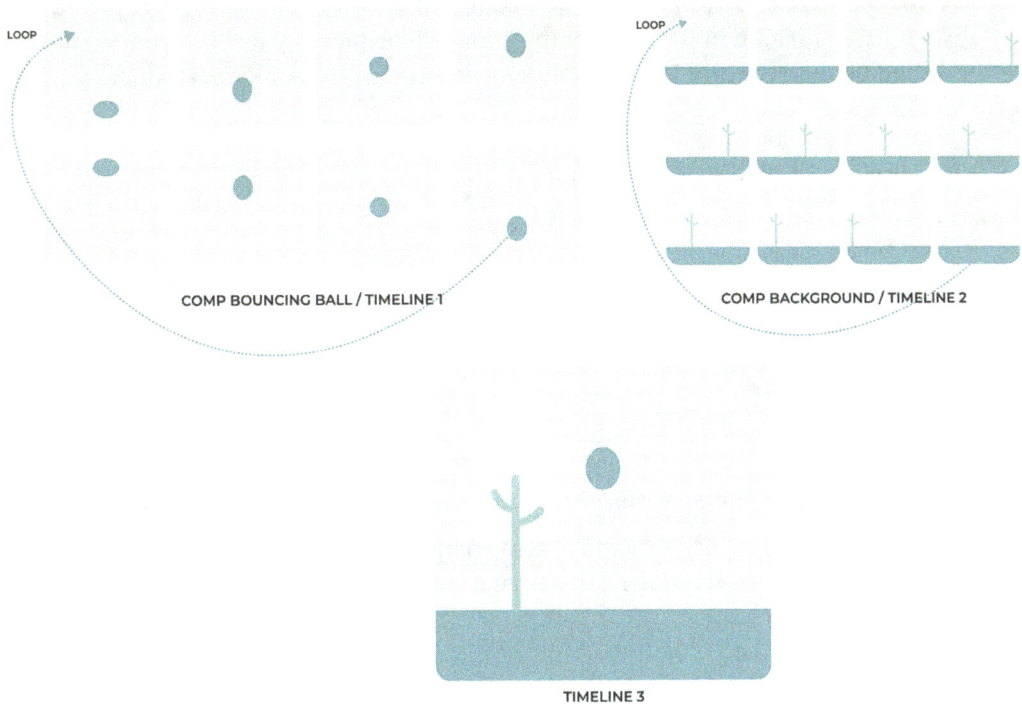

Figure 3.6 – One composition versus two compositions

Some advantages of having separated compositions are as follows:

- **Reusing a composition**: The same composition can be reused as many times as we want. Let's say I have a bunch of birds flying in the background; I only have to create one composition of a flying bird and duplicate this composition:

Figure 3.7 – A comp bird storyboard and a group of comp birds

- **Nested compositions**: You can have a composition inside a composition, which is usually called **a precomp**. Why is that so useful? Let's go back to our bird. We've got a bird moving its wings but not moving forward in space, and we want the bird to cross the screen. We can create a new composition with our moving-wings bird inside. The animation in the new composition will be moving the bird from point A to B, and because the bird is already moving itself, it will look like it is flying:

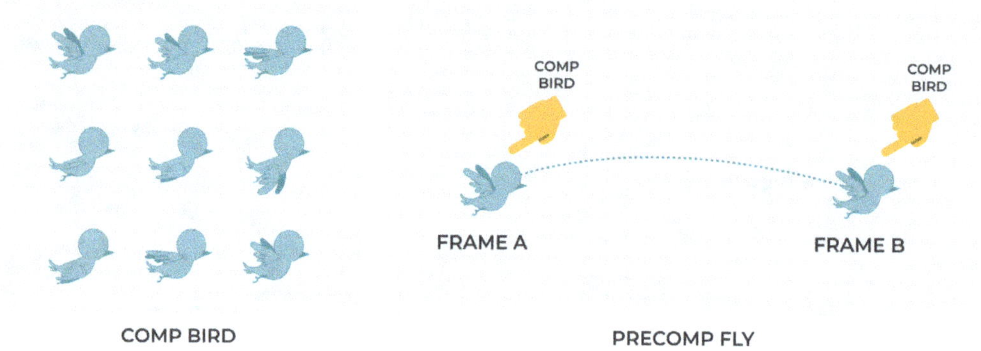

Figure 3.8 – A comp bird animation and a precomp of the comp bird flying animation

As you can see, reusing compositions and nested compositions is going to save us a lot of time and effort. So, now that we understand what a composition is, let's create one.

Composition settings

By now, we've got a clear idea of what a composition is, so let's see what we can do with it. Let's create one by clicking **Composition | New Composition...** on the top bar menu:

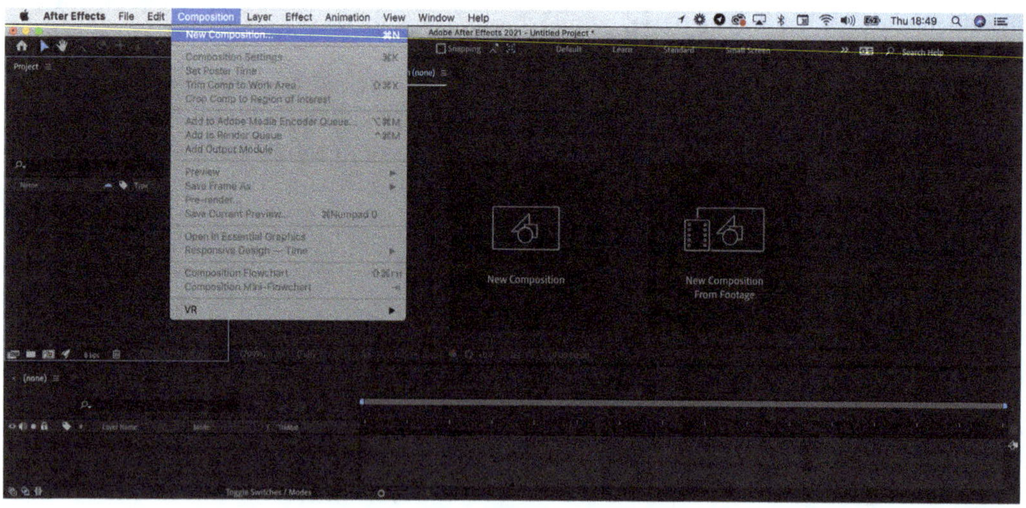

Figure 3.9 – Creating a new composition

The **Composition** panel opens up, as shown in *Figure 3.10*:

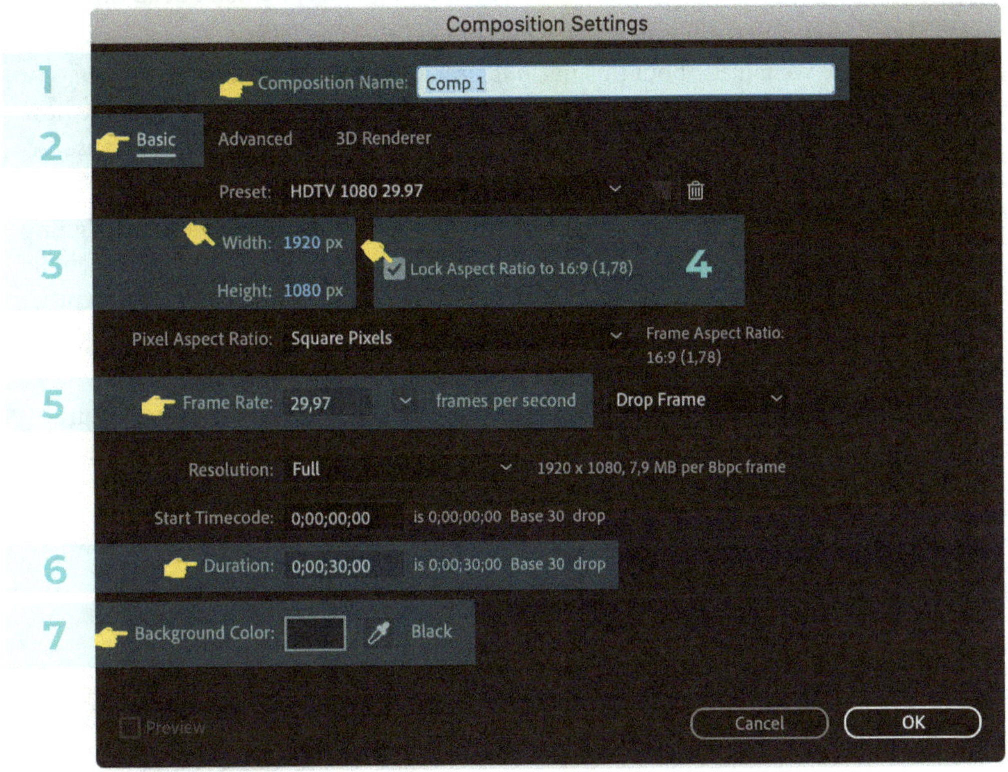

Figure 3.10 – The Composition Settings window

As you can see, there are a few settings to define here, so let's go through them one by one:

1. **Composition Name**: Here's where we can give our composition a name, so let's get creative here; let's name it `my_first_composition`.
2. The **Basic** tab: As you can see, there are three main tabs at the top – **Basic**, **Advanced**, and **3D Renderer**. We only need to know a couple of **Basic** options, so forget about the other two.
3. **Composition size**: Here is where we will give a specific size to our composition. We can change the size further in the process, but it is always better to set it up right from the beginning. If this is going to be the main composition of the project, I like to give it the size of my design, which matches the size of the place the Lottie file is going to be placed. Of course, Lottie is scalable and responsive, but we don't want a tiny icon of, say, 60 x 60 pixels in a container of 400 x 800 pixels. So, let's keep it tidy.

4. **Lock Aspect Ratio**: If this option is checked, the proportion of our animation will always be 16:9 by default. But since we are not doing video, we don't need this aspect ratio, so we can uncheck it and just put the size we want.
5. **Frame Rate**: We talked about this in *Chapter 2, Creating the Illusion: Get Rolling With the Basic Principles of 2D Classic Animation*. Here is where we will decide how many frames per second our animation is going to have. For websites and apps, I normally use 60 frames per second.
6. **Duration**: Here, we determine the duration of our composition. If we are designing an animated icon, this won't probably be longer than 3 to 5 seconds. And remember, each composition we have in our project will have its own duration independently.
7. **Background Color**: This is the color our composition will have as a background. However, this color is not going to show when rendering the movie; it is just a helpful aid for us to distinguish the design from the background. If we want our composition to have a background color, we will have to add a colored layer as a background.

So far, so good! We've just learned what a composition is, why it is so useful, and how to create and set up one, so let's move on to the timeline and layers.

Timeline

Timeline is the panel where we can control our animation. Move it back and forward, move to a specific part, to a second, or to a keyframe of our project. The timeline is also where we can find the **Layer** panel and where we will add our frames and keyframes.

Also, each composition has its own timeline, which means we can have a timeline within a timeline.

Let's see an example of how the **Timeline** panel looks in *Figure 3.11*:

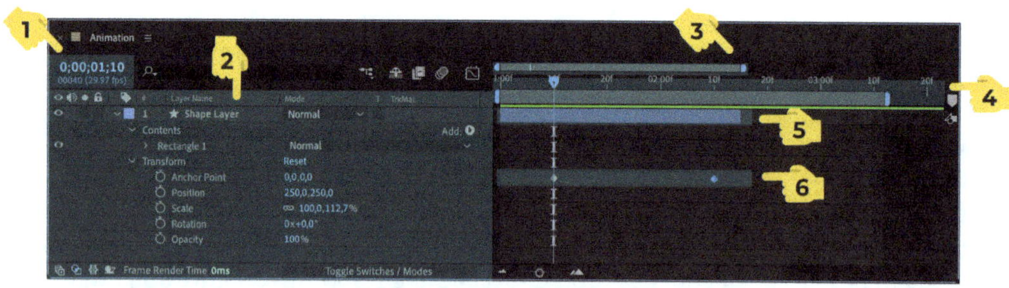

Figure 3.11 – The Timeline panel

By looking at the preceding screenshot, we can see there are a few key areas in our **Timeline** panel; let's look at each of these parts in more detail:

1. Indicates the current time in timeline.
2. This area is called the **Layer** panel, and as you can see, it is placed within the **Timeline** panel. We will be talking about this in the following section.
3. This is called the **timeline's zoom**. Drag it left to right to see how the timeline's frame area zooms in and out.
4. This gray line indicates the work area we are working on. Our composition can be 5 seconds long, but say we only want the animation to be 1 second. We don't need to change our composition settings. We can move the blue start and end points to adjust it to the time we need it to be.
5. This is the visualization of the layer in the timeline. If there's no color, it means the layer has ended or is starting later on the timeline, so it won't be showing at this specific time.
6. This is the area where keyframes and ease are represented.

Note the blue vertical line in the timeline's panel. This is the **time slider**, which indicates the current time at any point in the animation. Try to drag it left to right to move in time within our composition.

I must say, it is hard to talk about timeline panels without talking about layers, so I'm going to be mixing these two from now on. Let's introduce layers.

Understanding layers

A composition without layers would be just an empty frame. As we said earlier in this chapter, compositions are formed from one or more layers, and anything you add to it, such as shapes, text, images, and audio, will become a layer as well.

Let's see that in practice:

1. Open the `chapter03/AEbasics.ae` file that we provided with this book.
2. In the **Project** panel, you'll see a bunch of different compositions and files.

3. Double-click on the composition called **Animation**:

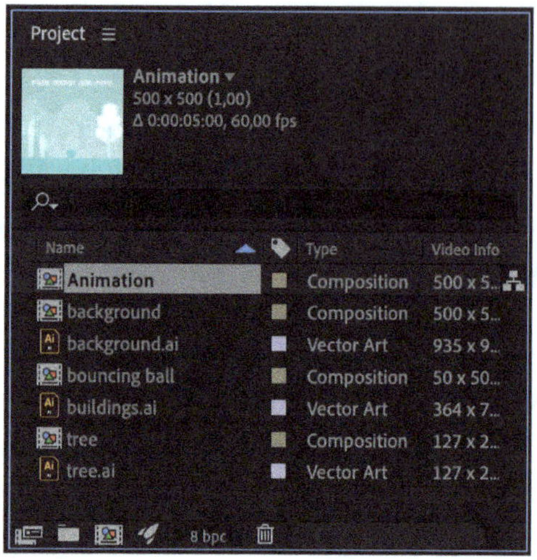

Figure 3.12 – The Project panel

Now, let's check what we've got in the **Layer** panel. As you can see, several different types of layers have appeared in the timeline, and each of these layers has its own properties as well, such as size, position, rotation, and opacity. These properties are very important as we'll see soon because by tweaking them, we will be able to start animating, but let's not rush.

The layer's position in the timeline is also important. The layers at the top will show in front of the layers at the bottom. So, we will normally put the background at the bottom and the objects we want to show on top at the top of the **Layer** panel. We can do that just by dragging layers around in the **Layer** panel:

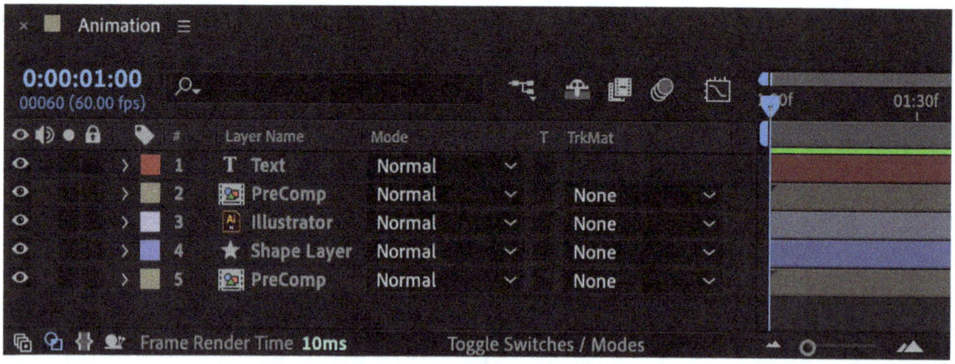

Figure 3.13 – The Layer panel

Let's learn about the different types of layers before we start messing around with properties.

Type of layers

As we are getting deeper into details about compositions, more and more options are opening in front of us. Now, we know a composition can contain as many layers as we want, including compositions as well. In AE, we can find different types of layers such as video, audio, light, camera, and GIFs. However, we are going to focus on the ones that we will be using for vector animations, which are **Shape**, **PreComp**, **Illustrator**, and **Text**, as shown in *Figure 3.13*.

Let's look at them more in detail.

Shape Layer

Even if it is not the best way to draw your assets (we will explore some other ways to do it further in this section), we can use the tools that AE provides us to create some illustrations. When we do that, we are creating a shape layer. Try to experiment yourself by using the tools you can find in the toolbar, at the top left of the screen:

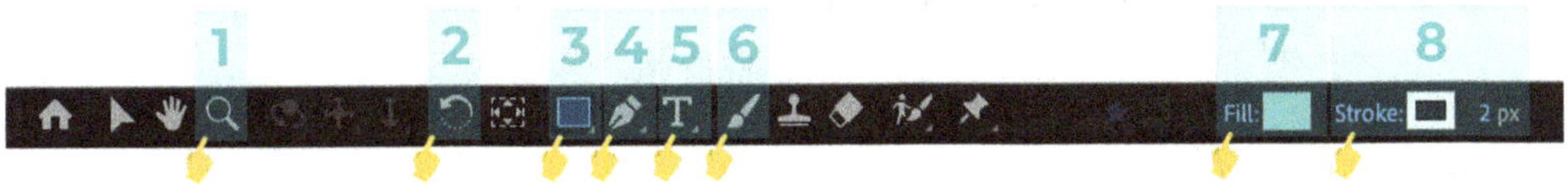

Figure 3.14 – Toolbar

1. The Zoom tool
2. The Rotation tool
3. The Rectangle tool
4. The Bezier tool
5. The Pen tool
6. The Brush tool
7. Fill color
8. Stroke color and width

Take the Rectangle tool, for example. Go to the composition screen and draw a square. You'll notice a new layer will appear on the **Layer** panel, which is a shape layer:

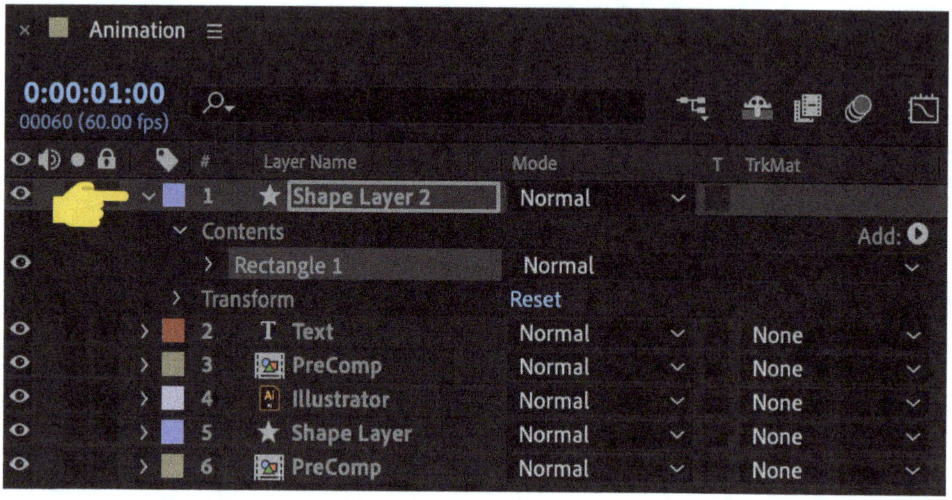

Figure 3.15 – The shape layer

The PreComp layer

Remember when we talked about **precomp** layers in the *Understanding compositions* section? A precomp layer is a layer formed by a composition inside another composition, otherwise known as a nested composition. But how do we create one? It's as easy as dragging the file into the layer's **Composition** panel. Let's see an example:

1. Go to the **Project** panel.
2. Double-click on the **Animation** composition.
3. Drag the **tree comp** file from the **Project** panel to the **Layer** panel.

4. That's it! You'll see that a new layer named **[tree]** appears in the **Animation** layer's panel:

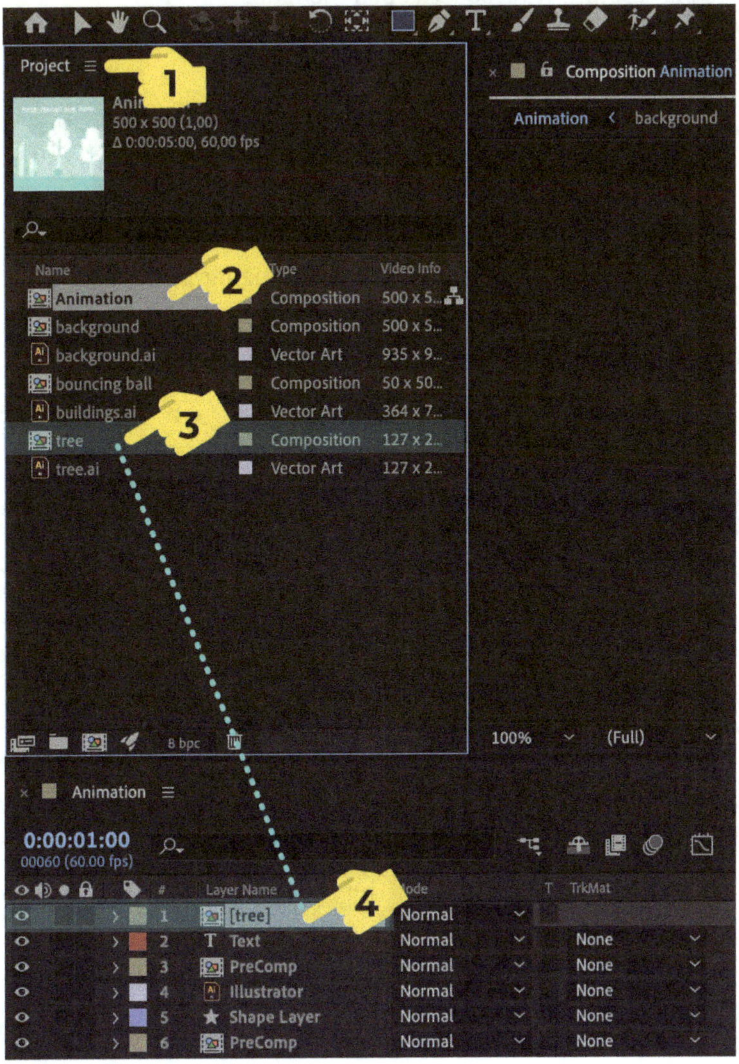

Figure 3.16 – tree is a precomp of the Animation composition

The Illustrator layer

As we mentioned earlier, AE is not the best way to create your graphics, as there are some other tools that will make your work easier – for example, Adobe Illustrator. Here's why. Files imported to AE from Illustrator will be linked, so any changes we make in the original file will be reflected in AE instantly, without the need to change them in AE.

It's like magic! Do you want to see how? Cool, but keep in mind then that to do this, we need Adobe Illustrator installed on our computer. Remember that we've provided you with some files to play around with, so let's open them up:

1. Open Adobe Illustrator.
2. Go to **File** | **Open** from the top main Illustrator menu.
3. Search for the `chapter03` folder from the provided files and open it.
4. Search for the `tree.ai` file and open it.
5. Change anything in the illustration – for example, I've changed the tree from white to pink, but you can do anything you like. Try changing the shape, adding some texture... whatever you like.
6. Now, this is very important – save it! Otherwise, your changes won't be reflected.
7. Go back to AE and see for yourself. As you can see, any changes you do in Illustrator will automatically be reflected in AE:

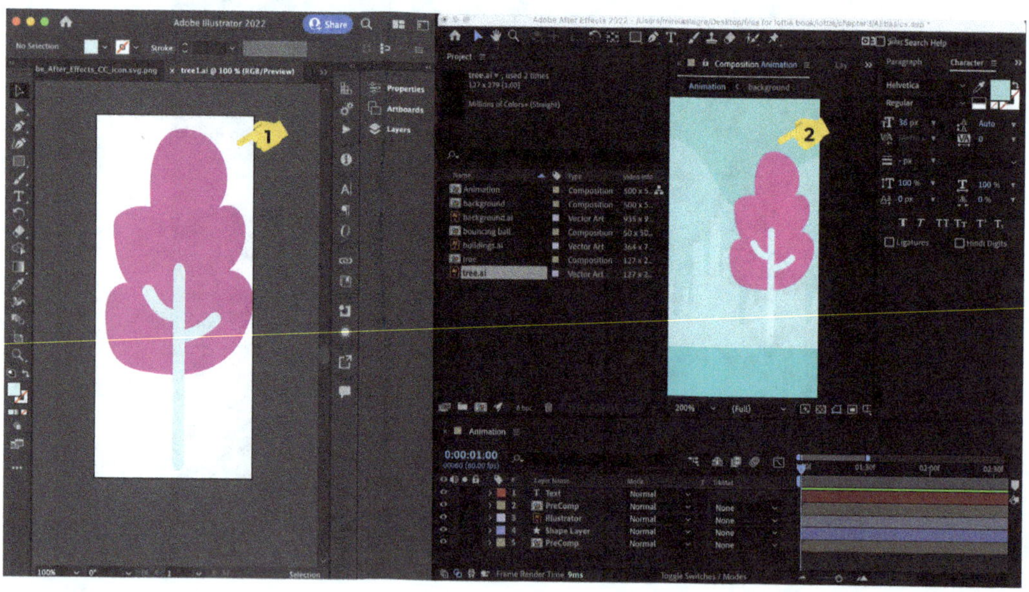

Figure 3.17 – A view of the tree.ai file in Adobe Illustrator and the Adobe AE window

The Text layer

If we want to include some text in our animation, we can do that directly in AE. Try the following:

1. Click on the **Text** tool, as shown earlier in *Figure 3.14*.
2. Click on the **Composition** panel and write something.
3. You'll see a new panel appear on the right side of the screen. In this panel, you've got plenty of options to personalize your text:

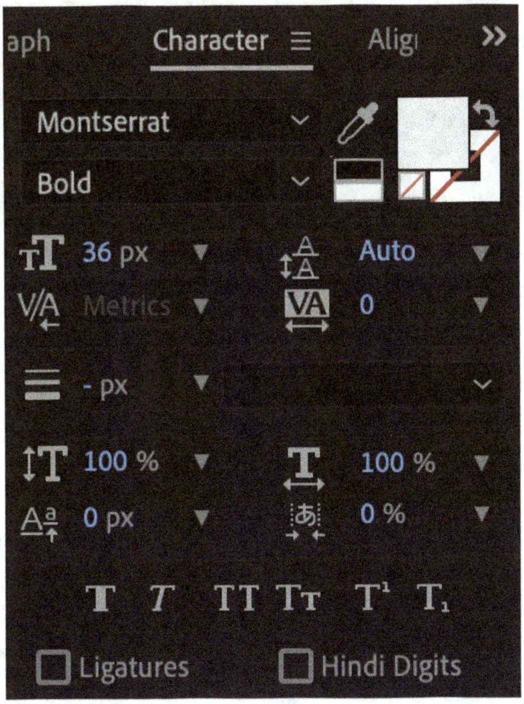

Figure 3.18 – The Character style panel

Cool, so we have covered the different types of layers that are best to use for our vector animations. Now, let's see in more depth what we can do with them.

Layer properties

As you know by now, each layer has properties. These properties can be modified and animated, which is how we will bring our illustrations to life.

So, this basic set of properties that each layer has is called the **Transform** group. This can be found by clicking on the little arrow each layer has on the left-hand side. So, let's expand them:

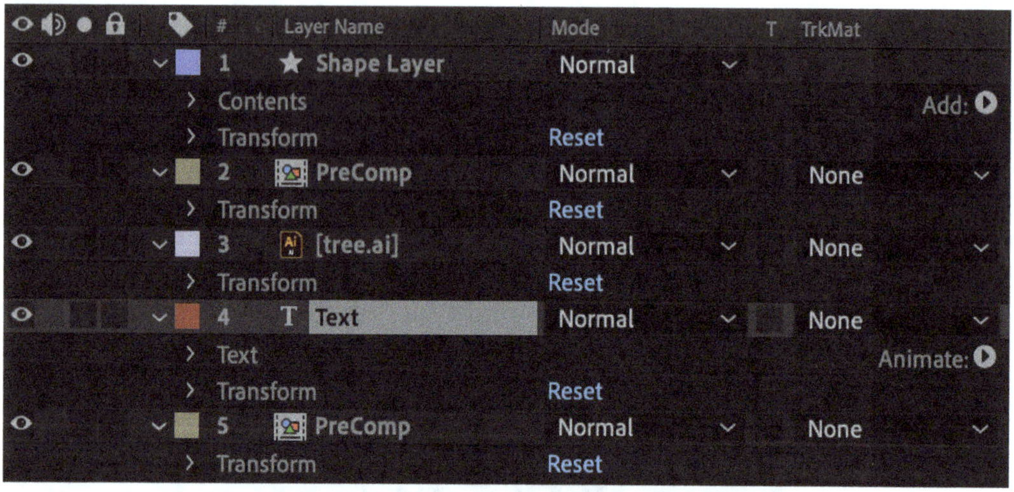

Figure 3.19 – A view of the Layer panel after clicking on each layer's arrow

As we mentioned, every layer has its own **Transform** group. We can also see that some types of layers have specific properties, but for now, we are going to just focus on the **Transform** group.

So, let's click, for example, on the transformation group of **Shape Layer** and see what happens… *voilá!* The **Transform** properties expand:

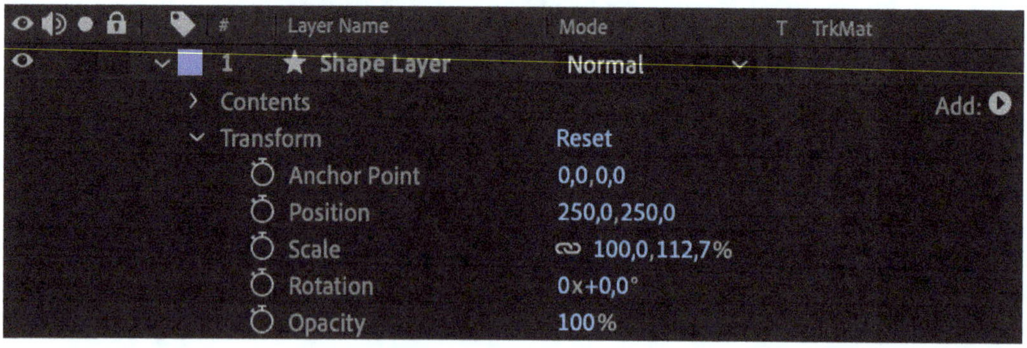

Figure 3.20 – A detailed view of the Shape Layer Transform group properties

Nice! We can see all the **Transform** properties now, and here's where we are going to be performing most of our magic. These properties are really powerful and will allow us to create our animations, by transforming, rotating, changing opacity, and moving the graphics on screen. We are going to create the illusion of animation. So, let's get into more detail and see what we can do with each property.

Anchor point

Transformations such as scale or rotation are done around an **anchor point**. The anchor point is, by default, at the center of a layer, as shown in *Figure 3.21*. Sometimes, we will need the anchor point to be placed somewhere else, maybe in one of the corners, or somewhere else in the layer.

If that's the case, I highly recommend doing it at the beginning before we start animating a layer, as when we change the anchor point position, the scale and rotation behavior is going to be different. See the following example in *Figure 3.21*:

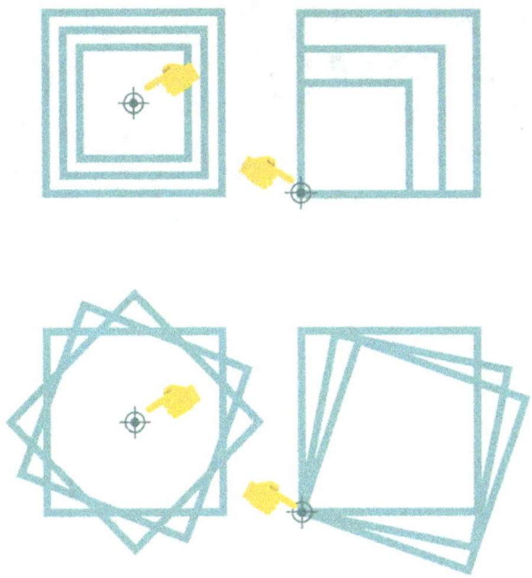

Figure 3.21 – A centered anchor point versus a bottom/left-hand-corner anchor point for the scale and rotation properties

We can choose the anchor point position by choosing the **Pan** tool from the tools panel, and just dragging and dropping it in the composition screen. We can also change its value in the **Layer** panel:

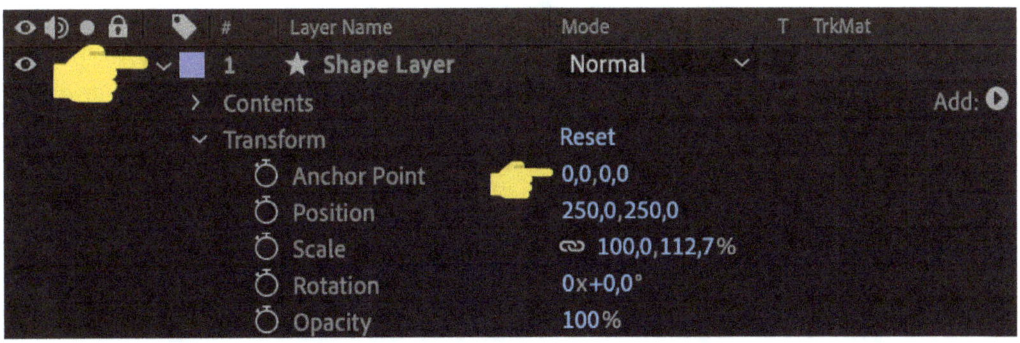

Figure 3.22 – The anchor point values are set to x = 0,0 and y = 0,0 by default

Position

Position is the place where our layer is going to take on a composition. We can move our layer around a composition and place it wherever we want, even outside the visible frame of the composition. Just try moving the layer around the composition screen or changing its values in the **Layer** panel:

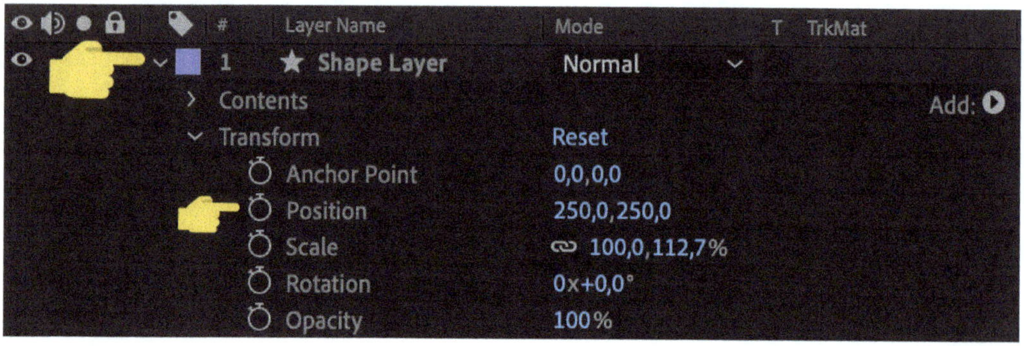

Figure 3.23 – The Position value based on the layer's position in the composition screen

Scale

It's the turn of **Scale**. Layers can also be scaled up or down. Remember when we talked about the anchor point and said our objects will behave depending on where the anchor point is positioned? We can change the size of a layer in the composition screen by pulling our layer handles up or down or changing them:

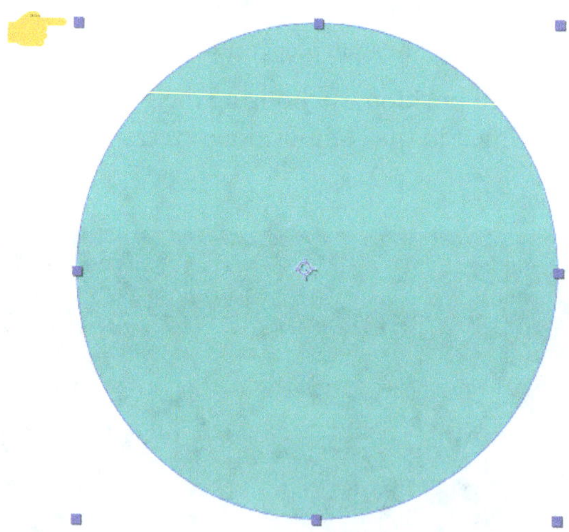

Figure 3.24 – Handles represented by little squares

We can change the scale from the **Layer** panel as well. Note the little icon at the left of the values. This is by default active and means our layer is going to scale up or down, keeping its proportions. Uncheck it if you want to scale the layer only on its vertical or horizontal axis:

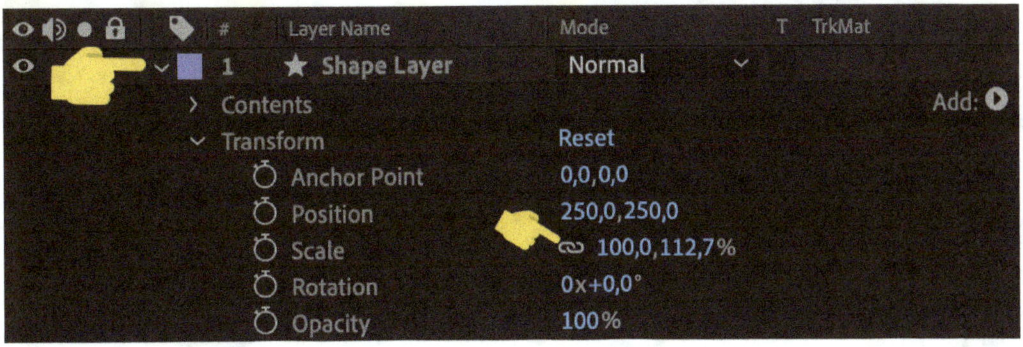

Figure 3.25 – Scale is set to x = 100% and y = 112.7% by default

Rotation

We can rotate our layer. To do that, we can select the **Rotation** tool on the tools panel and spin our layer around in the composition screen, or we can change values in the **Layer** panel. The first value shown in the **Layer** panel, which by default is **0x**, stands for the amount of turns we want our layer to make:

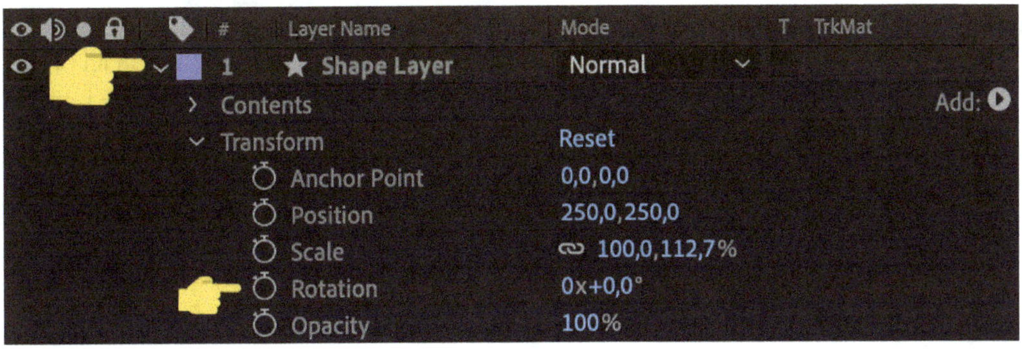

Figure 3.26 – Rotation is defined by 0x = number of turns and the degrees, set by default to 0,0 degrees

Opacity

Another interesting property is **Opacity**. We can change this from **0%** to **100%**, the former being totally transparent and the latter fully opaque. We can change opacity by changing the value directly in the **Layer** panel:

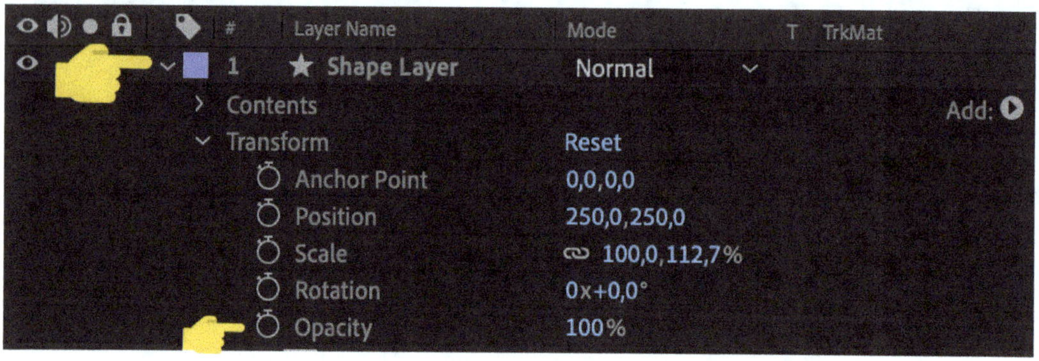

Figure 3.27 – Opacity set by default to 100%

Now that we've learned all about layers, types of layers, and their main properties, let's move on to the Parent and Link feature.

Animating using the Parent & Link option

In the last section, we learned how to apply properties to a layer. Now, what if we want different layers to behave in the same way? Do we have to change the properties in all of these layers? Well, not really!

In AE, we can link one layer to another one by **parenting**. The main layer is called a **parent** and the linked layer will be called a **child**. Simply put, we can say that parenting is a way to group layers.

Here are some aspects to keep in mind:

- A layer can only have one parent, but each parent layer can have as many children as we want.
- We can animate child layers on their own.
- When creating parenting, we can choose whether the child is going to adopt the parent's properties or not.

But where is the parent option? It is placed in the **Layer** panel; however, sometimes it can be hidden. If that's so, just right-click anywhere in the top bar in your **Layer** panel to reveal a new menu. Choose **Columns** | **Parent & Link**:

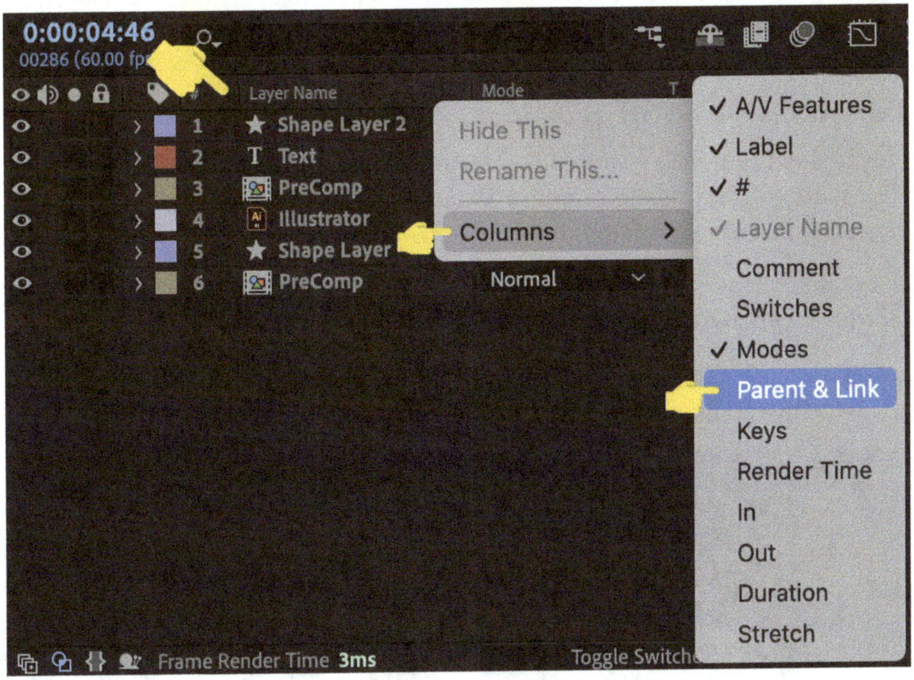

Figure 3.28 – The Layer panel view options

Now that we are sure we can see the **Parent** option in the **Layer** panel, let's see how to *parent* a layer.

Parenting a layer is really easy to do. Just drag the pick whip icon to the layer you want to link, as shown in *Figure 3.29*. And it's done!

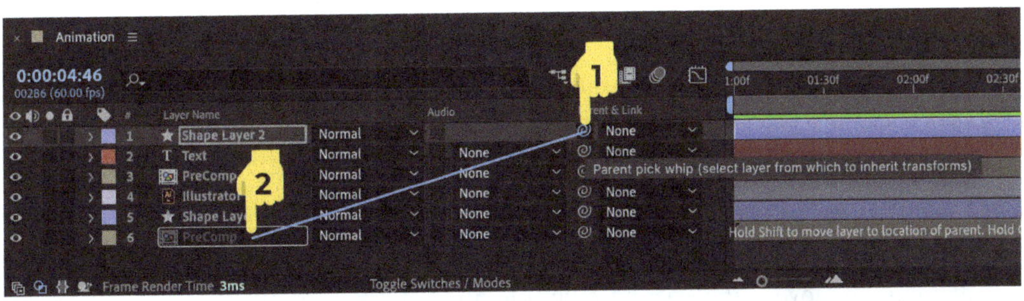

Figure 3.29 – Using the pick whip in the Parent & Link view

I would recommend you take your time to mess around with Parent & Link to get familiar with it.

So, now that we've learned what Parent & Link are and how to apply them to a layer, let's move on to keyframes and animation.

Keyframes and animation

Animation couldn't be possible without **keyframes**. As we mentioned earlier in *Chapter 2, Creating the Illusion: Get Rolling With the Basic Principles of 2D Classic Animation*, an animation is composed of keyframes and inbetweens.

AE generates the inbetween frames for us, so we don't need to create an animation frame by frame, which will save us a lot of time.

That said, let's see how this works. In the following screenshot, we have an example of a two-frame sequence and how it should look in the **Layer** and **Timeline** panels:

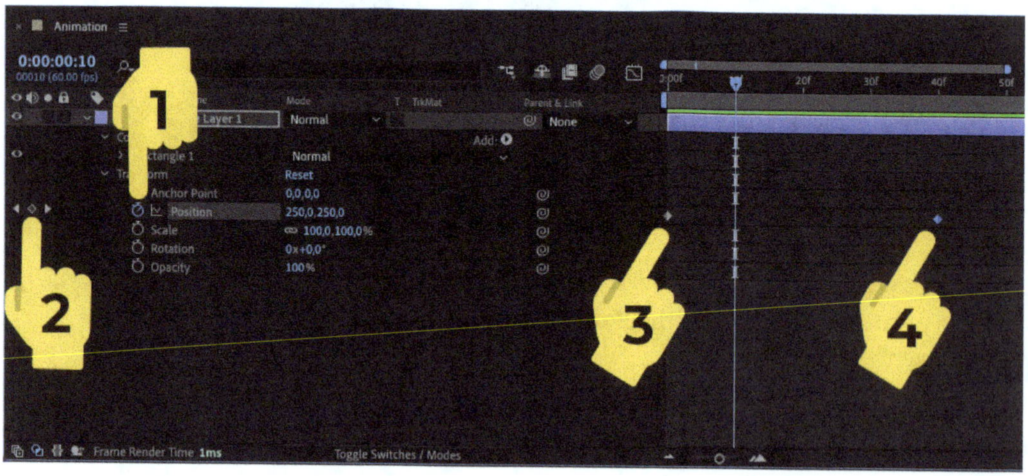

Figure 3.30 – A representation of frames in the Layer and Timeline panels

As you can see in the preceding screenshot, creating keyframes is just a matter of guided steps. Let's see how it is done:

1. Click **Stopwatch** to activate and create your first keyframe. If you click again, all keyframes will be erased.
2. Click the little diamond to **Add/Remove Keyframes**. Click arrows next to the diamond to move to the existing keyframes in the timeline.
3. Keyframe position A in the timeline.
4. Keyframe position B in the timeline.

We know we can animate a property when we see the little stopwatch icon next to it. When clicking on it (see **1** in *Figure 3.30*), little arrows and a diamond (see **2** in *Figure 3.30*) will appear.

When clicking on the stopwatch, our first frame will be created. Go on, try it! Let's do the following:

1. Let's go to the **Project** panel and double-click on the **bouncing ball** composition.
2. Let's place our time slider at **0** seconds (which we talked about in the *Timeline* section):

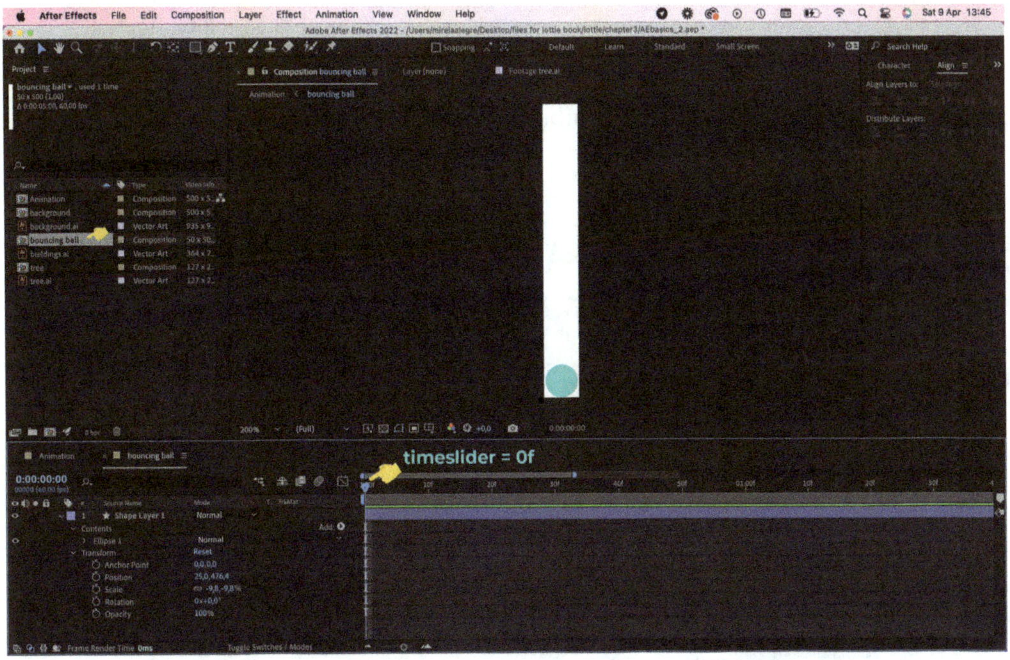

Figure 3.31 – The bouncing ball composition with the time slider at frame 0

3. Choose the **Position** property and click on the stopwatch next to it. Note that our new keyframe will be created just where our time slider is placed. We will call that **keyframe A**:

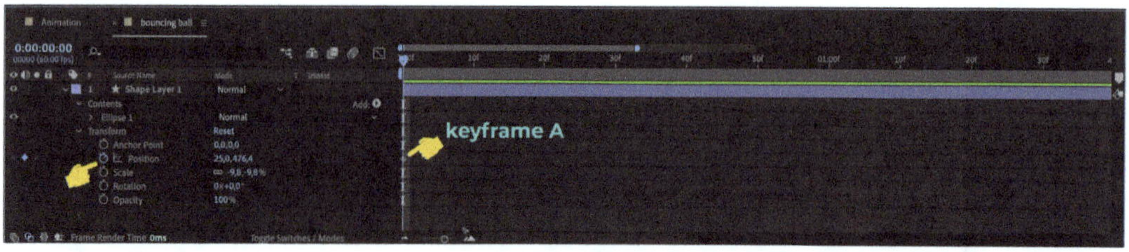

Figure 3.32 – A view of the Layer and Timeline panels after clicking on the position stopwatch

4. Now, let's move the time slider from **0** to half a second (**30f**).
5. Click on the diamond icon. Remember that if we click again on the stopwatch, we are deleting all keyframes in that property. We will call that **keyframe B**:

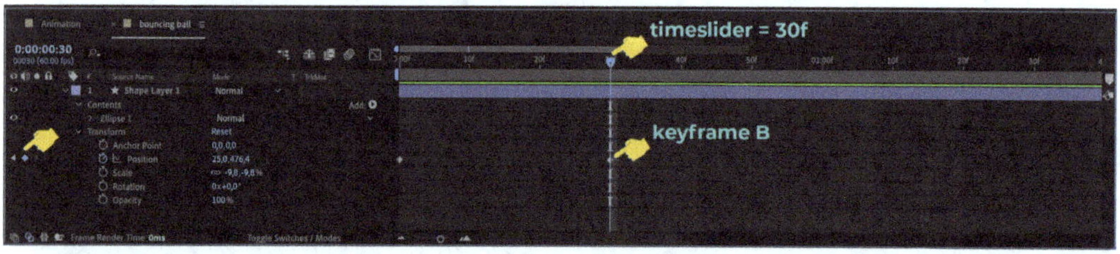

Figure 3.33 – A second keyframe is created after clicking on the diamond icon on the left

6. Now, let's move the time slider to **1** second.
7. Click again on the diamond to create our keyframe:

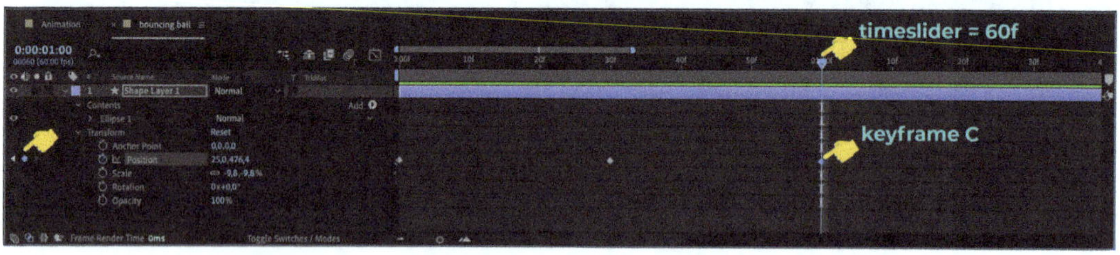

Figure 3.34 – The time slider at frame 60 and keyframe C

Cool, we've got our keyframes created, so now what? If we move the time slider from **A** to **C**, nothing is happening, right? Well, that's because our keyframes are exactly the same, with the same properties, color, and so on, so we don't see anything changing.

8. Now, move the time slider to **keyframe B** (**30f**).

9. Let's change its vertical position to **80**. Remember that you can do that by changing the property value in the layer's composition:

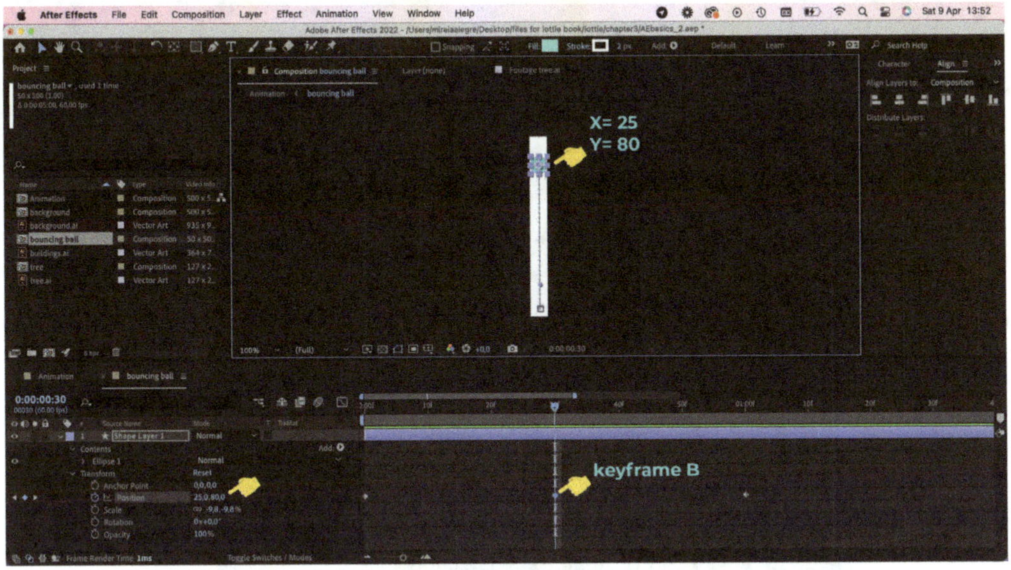

Figure 3.35 – Set position to x = 25 and y = 80

10. Drag the time slider from **A** to **C**. What's happening now? The ball is bouncing! Yes! We've just created our first animation!

You can press the *spacebar* as well to make the animation play in a loop. So, let's check a few things here. When pressing the *spacebar*, the animation plays one time, stops momentarily, and then starts again. Why is that?

It's because our animation is 1 second long but we decided our composition's length was going to be 5 seconds, remember? No problem – we can adjust that at any time. Let's open the composition settings.

Go to the **Project** panel, right-click on the **bouncing ball** composition, select **Composition Settings…**, and change the duration to 1 second, as we saw earlier in the chapter (**6** in *Figure 3.10*):

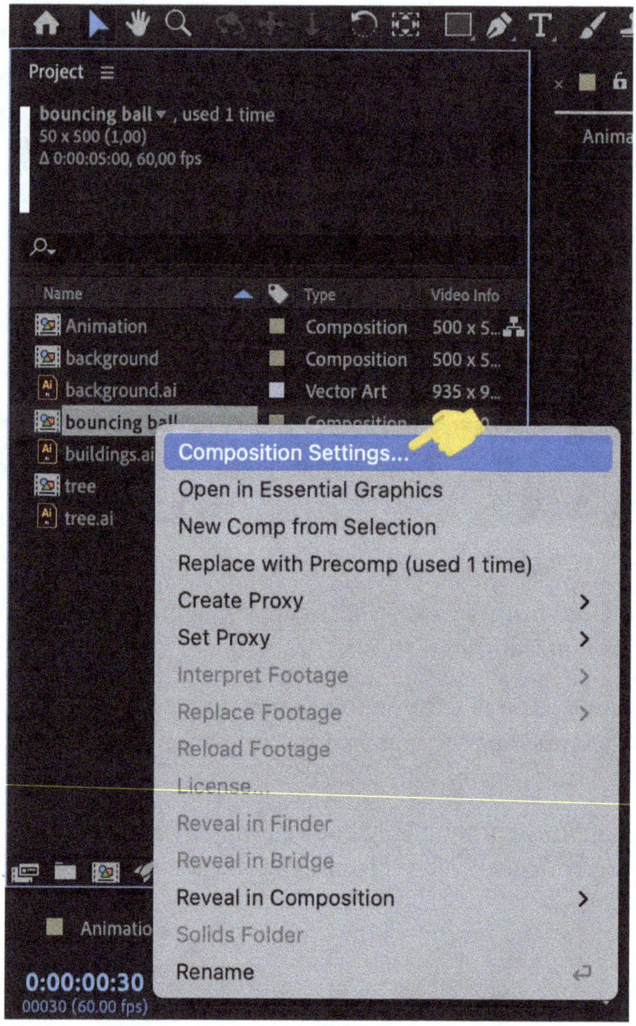

Figure 3.36 – The Project panel

Let's press the *spacebar* now. Cool! Our ball is moving up and down in an endless loop. It's still not quite a bouncing ball, but it will get there!

What else can we see here? If we check our ball on the compositions screen, we can see a line and a few dots:

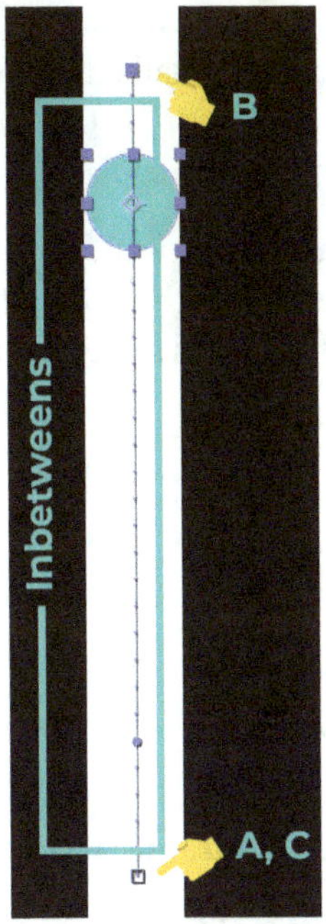

Figure 3.37 – Our bouncing ball view in the composition window

Let's see what all that means:

- The top square dot is our **B** keyframe.
- The little dots are the inbetween frames that AE creates for us.
- The bottom square dots are our **A** and **C** keyframes.

So, we've got our bouncing ball, but it still looks a bit weird, right? The timing doesn't seem right. I think we are ready to talk about ease now.

Exploring ease

As the name indicates, **ease** means moving carefully or gradually. In AE, ease is the effect that allows us to give the impression that our object is moving at different speeds within the same animation. It accelerates or slows down, depending on the effect we want to achieve.

How do we add ease to our animations? Easy – we will add ease by selecting the diamond keyframe in the timeline. Let's try it out!

Remember in the last section when we animated our ball? Let's run it a few times just to remember how it looks (press the *spacebar*). What's happening?

We can see the ball moving up and down at a constant speed, which looks unnatural. Remember the 12 principles of animation we talked about back in *Chapter 2, Creating the Illusion: Get Rolling With the Basic Principles of 2D Classic Animation*? Ease is one of the 12 principles; real-life objects don't move at a regular speed.

To make the movement look more natural, we want our bouncing ball to slow down when it reaches the top and slow down when it hits the floor. That involves using the ease effect, which uses acceleration and deceleration. Let's start playing around with ease, first with easy ease.

Easy ease

Easy ease is an option that AE offers to add ease quickly and effortlessly. So, let's move to the timeline and do the following:

1. Select the **0** keyframe (remember that we can use the timeline's zoom to adjust our view).
2. Right-click the mouse and select **Keyframe Assistant | Easy Ease**:

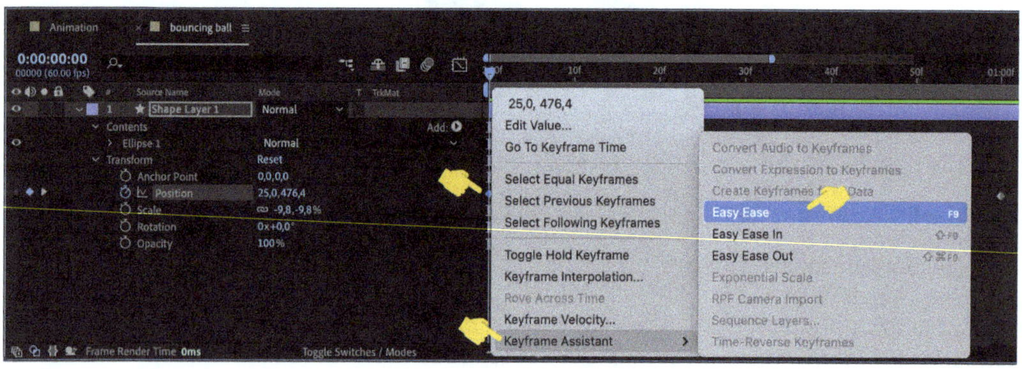

Figure 3.38 – Right-click on the keyframe menu

3. Let's have a look at our timeline; you'll notice the diamond figure has changed to a different one. That means that this frame has the ease effect on it.
4. Now, let's select the second keyframe (**30f**). Remember that you can also navigate through keyframes by clicking on the little arrows next to the diamond. This may come in handy when working with long timelines.
5. Right-click and select **Keyframe Assistant | Easy Ease**. Why are we choosing this? Because we want our frame to slow down when entering and when exiting the keyframe, from both sides.

6. Now, let's have a look at our timeline again; you'll notice this keyframe looks different from the first one, which indicates that it has the ease effect active on entering and exiting the frame, from both sides:

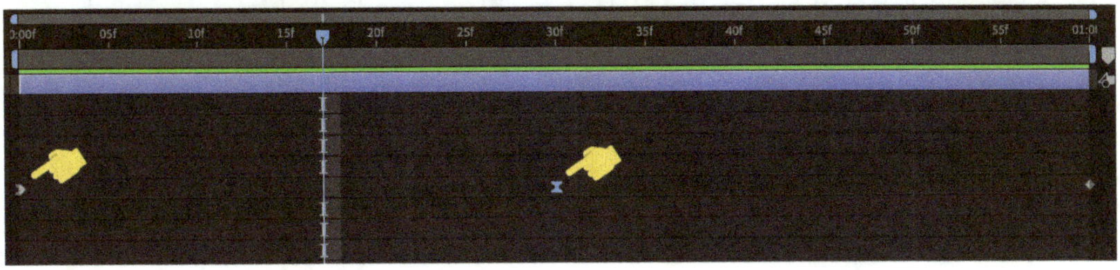

Figure 3.39 – Easy ease in and easy ease keyframe representations

7. Finally, let's click on the third frame.
8. Right-click **Keyframe Assistant | Easy Ease Out**, as we want our ball to slow down before hitting the floor.
9. Check the keyframe; it looks different from all of them. The shape that appears indicates ease out:

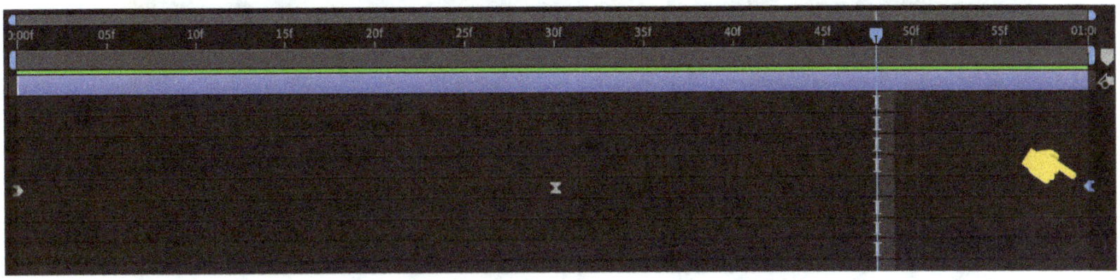

Figure 3.40 – Easy ease out

Now, let's play it! What do you think? The animation looks much better now; the acceleration and deceleration of the ball make a lot more sense, and it looks more real. What now? We can add a **squash and stretch** effect.

Just to refresh your memory, back in *Chapter 2*, *Creating the Illusion: Get Rolling With the Basic Principles of 2D Classic Animation*, when we talked about the 12 principles of animation that help our animations look more realistic, we gave an example of a bouncing ball that stretches and expands along the way to give a more realistic effect.

Now, I encourage you to experiment on your own with squash and stretch and apply it to a bouncing ball animation. If you want to see the final results, you can open the example provided with this book, `chapter03/ AEbasics_bouncingball_squash_stretch`, to check how the animation is done and play around with keyframes, width, height, and also ease.

But let's go a bit deeper into ease. Let's talk about the Graph Editor.

Graph Editor

The **Graph Editor** is the window where we can see a graphical representation of ease, and it is also where we can create and edit ease by hand and adjust our animation's speed.

Let's have a look; click on the following little icon in the **Timeline** panel:

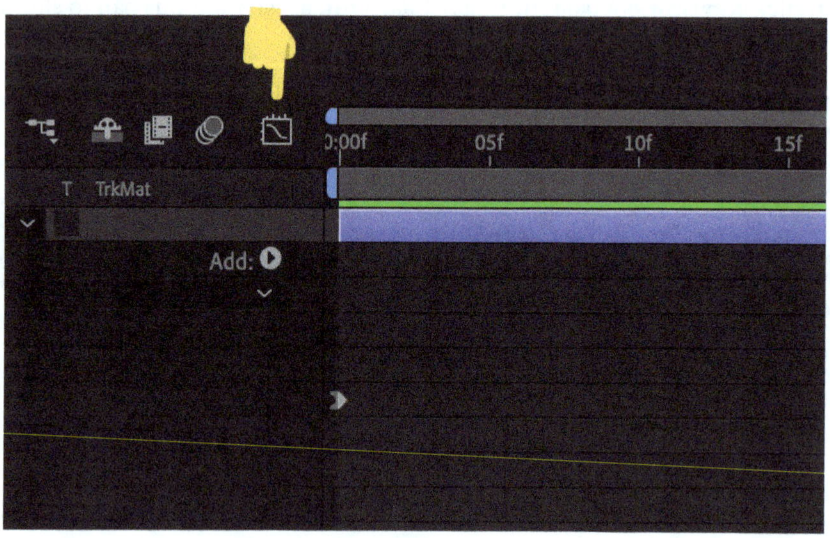

Figure 3.41 – The Graph Editor icon

When clicking on it, you'll notice that the timeline changes to a kind of graph. This is the Graph Editor. You can click again to go back to your timeline. In the **Graph Editor** panel, note a few things:

- The yellow squares represent our keyframes; as you can see, they are placed in the same timing as in our timeline (**0**, **30**, and **1**).
- The green curve represents the inbetweens on the *y* axis or, in other words, the speed of the vertical movement of the ball. By looking at the chart, we can tell that our ball decreases in speed until it hits the top and then accelerates until it hits the floor.

- The red straight line represents the inbetweens in the *x* axis. But why is it flat? Because there is no movement on the horizontal axis. Our ball is only moving up and down:

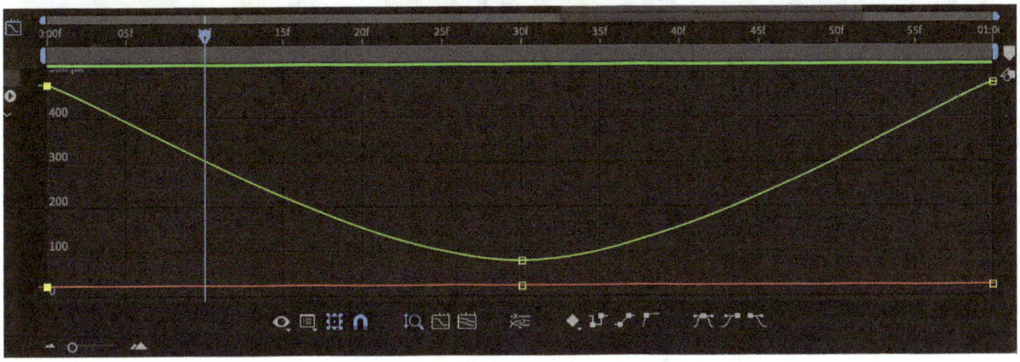

Figure 3.42 – The Graph Editor value's view

I invite you to play around to get familiar with the Editor. You'll see that you can move the keyframes around the panel by dragging them. That will change the speed and the position of the ball to create a different effect. You can also change the curves by dragging the handles and adjusting your animation.

Also, you can change the editor panel's view from **Values** to **Speed**. Just right-click anywhere in the **Graph Editor** panel to reveal a new submenu and select **Edit Speed Graph**:

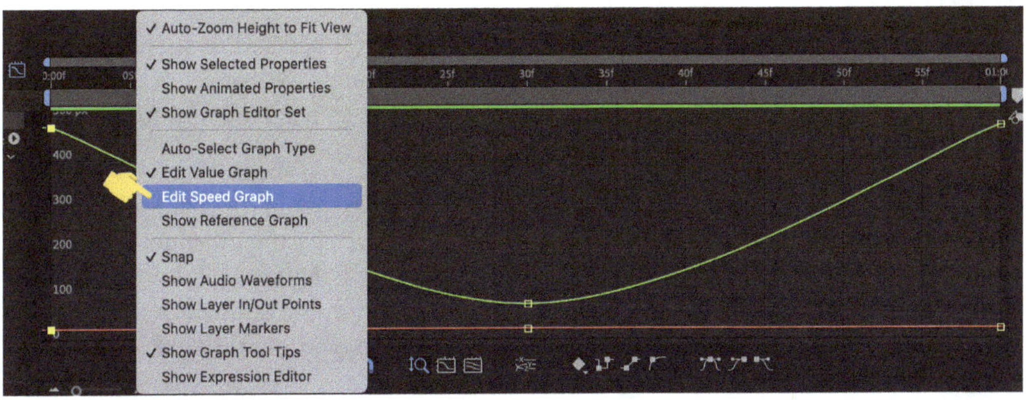

Figure 3.43 – The Graph Editor hidden menu

When selecting **Edit Speed Graph**, we can see that our panel changes to a different view. Now, instead of seeing the *x and y* axes, we just see one gray line, which represents the variation of the speed in our animation.

Again, play around with the handles and keyframes and choose the visualization you feel more comfortable working with:

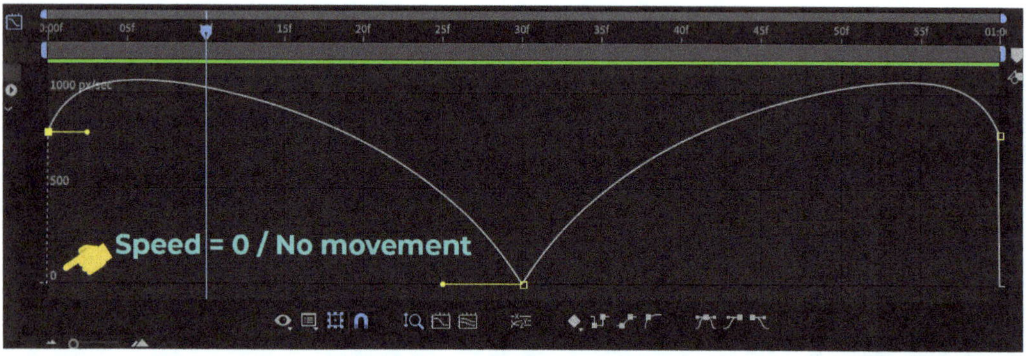

Figure 3.44 – The Graph Editor speed view

What we've just shown you, easy ease, is an ideal way to start understanding what ease is and how it works. However, once you start getting familiar with it, you'll see that it is much better to create ease on your own directly in the **Graph Editor** panel. But at this stage, we are just going to be focusing on this, which is enough for us to make our animations look better and give us enough knowledge to keep us going and learning at our own pace.

Summary

We are done! Yes, in just one chapter. Don't be surprised; as we said earlier, we've got to be practical here. There's no need to start learning every single tool, panel, action, or expression available in AE, as there are so many things we don't need to know for our Lottie animations. So, we wanted to keep it simple for you.

In this chapter, we've discovered the AE workspace area, talked about the main panels, and got experience with real files with working with compositions, the timeline, and layers. We've been through layer properties, learned what the Parent & Link feature is and how to apply it to our layers, and learned how to create our first animation while explaining how to use keyframes to finally refine it, thanks to ease and the **Graph Editor** panel.

Looking back to the first part of the book, we've come a long way. We've learned what Lottie is, the principles of animation, and the basics of Adobe AE; we are now ready to move on to the second part of the book and perform some magic. Let's get started with our animated icon! I invite you to follow me to the next chapter.

Part 2 - Cracking Lottie Animations

We will learn how to create animations in After Effects and Lottie, final Lottie deliverables and applying best UX/UI practices.

We will cover the following chapters in this section:

- *Chapter 4, Move It! Animating Our First Lottie With After Effects*
- *Chapter 5, Share It With the World: Working With LottieFiles*
- *Chapter 6, Don't Stop! Exploring Plugins and Resources That Will Keep You Going*

4

Move It! Animating Our First Lottie With After Effects

And... here we are! Ready to start our own first animated project in Adobe After Effects! Yes! It has been an exciting journey, and we've learned loads of new words, concepts, and tools. Looking back, it seems like ages ago when we started talking about Lottie, don't you think? Not because of the matter of time, but because we've learned so many new things! In the first part of the book, we learned what Lottie and LottieFiles are, we went through the history and principles of 2D classic animation, and got our hands on the Adobe After Effects working area and main animating features. Now, we are all ready and set to animate our icon.

In this chapter, we are going to go step by step through creating our animated icon. Get ready, as we are going to put everything we've learned so far on the table, all the knowledge we've gained about Lottie, classic animation, and Adobe After Effects. We will learn how to import our assets from different vector-based tools, we will create and adjust our composition, create keyframes, and change layer properties to give the illusion of animation. We will also learn how to animate a path, adjust the timing, and apply ease, based on classic animation concepts, to give our icon a more trustable movement. So, by the end of this chapter, we will have our first animated icon ready to be exported for LottieFiles.

In this chapter, we are going to cover the following topics:

- Importing vector files into our Adobe **After Effects** (**AE**) project from different design tools such as Sketch, Figma, and Adobe XD
- Setting up the composition for our animated icon
- Creating keyframes
- Animating our icon by changing layer properties
- Being time efficient by learning how to use Trim Paths and radial burst effects
- Adding ease and adjusting timing to polish our animation

Technical requirements

Remember that this chapter is a hands-on project, and in order to be able to complete it successfully, it is important you have the following tools up and running:

- Adobe AE.
- A vector illustration software of your choice. We will be focusing on Sketch, Figma, and Adobe XD:
    - **If you use Sketch**: You need the AEUX plugin for Sketch installed.
    - **If you use Figma**: You need the AEUX plugin for Figma installed.
    - **If you use Adobe XD**: There's no need to install any extra plugins.

Creating your first project in Adobe AE – an animated check icon

Cool, let me recap a bit here. Sometimes you may think, why go through all this effort to create an animation if we could just have a text or an illustration instead? Well, as we mentioned earlier, animations can be so helpful in terms of UX. They help us to talk to our users; we've learned how animation can communicate so many things, such as actions or emotions.

If we go back to our brief, remember we've decided to create a check icon that will show the user the purchase has been successfully made and the money is safe and well spent.

So, in UX terms, what sort of emotions do we want our users to feel? I guess something like the following:

- **Safety**: The purchase has been made correctly.
- **Relief**: The money hasn't been lost in the middle of the transaction.
- **Excitement**: Imagine the feeling you have after treating yourself to a new T-shirt. Exciting, right?

When animating, we are not just talking about some cool motion graphics that will show up in our app to make it look better; instead, we are talking about making our users' lives easier and happier. We are talking about making people feel better! Can you see the power we've got in our hands? So, let's not waste any more time. Let's make our users feel great!

Importing our icon to After Effects

Let's start by importing our assets to AE. To do that, we assume you already have your icon design ready in any of these three vector-based tools: Sketch, Figma, or Adobe XD.

> **Important**
> If you don't have any vector-based tool chosen yet, I would recommend using Adobe XD, which will save you time and effort. The exporting option for XD is already included in XD and there is no need to add any extra extensions or plugins. However, if you already use Sketch or Figma, no worries, we will cover that too. Also, you can find more information about how to install the plugins in *Chapter 6, Don't Stop! Exploring Plugins and Resources That Will Keep You Going*, of this book.

Importing files from Sketch to AE

In order to avoid some animation issues, I always recommend keeping the illustrations as tidy and as simple as possible. For example, some Boolean operations, text layers, or symbols can generate problems when exporting to AE.

That said, let's open our icon in Sketch. Go to the top bar menu and select **File | Open Local Document**:

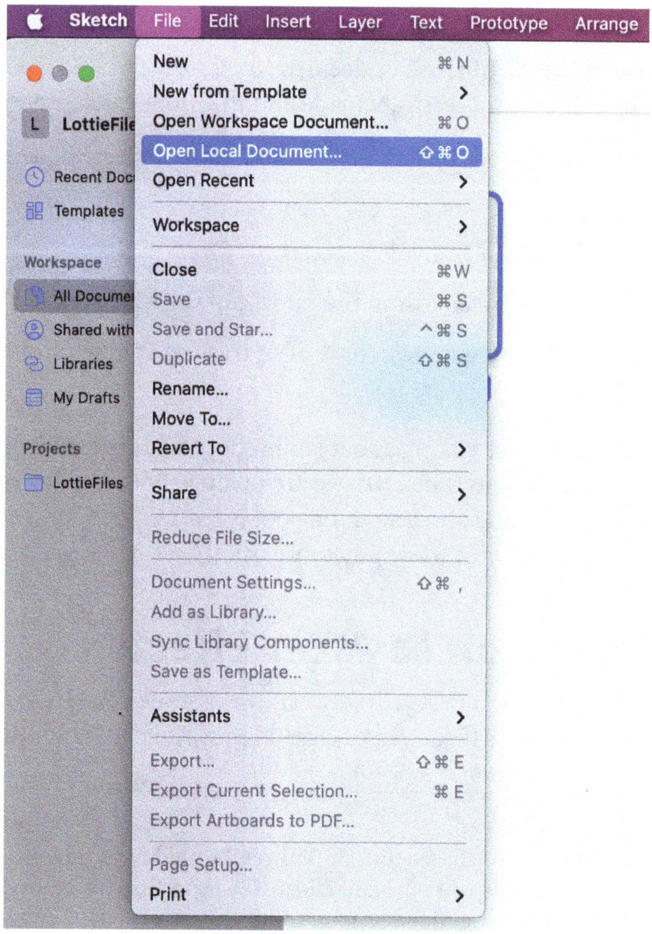

Figure 4.1 – Sketch File menu

Go to the `Files` folder provided with this book and open `lottie/chapter04/sketch/lottie_sketch`.

Now is the time to install the AEUX plugin for both Sketch and AE. You'll find more information on how to install AEUX for Sketch and AE in *Chapter 6, Don't Stop! Exploring Plugins and Resources That Will Keep You Going*.

> **Important**
>
> If you installed the plugin without following our instructions, please check the *How to set up AEUX in AE* section in *Chapter 6, Don't Stop! Exploring Plugins and Resources That Will Keep You Going,* as some options have to be selected.

Once we have our AEUX plugin installed in Sketch, let's open it up and check the panel. To do that, go to the top bar menu and select **Plugins** | **AEUX** | **Open panel**:

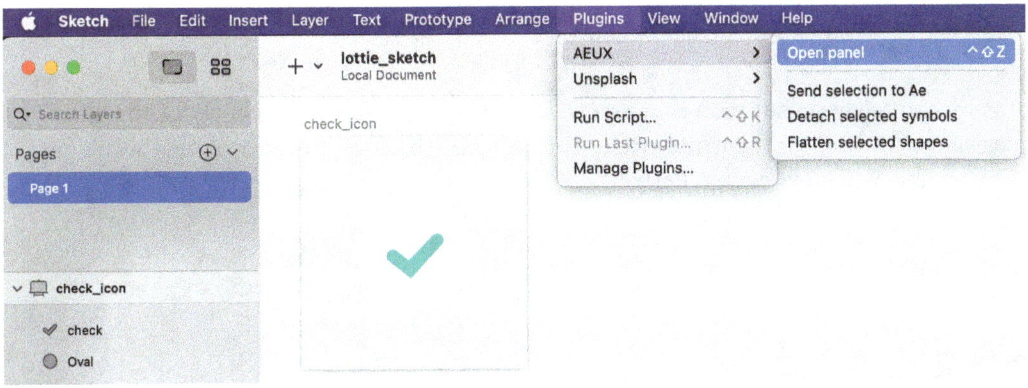

Figure 4.2 – AEUX plugin panel window

As we can see in *Figure 4.3*, this is a very simple panel with just three different options:

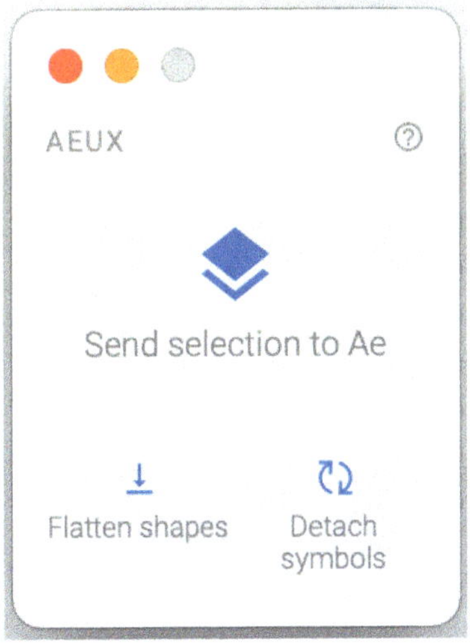

Figure 4.3 – AEUX for Sketch plugin window

- **Send selection to Ae**: This is pretty straightforward; by selecting the layers and clicking this option, we will export our illustration to AE.
- **Flatten shapes**: As we mentioned earlier, when exporting for AE, it is always a good idea to keep our illustration and layers tidy. With the **Flatten shapes** option, we can flatten our grouped or Boolean layers into a flat vector single shape and avoid AE layer issues.
- **Detach symbols**: Symbols may be confusing for AE to represent. With the **Detach symbols** option, we will remove the symbol dependence from its master so it will work better in AE.

So, as we can see here, our icon is composed of just two single layers: **check** for the blue check sign and **Oval** for the white circle. The layers are basic simple shapes that won't give us any trouble when exporting. Perfect!

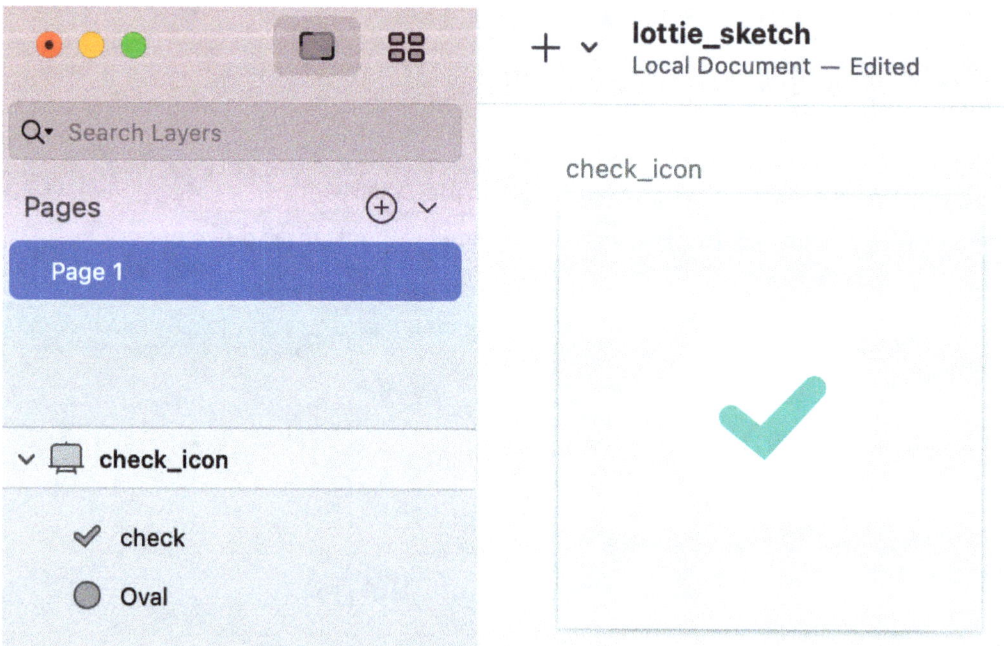

Figure 4.4 – Layers panel

Now that we've got our icon ready and tidy, let's export it to AE:

1. Open Adobe AE if you haven't done that yet.
2. Go back to Sketch and select both layers at the same time: **check** and **Oval**.
3. Click **Send selection to Ae** in the AEUX panel.

4. Go to Adobe AE and check that the files have been imported:

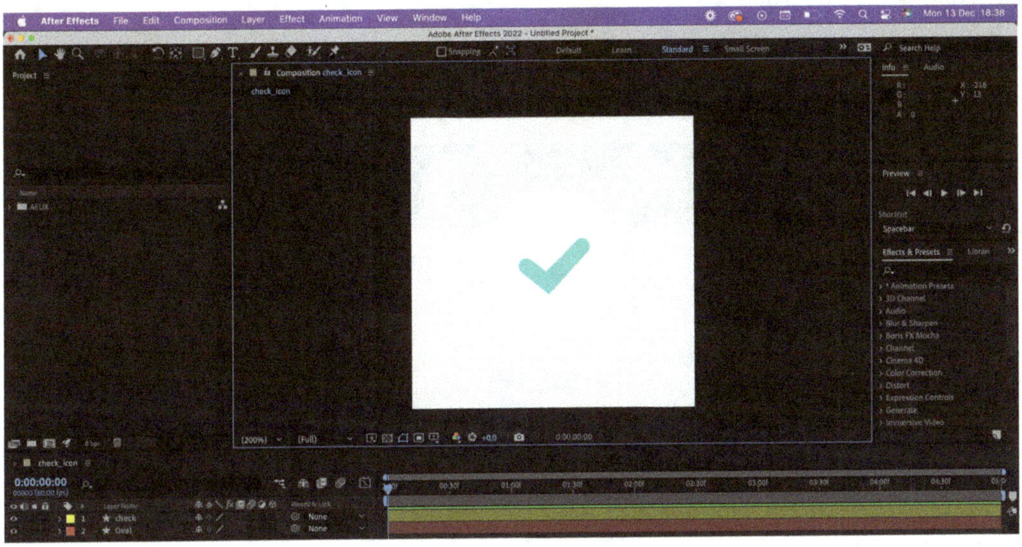

Figure 4.5 – Imported layers from Sketch to AE

Great! We've got our icon perfectly imported into AE and ready to be animated. Just save it! Now, let's see how to do the same using the Figma tool.

Importing files from Figma to AE

To export your illustrations from Figma to AE, the process is quite similar. You can go to *Chapter 6, Don't Stop! Exploring Plugins and Resources That Will Keep You Going*, where you'll find a guide on how to install the plugin for Figma and also AE. Remember, if you have installed the plugin on your own, please check the *How to set up AEUX in AE* section to be sure the selected options are the same as you have.

Now that you have your plugins up and running, let's open the icon in Figma. How to do that? Follow these instructions:

1. Open Figma.
2. Choose the **Import file** option from the home page:

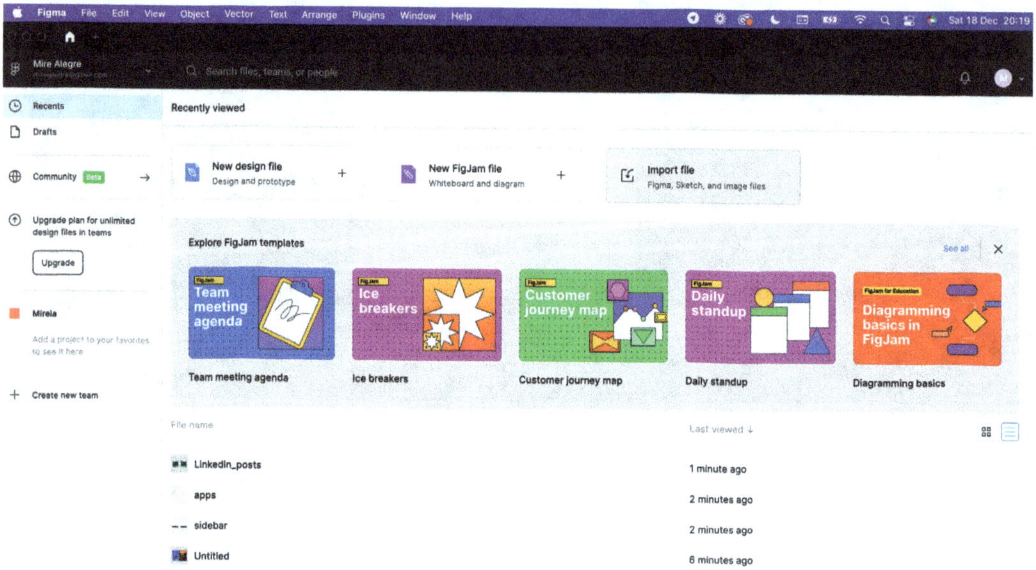

Figure 4.6 – Figma home page

3. Search for the `lottie/chapter04/Figma` folder from the provided files.
4. Open the `lottie_Figma.fig` file.
5. Click the **Done** button. The file will appear on Figma's home page, as shown in *Figure 4.7*:

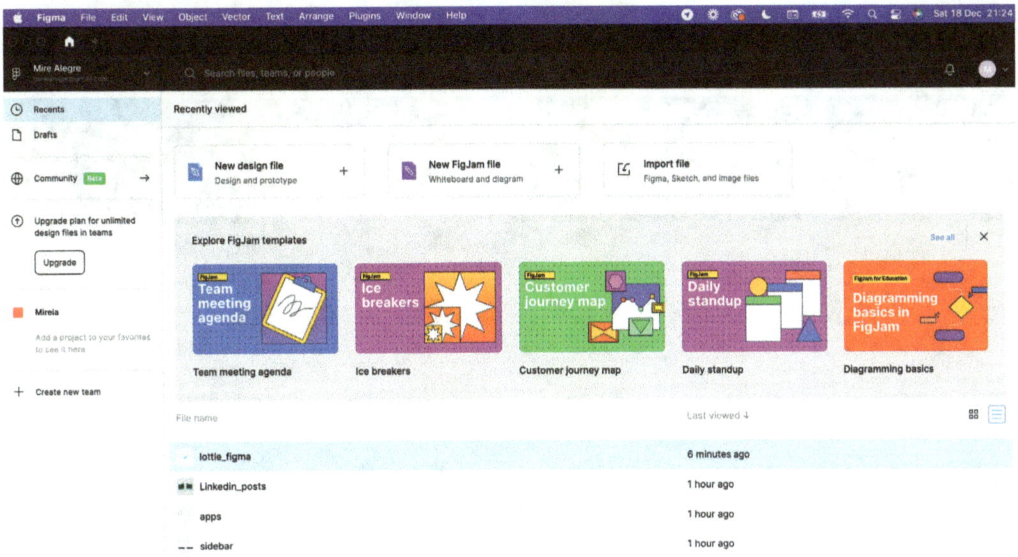

Figure 4.7 – Figma home page and provided Figma imported file

6. Double-click on `lottie_Figma` to finally open the file, as shown in *Figure 4.8*:

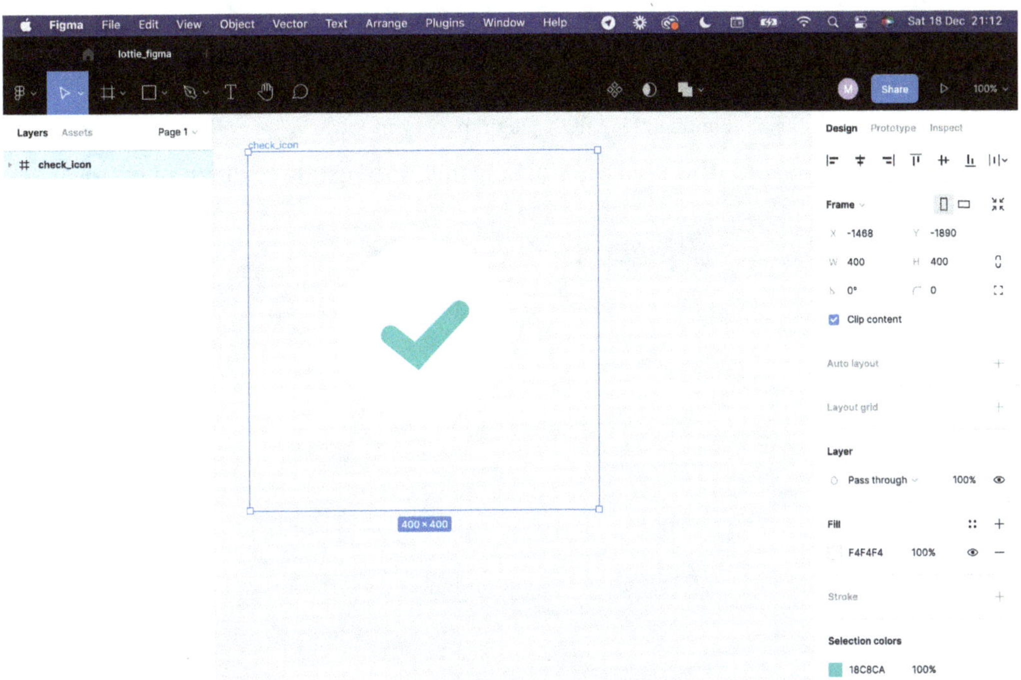

Figure 4.8 – Icon file

Cool! Now, we've got `lottie_Figma.fig` imported.

7. Let's open the AEUX panel and check out the options available to export our icon to AE. Go to **Plugins | Development | AEUX**.

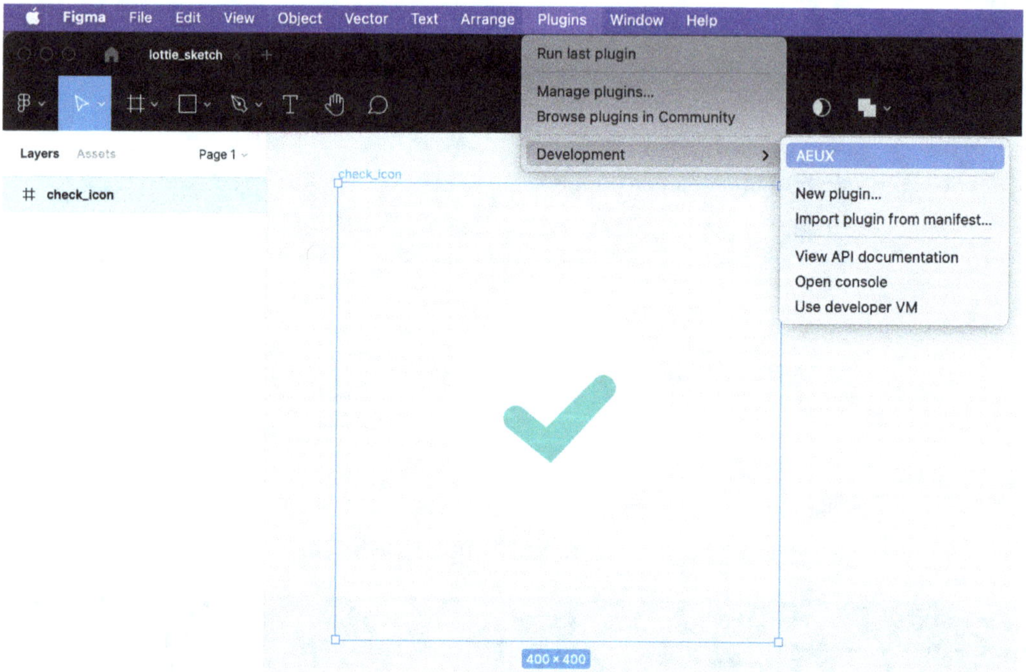

Figure 4.9 – AEUX plugin panel window

As we can see in *Figure 4.10*, this is a very simple panel with just three different options:

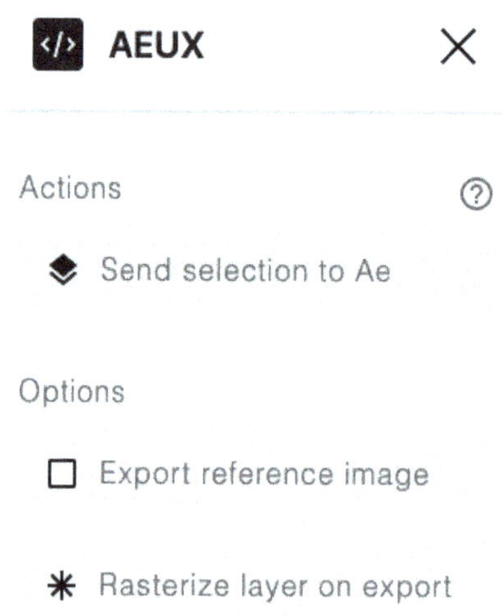

Figure 4.10 – AEUX for Figma plugin panel window

- **Send selection to Ae**: This works the same way as in Sketch. It is pretty straightforward; by selecting the layers and clicking this option, we will export our illustration to AE.
- **Export reference image**: There are a few known alignment issues with layers from Figma, such as text layers and rotated images. Enable this checkbox to generate an image overlay of the Figma frame to allow for manual alignment.
- **Rasterize layer on export**: It is possible to automatically send anything in Figma to AE as a PNG file. This becomes very useful for anything that doesn't need to be animated and could be optimized by flattening it down to a single image.

As we mentioned earlier, it is very important to keep our illustration as simple as possible, as some effects can generate issues. You'll notice our illustration is very simple; it is made of just two layers named **check** and **Oval**, and that's all we need.

Now that our icon is done and tidy, let's export it to AE:

1. Open Adobe AE if you haven't done that yet.
2. Go back to Figma and select both layers at the same time: **check** and **Oval**.
3. Click on the **Send selection to Ae** AEUX panel option.
4. Go to Adobe AE and check that the files have been imported:

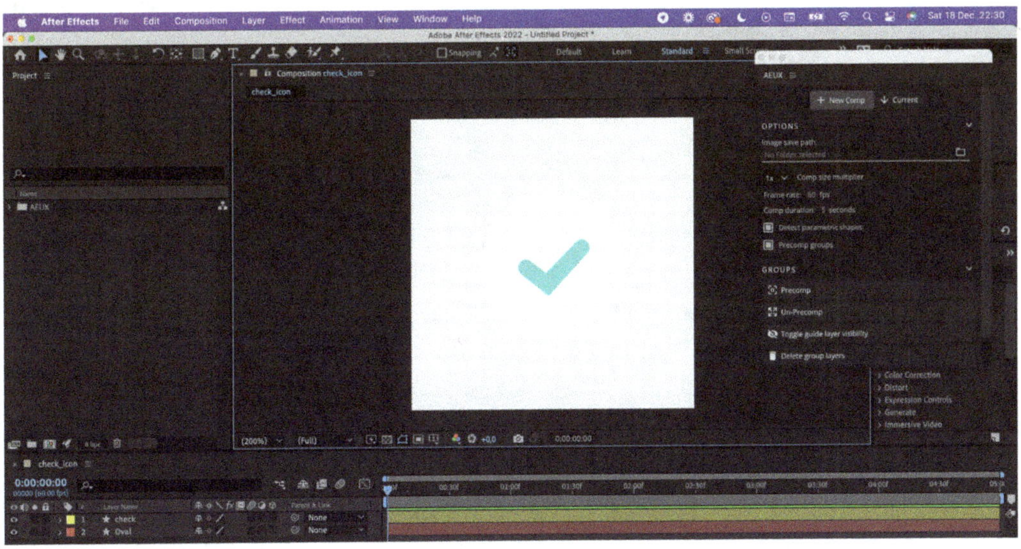

Figure 4.11 – Imported files from Figma to AE

Cool! We've got our icon ready to go in AE; now, remember to save it! Let's see how to do the same with XD.

Exporting assets from XD to AE

Exporting your icon from XD to AE is probably the easiest way that exists right now. There is no need to install any plugin as Adobe XD already includes an exporting option for AE. Let's have a look. Let's open the XD file provided with this book.

Let's open our icon in Adobe XD. To do this, just follow the next steps:

1. Open XD.
2. Go to **File** | **Open from Your Computer...**.

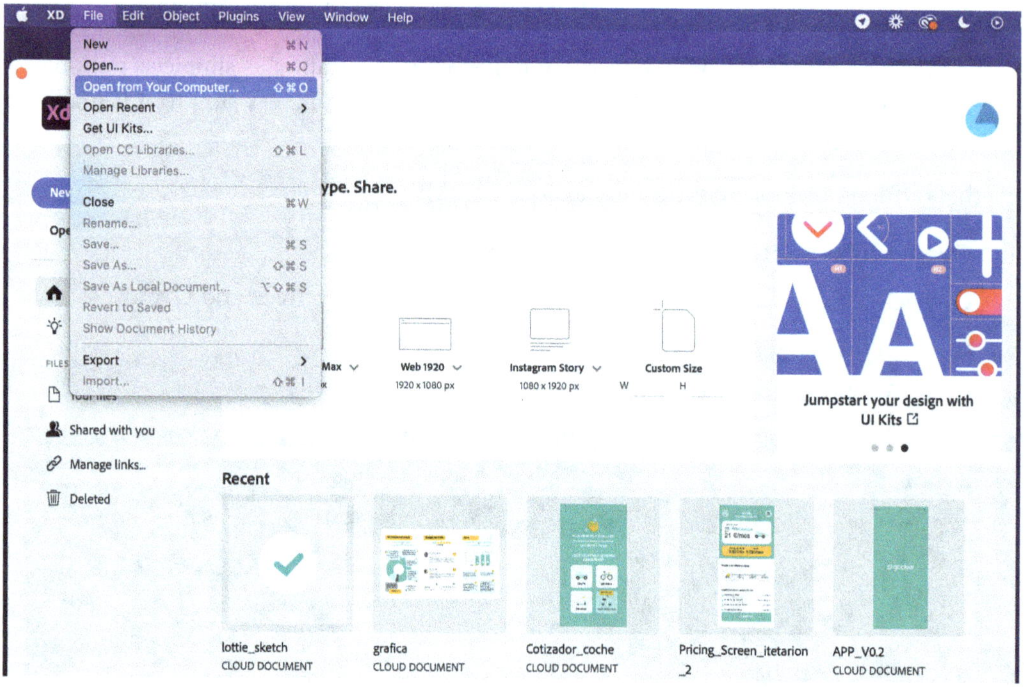

Figure 4.12 – XD home page

3. Search for the `lottie/chapter04/xd` folder from the provided files.

4. Open the `lottie_xd.xd` file:

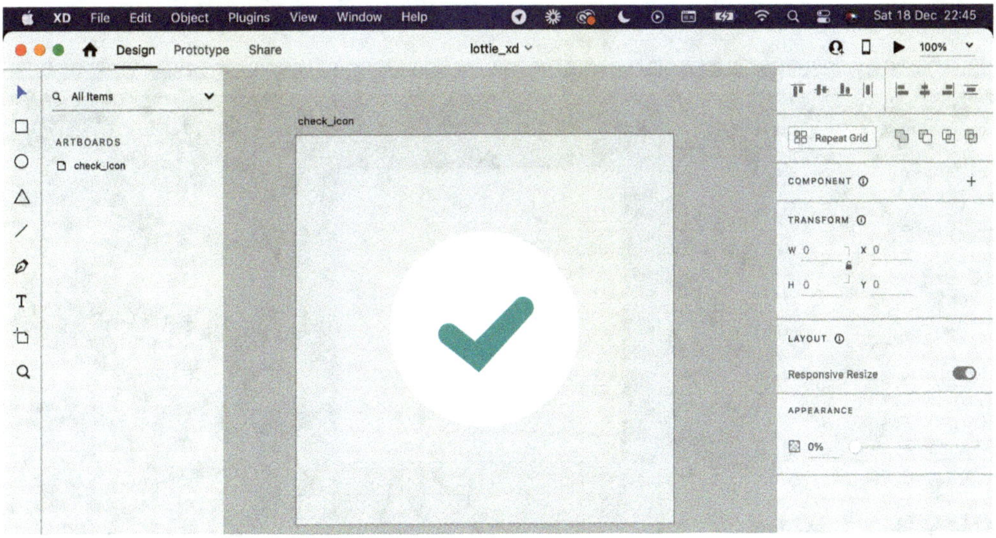

Figure 4.13 – XD lottie_xd icon file

Now, you'll see how easy it is to export our icon to AE:

1. Select the entire layout area by clicking on its name.
2. Go to the top bar menu and select **File | Export | After Effects...**:

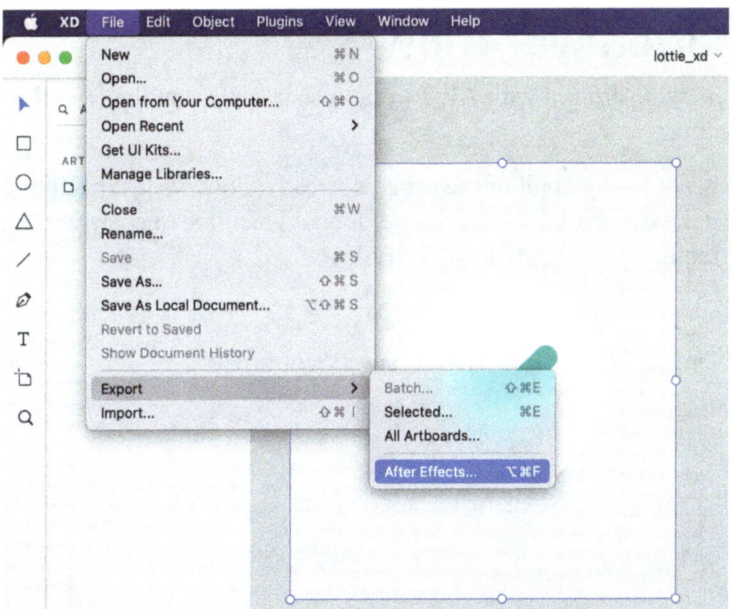

Figure 4.14 – Export option from XD

And, voilà! AE will open automatically, and our icon will be ready to be animated. Easy, right?

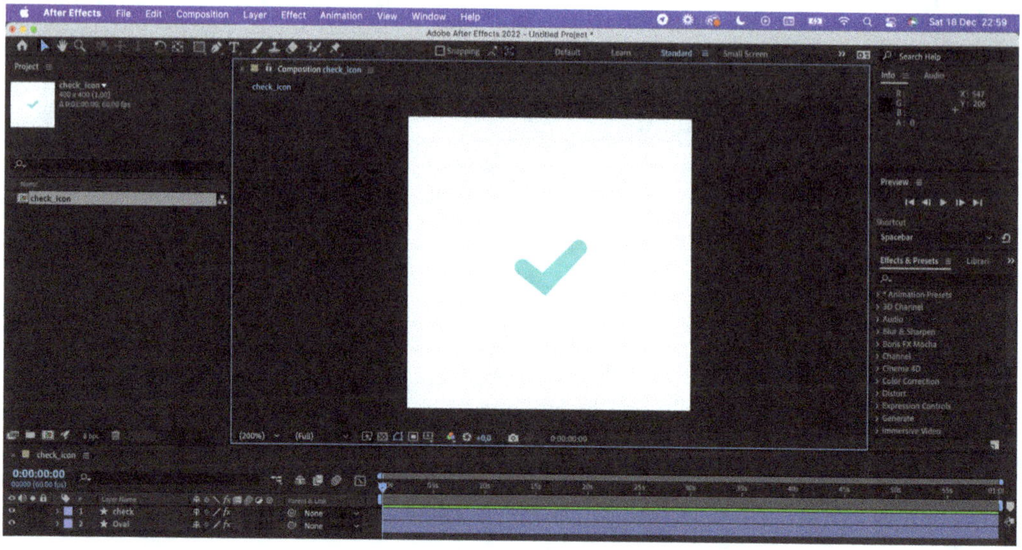

Figure 4.15 – XD icon imported to AE

Save the project and let's start animating!

UX animation workflow

Before we start messing around with AE, I want to share with you the workflow I normally use when animating.

You'll see we've been through half of the process already; now, we just need to bring it to life. And please, take this workflow as a suggestion and feel free to change it in any way to meet your own requirements. Here is my workflow:

1. UX research to find user pain points.
2. Spot problems/find solutions based on users' comments.
3. Wireframing.
4. Storyboard.
5. Low fidelity design to test again.

6. Design.
7. Export assets to AE.

We have already covered all of these:

1. Set up compositions.
2. Create keyframes.
3. Modify layers.
4. Adjust timing.
5. Add ease.

We will cover the following in *Chapter 5, Share It With the World: Working With LottieFiles*:

1. Export as `.json` for LottieFiles
2. Preview in LottieFiles
3. Hand off to developers

I know, this process might look a bit long, but this is just an example that covers the whole process of a complex project. Sometimes, there won't be any need to run user interviews, or at some point, you won't need to draw a storyboard or wireframes as these will be in your head.

Let's go back and see where we were, let's see where we left our storyboard. Let's recap; what was our icon doing?

1. Our icon will increase from 0% to 110% approximately.
2. Bubbles come out from the Oval-like sparkles.
3. Oval goes back to real size (100%) and the bubbles start to disappear.
4. While the bubbles disappear, the *check* symbol starts to draw.

5. Finally, the *check* symbol is revealed at 100%:

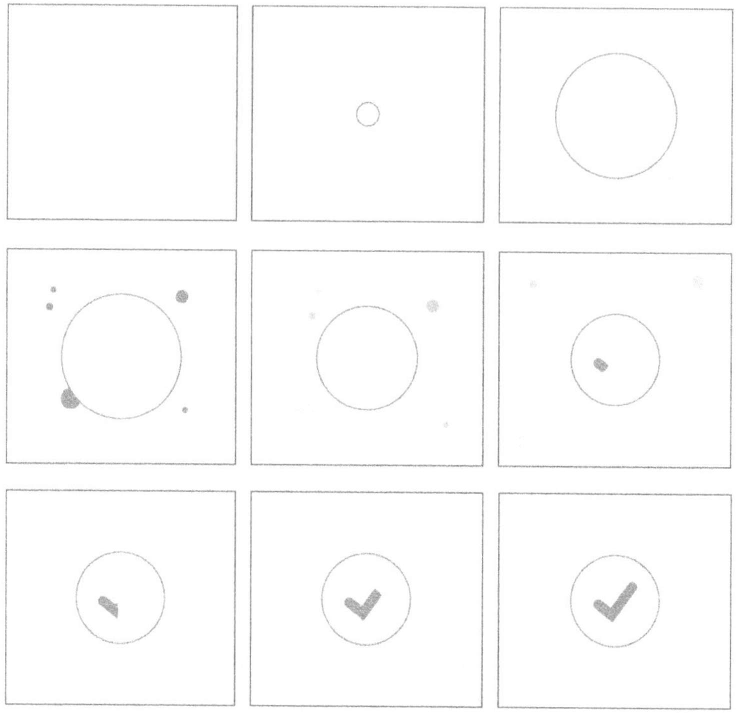

Figure 4.16 – Our storyboard

At this point, we have given you all the elements, resources, and tools necessary to have everything ready to start animating. We've been through a few main UX concepts, learned how to import our files to AE, checked one of many animation workflows, and gone through the storyboard again to refresh our minds.

So, now that we've got a pretty clear idea in our heads and on paper about how the animation is going to look, what needs to be done, and the steps to follow, let's start animating! Let's create our compositions.

Adjusting our icon composition settings

Remember back in *Chapter 3, Learning the Tools: Getting Familiar With After Effects*, we talked about compositions, what they are, and what we use them for? Cool. Now is the time to start putting everything we've learned into context.

When we import our icon to AE, it normally gets imported as a **composition**. Remember, compositions are shown in the **Project** panel, and to open one, we just need to double-click on it.

Now, how is this composition imported to AE? Are the main specifications of this composition the ones we want? Let's check it out. Let's check our **Composition Settings** icon:

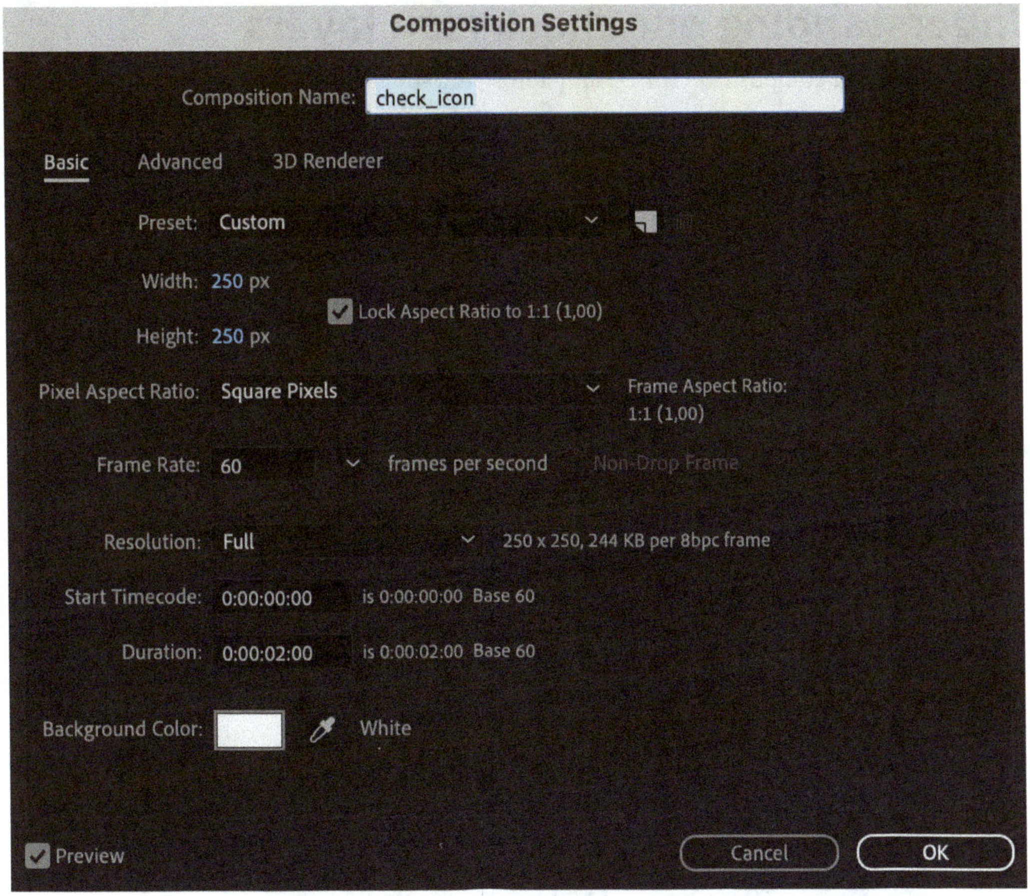

Figure 4.17 – Composition Settings window view

Let's adjust some of these settings. Remember how to do that? Here are the instructions:

1. Select your composition from the **Project** panel.
2. Select **Composition** | **Composition Settings** from the top menu.
3. Adjust the composition size to **250** x **250** px.
4. Set the frame rate to **60** frames per second.
5. Set the duration to **2** seconds.
6. Change the background color to `#989898`. Notice that the background color won't be exported, but I'm changing it so we can see the white circle better.

That was easy, right? Now that we've got our composition ready, let's move to the **Layers** panel.

Understanding our check icon layers

We've got our icon composition sorted and adjusted to our needs; now is the time to understand how our icon is built in terms of layers, so, let's check what we've got in our layers panel.

As you can see in *Figure 4.18*, when we check the Layer panel, we find the same two layers we had in our illustration file that we just imported, **check** and **Oval**.

Just to be clear, **check** is a *stroke* and **Oval** is a *shape*. This is important and will help us to give the effect that we want to the **check** layer. But, don't worry for now; we will see that a few steps further in this section.

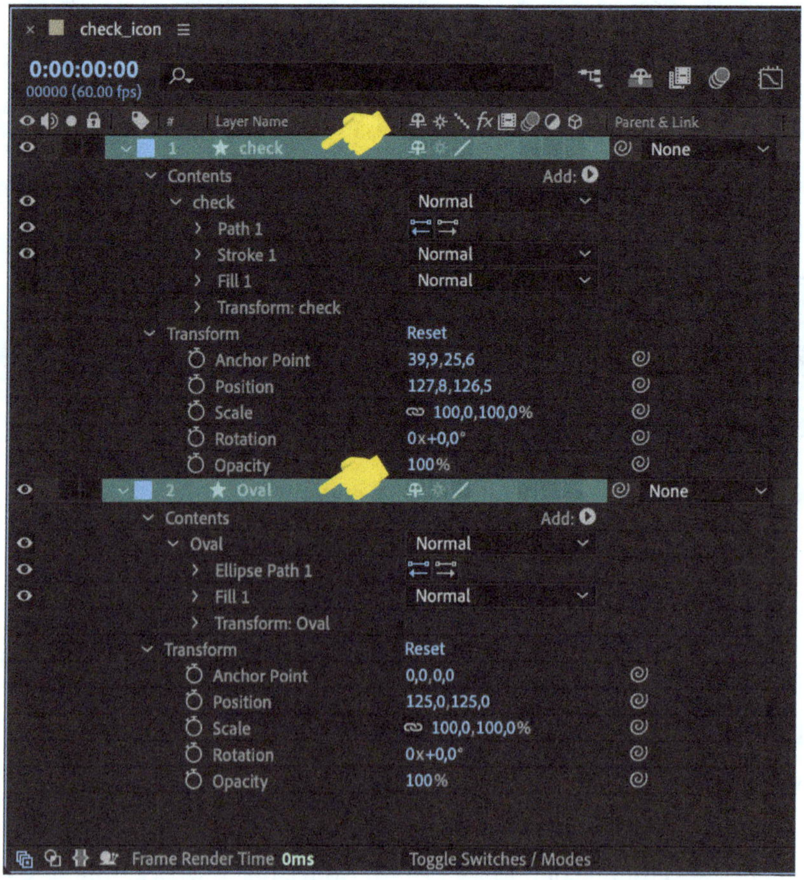

Figure 4.18 – Layer panel with check and Oval layer properties

Also, as you can see in the preceding screenshot, each of our layers has a lot of sub-layers. We are going to be seeing this in the next steps.

But first, let's recap. Remember, our animation will start with the oval getting bigger.

> **Suggestion**
>
> Since we are going to be focusing on the **Oval** for now, I recommend blocking and hiding the **check** layer as it is not relevant at this stage. Of course, we've just got two layers and there's probably no need to start hiding or blocking other layers, but when we start working with some more complicated projects, this is good to have as a habit.

Click the little eye and lock icons from the Layer panel to hide and block any layer you want, as shown in the following screenshot:

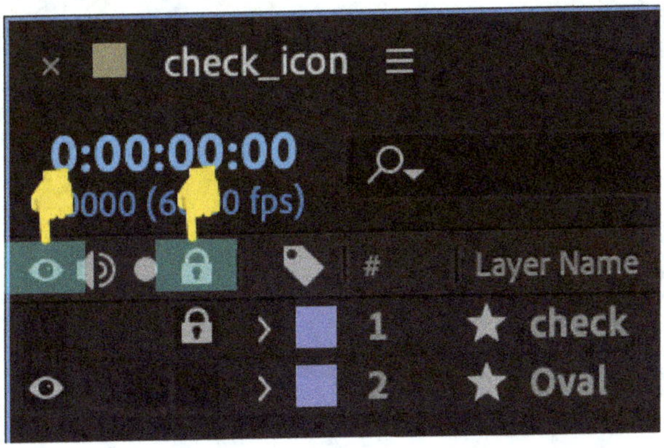

Figure 4.19 – Eye and lock icons

Adding Keyframes

Great! Now that we are more familiar with our layers, and the **Oval** is on its own, and there's no danger that we are going to move the **check** icon, even by mistake, let's start creating some movement.

Remember back in *Chapter 3, Learning the Tools: Getting Familiar With After Effects*, when we talked about keyframes? Exactly! Keyframes are used to create movement and to do that, we need at least two of them: one keyframe as a starting point and one as an ending point.

That said, we want our **Oval** to grow from 0 to 100%, right? Any idea about how to do that? Sure, we will create two keyframes and change the scale of the **Oval**, so one keyframe will be 0% and the other 100%. Let's do that now.

Changing scale

We are going to start by animating the scale. How do we do that? By adjusting the scale's **Oval** properties, at specific keyframes. Here's how to do it:

1. Go to the **Layer** panel.
2. Open the **Oval** layer's **Transform** properties. You could do that by selecting the layer and pressing *S*, but we will talk more about shortcuts in the following sections.

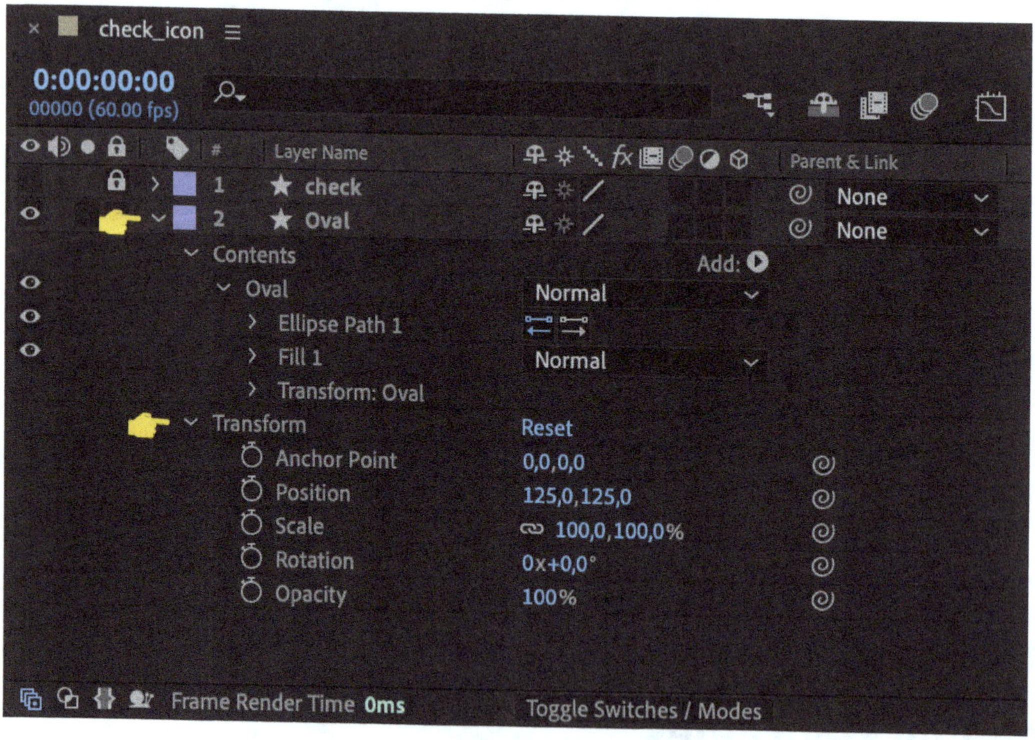

Figure 4.20 – Scale values for the Oval layer

3. Place the time slider at **0** frames.

4. Click on the stopwatch of **Scale** to create our first keyframe:

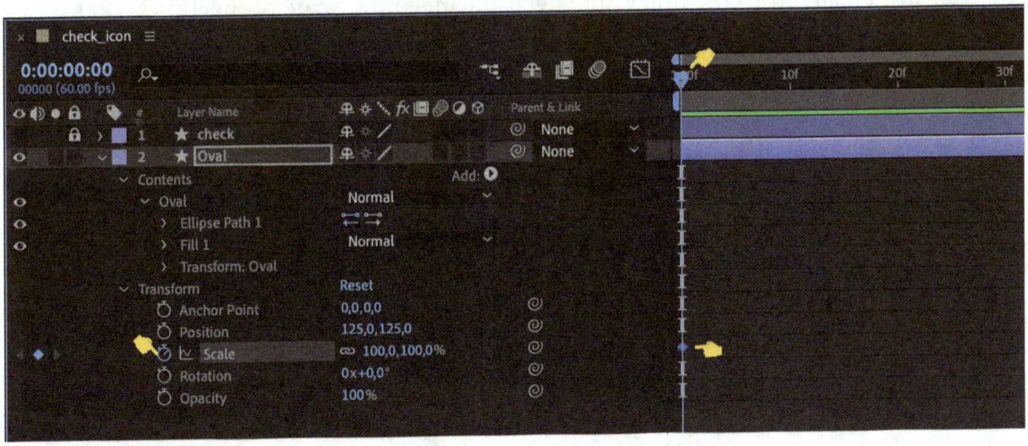

Figure 4.21 – New keyframe for the Scale property

5. Move the time slider to frame **30**.
6. Click on the little diamond at the left of the **Scale** property to create our second keyframe:

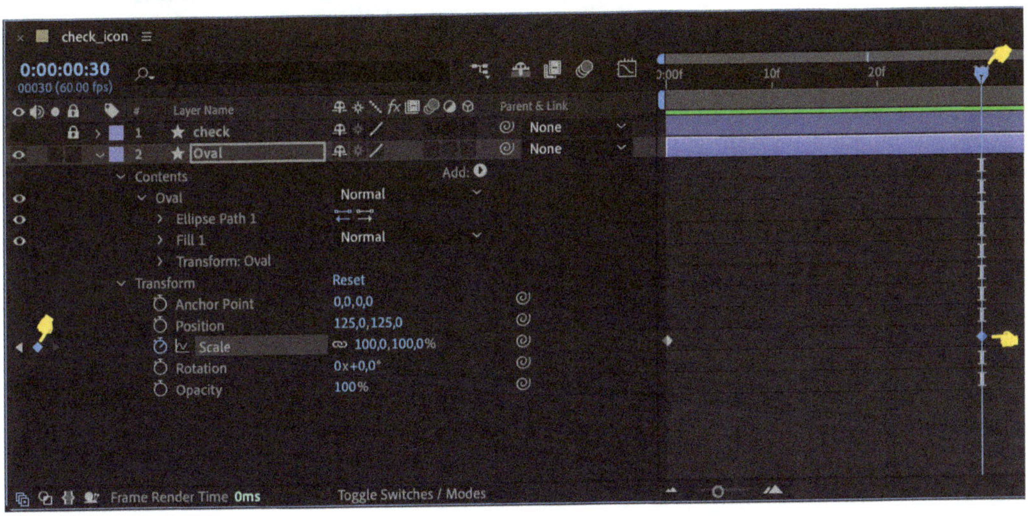

Figure 4.22 – Second keyframe

Now, let's move the time slider left and right; can you notice anything different? Of course not. We've just created the keyframes but haven't changed the **Scale** property yet. Let's do that as follows:

1. Move the time slider to frame **0**.
2. Click on the keyframe we've just created.
3. Set the **Scale** property's percentage to **0%**:

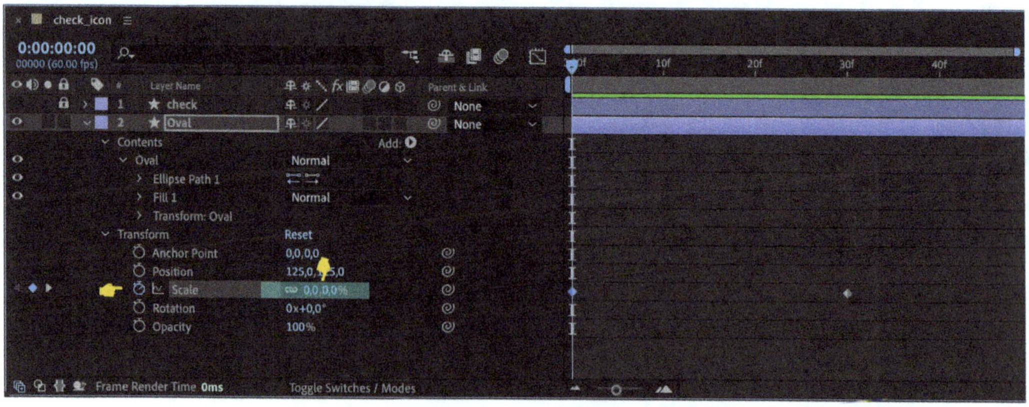

Figure 4.23 – Scale value to 0%

4. Press the spacebar or move your time slider from left to right; is anything happening now? Yes! Our icon is finally doing something!
5. Place the time slider back at **0** and press the spacebar. Do that a few times to check the animation; what do you think? Is the timing correct? It is maybe too slow? No worries, we will adjust that later when we talk about Ease.

Now, going back to our storyboard, we've defined the **Oval** as scaling up to 110-120% and then going back to 100%. But, why are we doing that? Remember when we talked about 2D animation principles? For this little icon animation, we will be applying the **Exaggeration** and **Stretch and Squash** principles to our **Oval**, to give an idea of flexibility, mass, weight, and speed. So, simply exaggerating the size of it will give this impression.

How to do that? Easy. Follow these steps:

1. Move the time slider to frame **25**.
2. Click on the diamond to create a new keyframe.
3. Set the scale to 120%.

Press the spacebar to play our animation again. What do you think? With just this little tweak, our animation looks more real now; of course, the timing is still not good and is missing some **Ease**, but we are getting there.

Let's stick to the **Oval**. Let's adjust the timing. To do that, we just need to drag our keyframes. I encourage you to play around and move them around the timeline to see how **Oval** behaves. I'll set my **Oval** keyframes between frame **0**, frame **18**, and frame **21**:

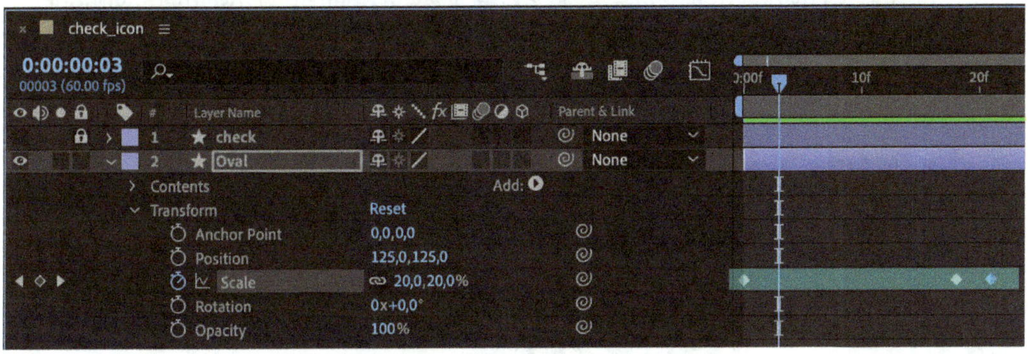

Figure 4.24 – Scale keyframes

Let's move the time slider to **0** and play it again a few times. What do you think? It looks better now, right? What about scaling up and down, maybe we could adjust the size a little bit? Let's adjust the second keyframe to make it subtle, the one that scales up to 120%, and take it down to 110%. Play again, and... it now looks smoother. Right! Let's keep moving! Let's tweak the **Opacity** property to make our illustration even smoother.

Adjusting the Opacity

Now that we've got the **Scale** property as we want it, let's adjust the opacity. To do that, we are going to follow the same steps as we did in the previous section. Of course, we could have done both at the same time, but I preferred to show you step by step; there will be plenty of time to do things quicker, but we want to have the basics clear, right?

> **Important**
>
> From now on, I'm going to start introducing some shortcuts that will save you tons of time and will help you be more productive. The shortcuts I'm using here are for macOS. Most of them are the same for macOS and Windows; however, if you are using a Windows system and you are not sure which shortcut to use, check *Chapter 6, Don't Stop! Exploring Plugins and Resources That Will Keep You Going*, for a list of the most common and useful shortcuts for macOS and Windows.

That said, let's change the opacity:

1. Select the **Oval** layer.
2. Press *T* to reveal the **Opacity** property (*T* stands for **Opacity**, *A* for **Anchor Point**, *S* for **Scale**, *P* for **Position**, and *R* for **Rotation**).
3. Press *Shift* + *S* to show the **Scale** keyframes as well. We want to have that layer visible too, so by pressing *Shift* + *A*, *S*, *P*, or *R* we will open and close them without closing the rest.
4. Place the time slider at keyframe **0**. We can move backward and forward between keyframes by pressing *K* to move to the next keyframe and *J* to the previous one.
5. Press the **Opacity** layer stopwatch to create our keyframe. We can also do that by pressing *Option* + *T*.
6. Change the **Opacity** value down to `40`%, for example:

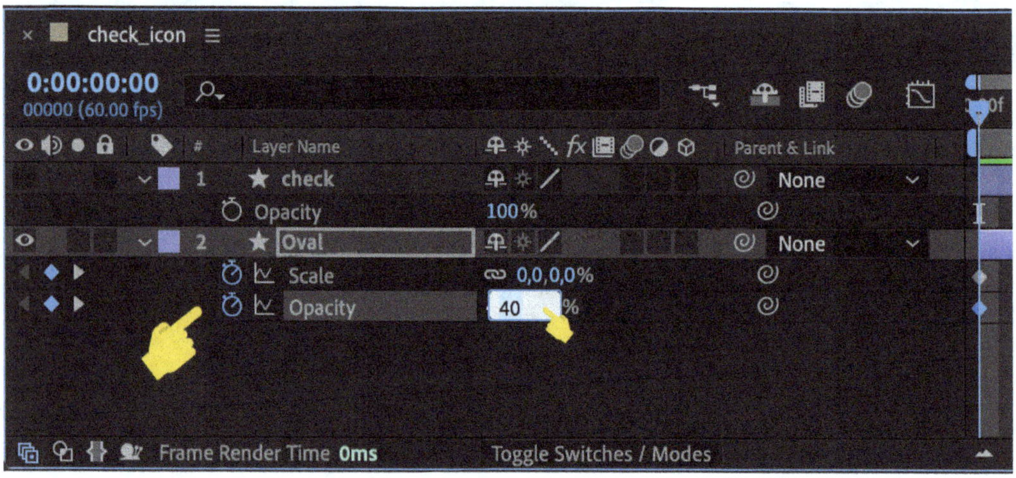

Figure 4.25 – Opacity value

Nice! That's the first keyframe created with a value of 40% opacity. Let's create a second keyframe:

1. Move the time slider to the next keyframe by pressing *K*.
2. Press ⌘ + *T* to create a new keyframe or click on the little diamond icon as we did earlier.

3. Set the **Opacity** value to `100%`.

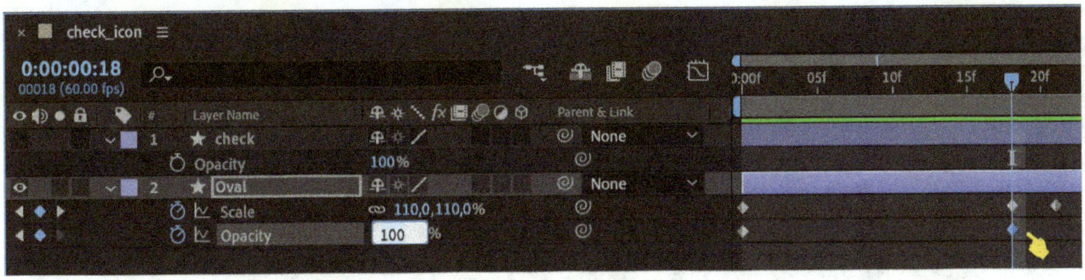

Figure 4.26 – Second keyframe opacity property value set to 100%

4. Let's move the time slider to **0** and press the spacebar to check our animation again.

Looks good to me, at least for now. Once we add some ease to the animation, it will look much more realistic and flexible. But, let's go first to animate **check**.

So, **check** behaves differently; it doesn't scale up or down or fade in, and is not rotating or moving either. What we've decided **check** will do is draw itself. How do we do that? Well, I'm going to show you how to use **Trim Paths**.

Trim Paths

To show and hide a path or reveal a part of it, we could be working with masks; however, Lottie doesn't work very well with them, at least not yet. Using masks can get us in trouble so we are going to try to avoid them and try something else.

Another option could be to draw our **check** animation frame by frame, so the following keyframe always shows a little bit more of the drawing than the first one, but this would be very time-consuming!

This is where Trim Paths comes into the picture. Using this option can be very helpful and time-saving. Let's see what this can do for us:

1. Block the **Oval** layer. In that case, we are not going to hide this layer as it is behind the **check** layer.
2. Show and unlock the **check** layer by pressing the little eye and lock icon.
3. Open the **check** layer.

4. Open the **Contents** properties and close everything else:

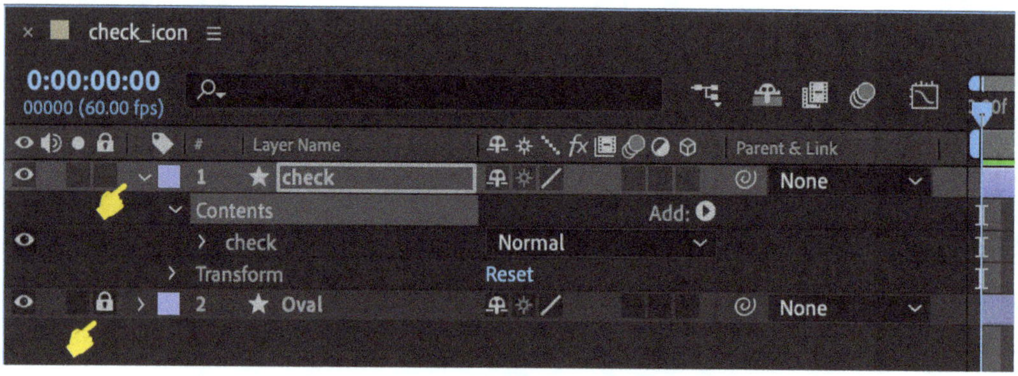

Figure 4.27 – Contents properties

5. Click on the **Add arrow** button and select the **Trim Paths** option:

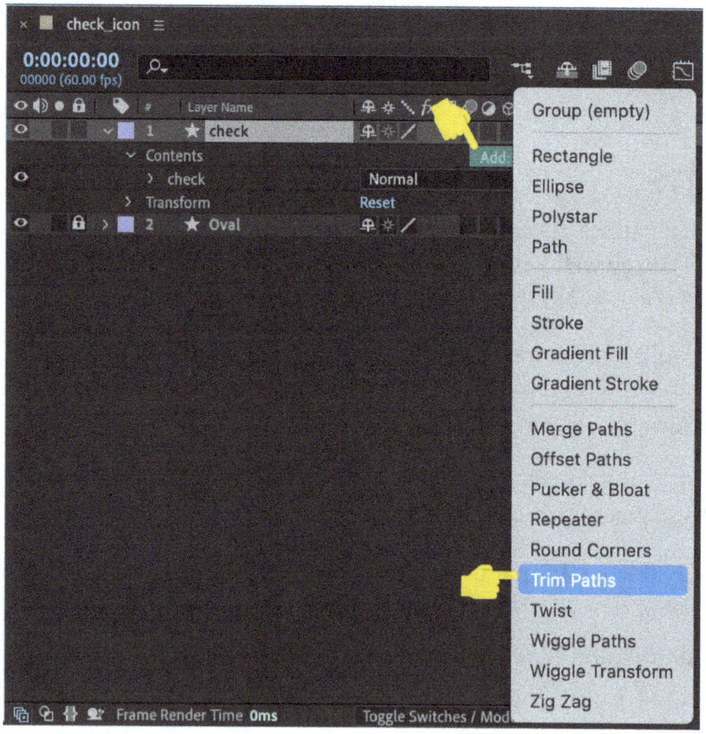

Figure 4.28 – Selecting Trim Paths

Now, let's check our Layer panel; what happened there? As you can see, a layer called **Trim Paths 1** has appeared. Let's open it up by clicking on the little arrow. A few different options come up; what are these?

These new options will let us decide whether the **check** path starts drawing itself from the beginning of the path or the end. Instead of a drawing effect, it is more of an erasing effect.

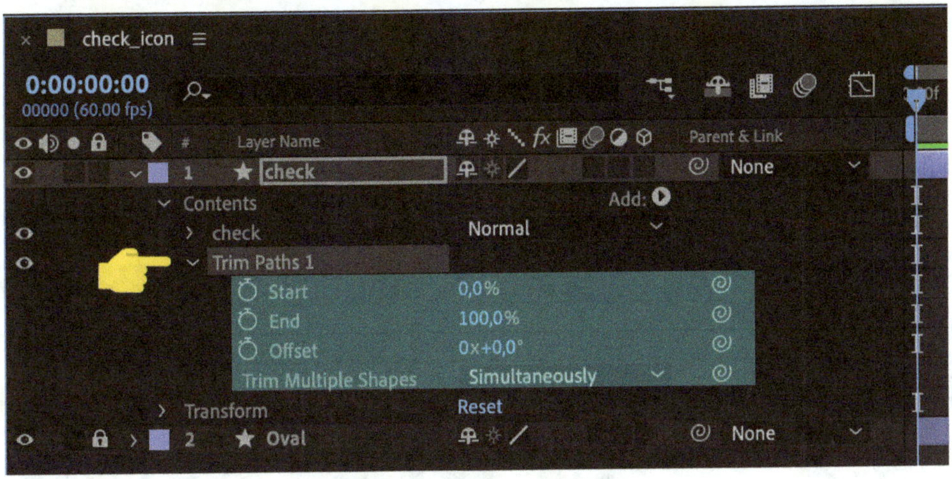

Figure 4.29 – Trim Path options

Let's mess around a bit with these options:

1. Place the time slider on keyframe **0**.
2. Create a new keyframe at the **Start** layer.
3. Set the **Start** value to **0**.
4. Place the time slider on keyframe **30**.
5. Create a new keyframe.
6. Set the **Start** value to `100%`.
7. Move the time slider back to **0**.
8. Press the spacebar to check the animation.

What's happening here? It looks like **check** is doing what we wanted but the other way around. Instead of drawing itself, it is erasing itself. Right, this feature can be a bit confusing sometimes, but don't get frustrated! It took me a while to understand the logic behind it, and even now, sometimes I have to try it a few times to get it right. So, I encourage you to play around with the **Start** and **End** values to get used to the effect and its behavior.

Now let's swap the values and try to get it right:

1. Let's set up the **Start** value at keyframe **0** to `100%`.
2. Move to the next frame and set the **Start** value to **0**.

3. Press the spacebar and check it out.

   Great! Now, the **check** icon is doing it right. It starts from nothing to drawing itself, as if someone was writing it, right? We've got it! However, the animation is not placed in the right place.

   Notice that the **check** animation is starting before the **Oval** is 100% on screen. If we take a look at our timeline (see *Figure 4.30*), we can see that both layers have the keyframes within the same time. Both are starting at frame **0**, which is why the check icon is playing at the same time as the **Oval**.

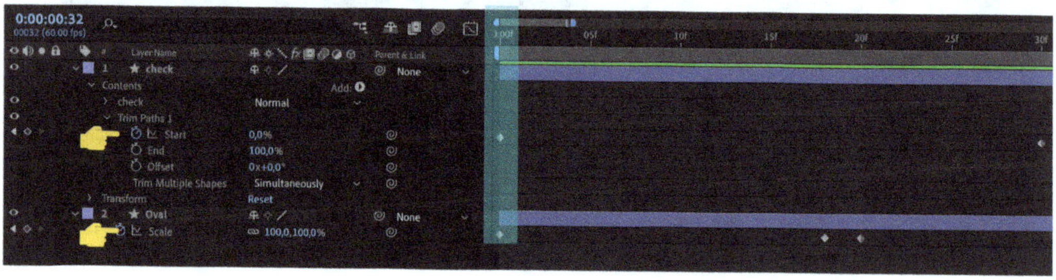

Figure 4.30 – Keyframes position on the timeline

   Remember that when we defined our storyboard, we decided **check** was going to be drawn after the **Oval** was shown on screen. So, to do that, we need to adjust a couple of things:

4. Unlock the **Oval** layer.
5. Select the **Oval** layer and press *S* to show the **Scale** property.

Let's check our keyframes on the Layer panel. We can see both animations are starting at frame **0**. Instead, based on our storyboard, the **check** animation should start once the **Oval** is fully 100% on screen. That means, we need to move the **check** keyframes to the end of the **Oval** animation. We can do that by selecting both the **check** keyframes and just dragging them to the right. You'll know both keyframes are selected as they both will be blue:

1. Select both keyframes and drag them to the right.

2. Press the spacebar and check the animation:

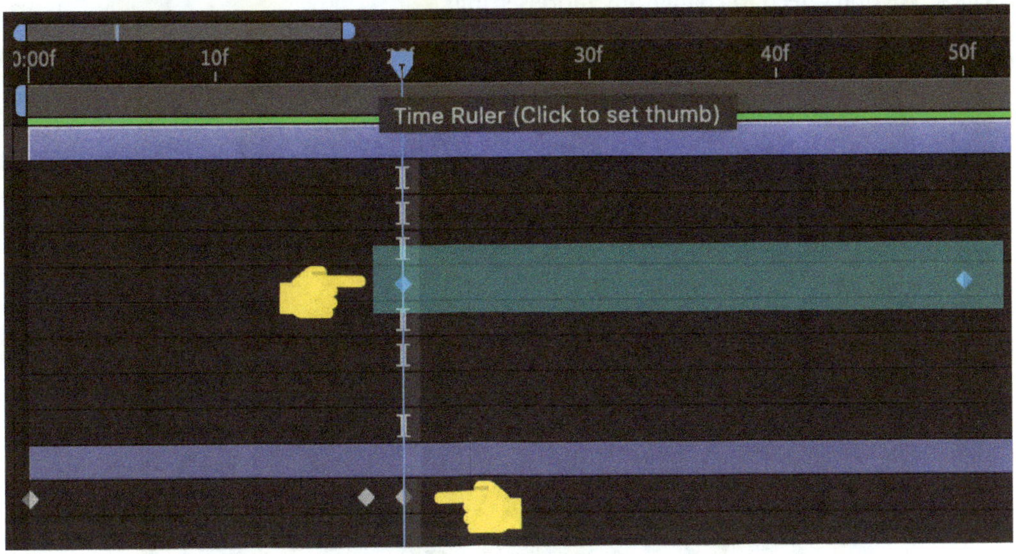

Figure 4.31 – Check keyframes

Cool! Looks perfect to me now! However, it looks a bit slow, don't you think?

3. Select the second **check** keyframe.
4. Drag it to frame **35** approximately.
5. Press the spacebar to play the animation.

Perfect, we've got it! We are getting there. Now, we are going to add the sparks.

Working with radial bursts

To add some fun to our animation, we are going to add little sparks coming out of **Oval**. To do that, we could animate each individual sparkle on its own, drawing little circles, and changing the **Position**, **Scale**, and **Opacity** values for each of them. However, we are going to try something different here. I'm going to teach you how to create a **radial burst**, a really cool effect that is going to save us a lot of time.

So, let's do it! Let's start by creating a new composition by pressing ⌘ + *N* and naming it `Sparks`. We don't need to change any more settings.

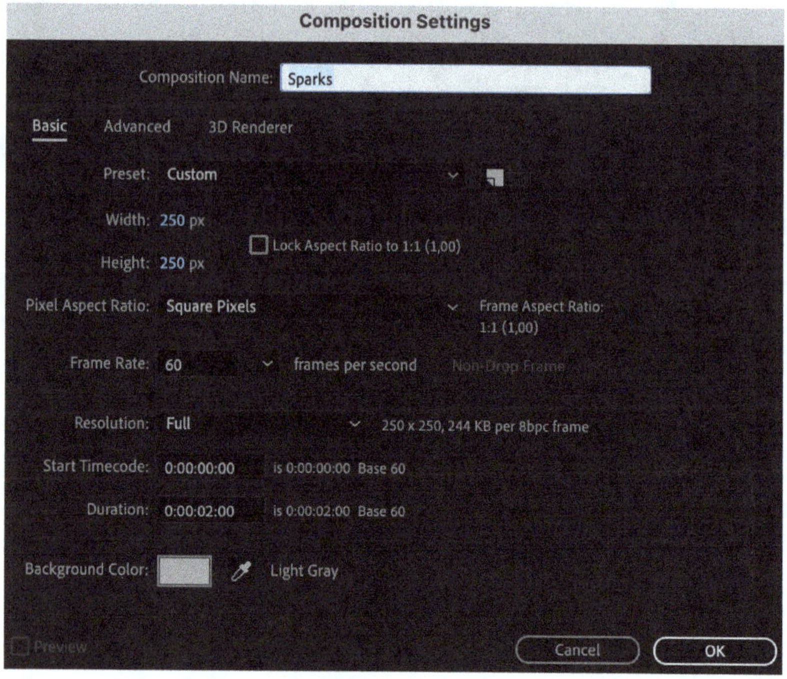

Figure 4.32 – Composition settings

Follow these steps:

1. Now, let's draw a shape layer inside our `Sparks` composition. Let's do a circle.
2. Grab **Ellipse Tool** from the top menu.

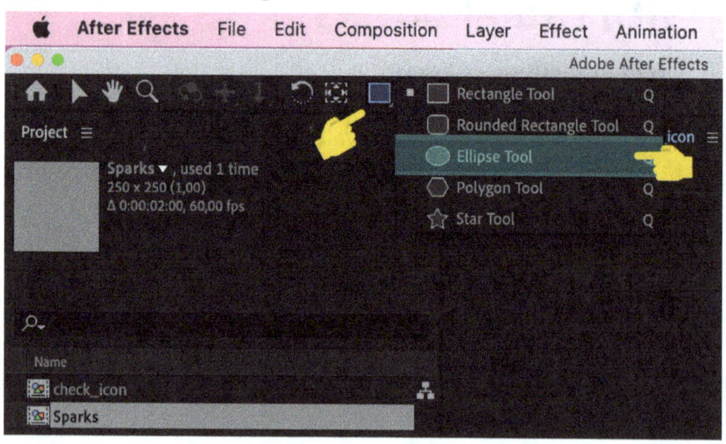

Figure 4.33 – View of the Project panel with a new composition called Sparks

3. Draw a circle in the **Stage** panel.
4. Let's draw a small circle. Let's name the **Shape** layer as `circle` by right-clicking on the shape layer's name, `Shape Layer 1`.

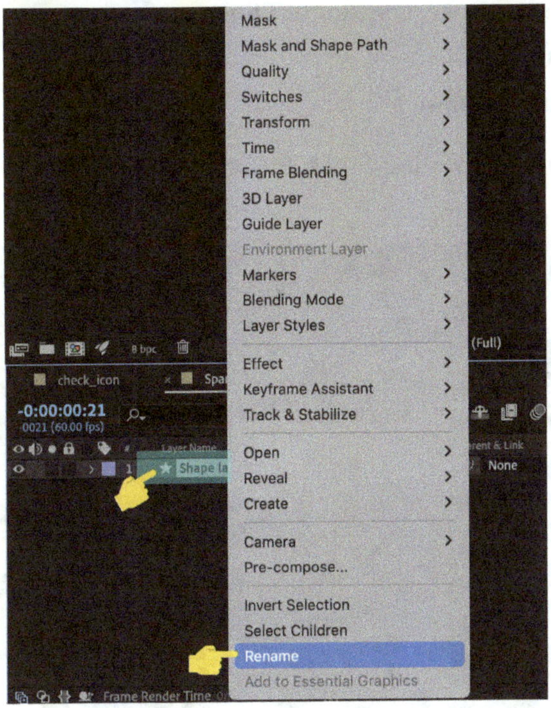

Figure 4.34 – Renaming the layer

5. Let's open up the **circle** layer and see what we've got there. As you may notice, we can see two different **Transform** options:

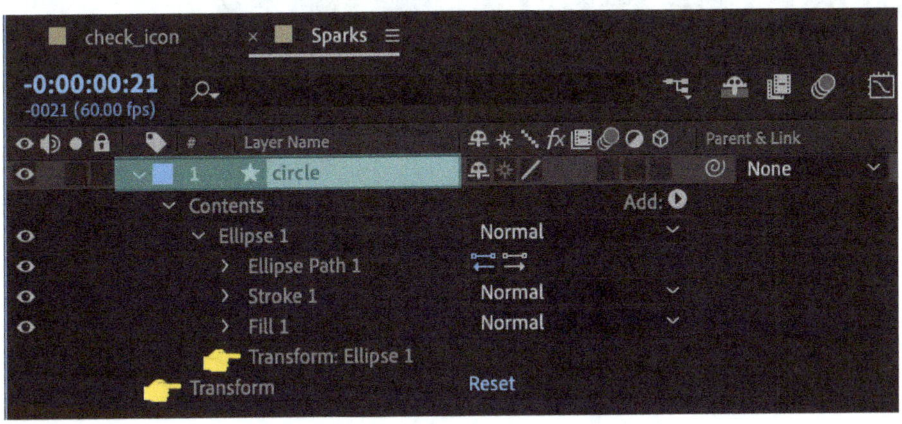

Figure 4.35 – Circle layer Transform options

For this effect, we are not going to use the **Transform** options we've been using up till now; instead, if we want the radial burst effect to work, we are going to be working with the **Transform** options we can find inside the **Contents** option:

1. So, let's open that up. Open **Transform: Ellipse 1**.
2. Click on **Contents**.
3. Click on **Transform: Ellipse 1**.

As you can see in *Figure 4.36*, we find almost the same options as we found earlier in the **Transform** tools:

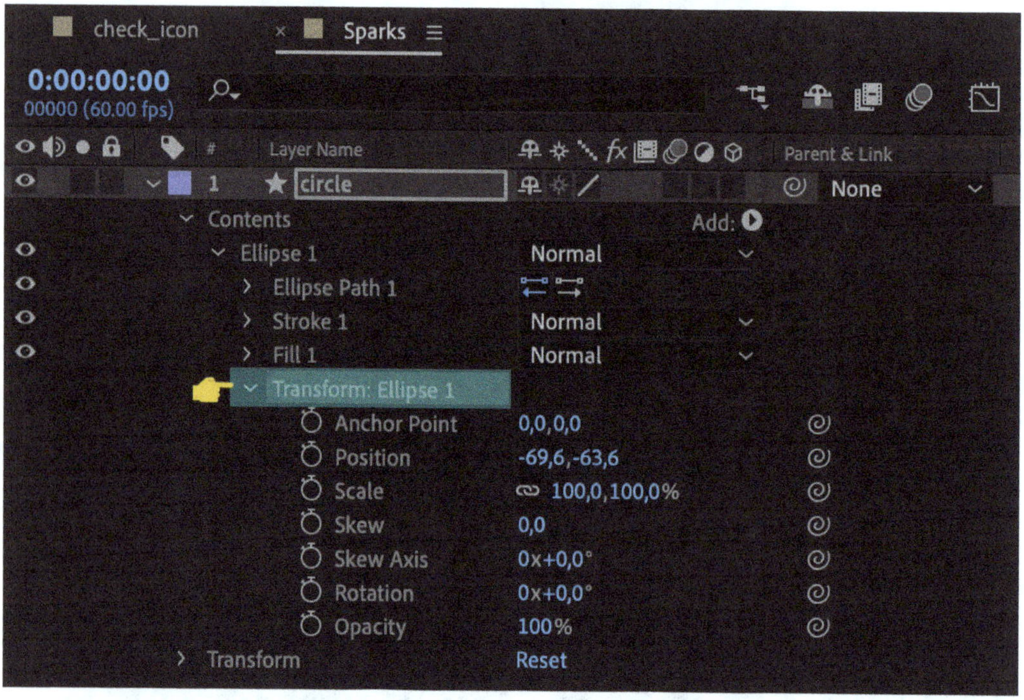

Figure 4.36 – Transform Ellipse 1 options

Let's animate its position:

1. Select the **Position** property.

2. Create a keyframe on frame **0**.

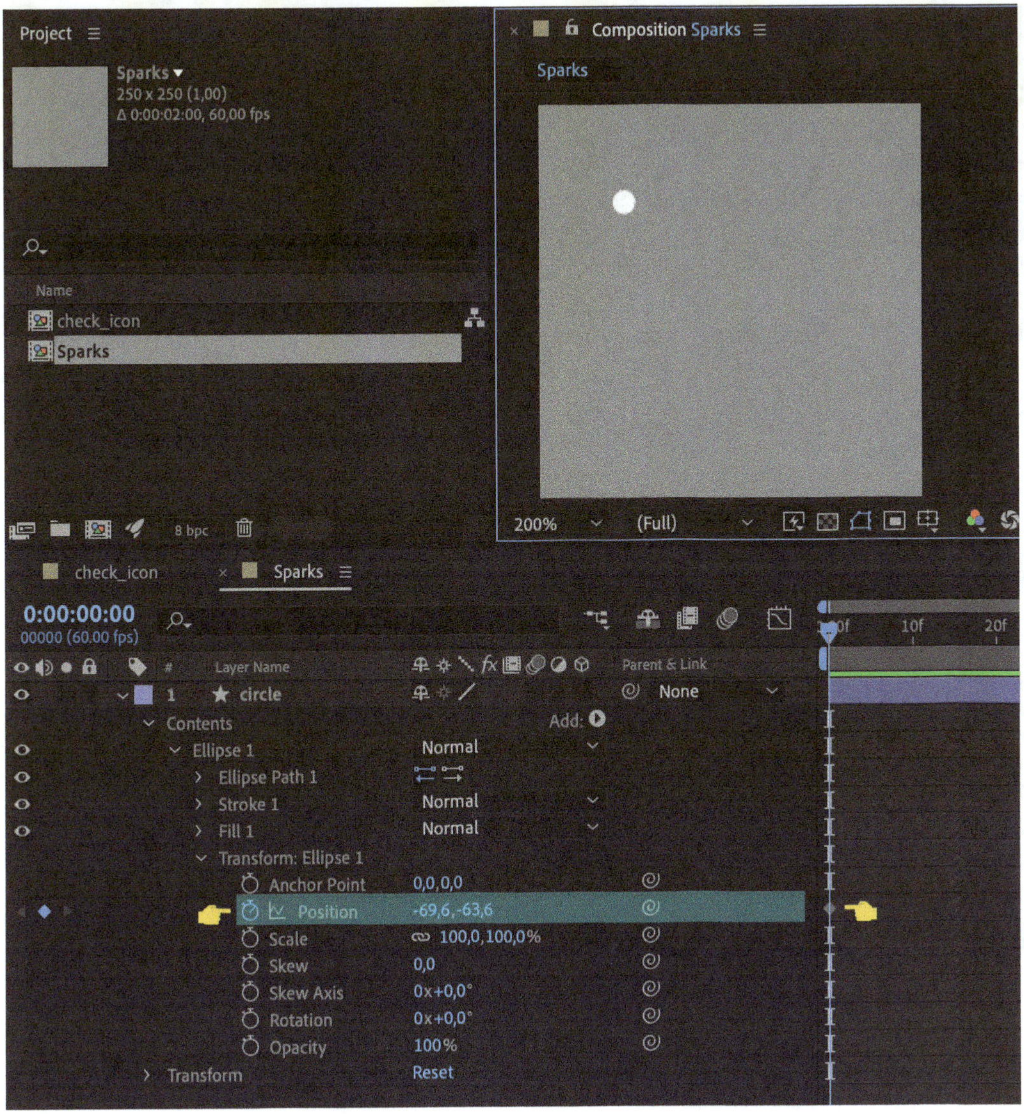

Figure 4.37 – Layer and Timeline view of a new keyframe for the Position property

3. Now, hold down *Shift* + ⌘ and press the right arrow three times; that will move our time slider to frame **30**. Or, just drag and drop the time slider.

4. Create a **Position** keyframe.

5. Move **circle** a few pixels up, and a few pixels right.

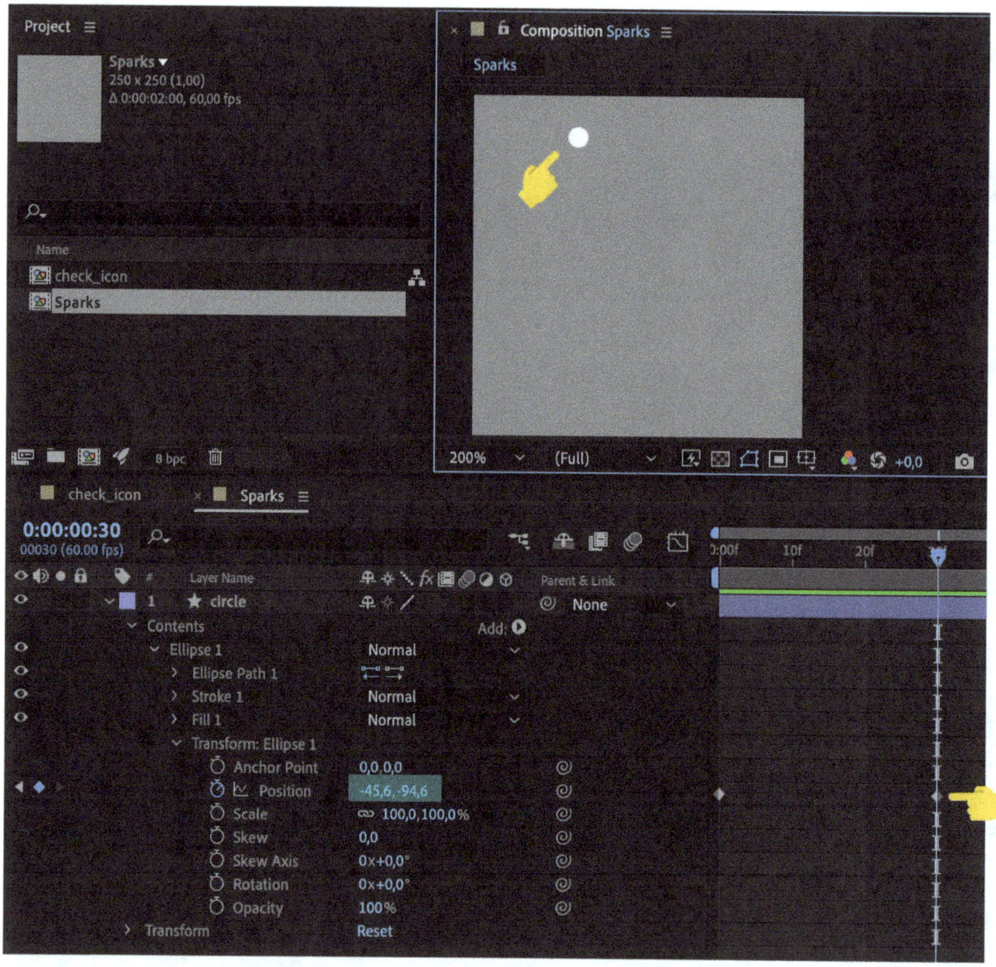

Figure 4.38 – Layer and Timeline view of a second new keyframe for the Position property

Now, let's change the **Scale** property so it will scale out at the end:

1. Move the time slider to **0**.
2. Create a **Scale** keyframe.
3. Move the time slider to frame **30**.
4. Create a second **Scale** keyframe.

5. Scale down the circle to **0**.

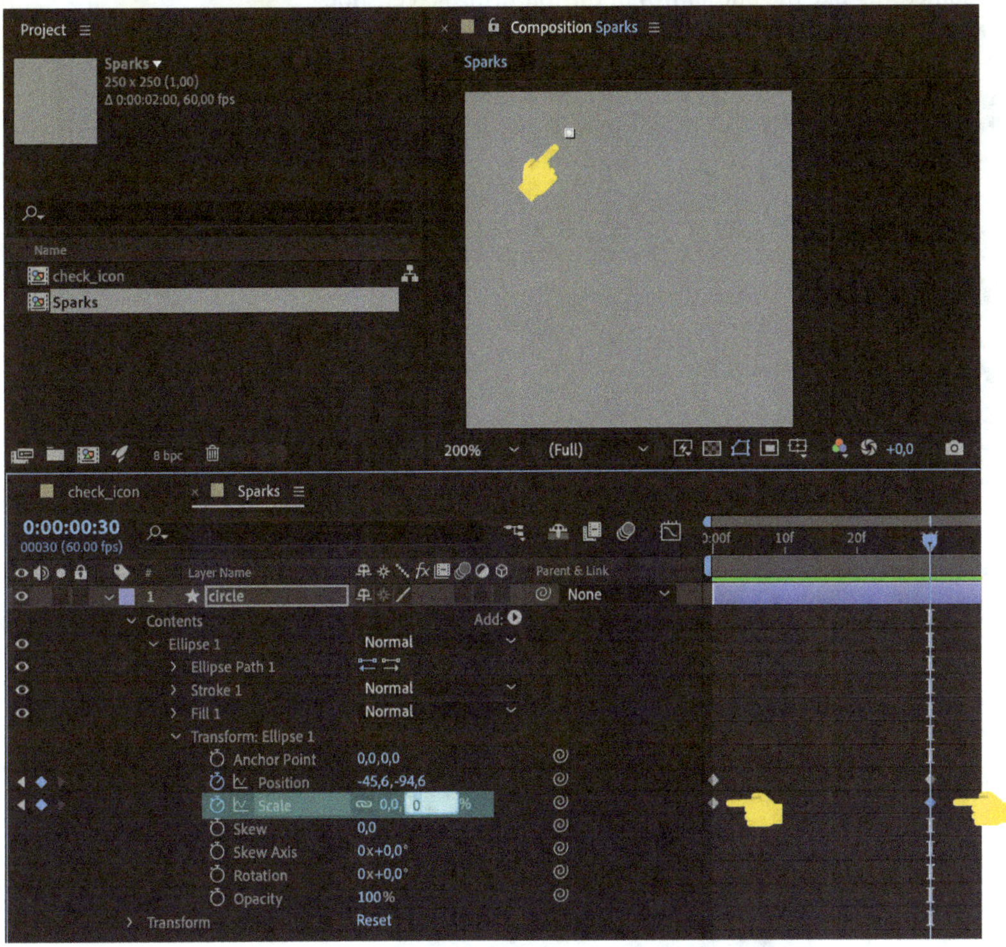

Figure 4.39 – Timeline view of the Scale keyframes

While we are at it, let's make our circle fade out, so let's change **Opacity**:

1. Move the time slider to **0**.
2. Create an **Opacity** keyframe.
3. Move the time slider to **30**.
4. Create a second **Opacity** keyframe.
5. Set the **Opacity** property to **0**.

Good! Can you feel it? We are animating with no effort at all! Now, your timeline should look something like the one shown in the following screenshot:

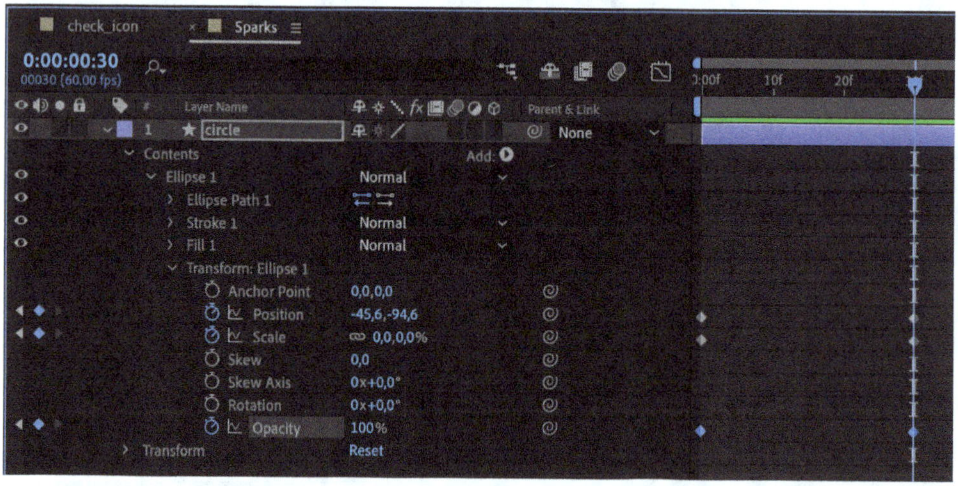

Figure 4.40 – Timeline view of the Opacity keyframes

Let's add the magic:

1. Let's select **circle**.
2. Click the **Add** button.
3. Select the **Repeater** option:

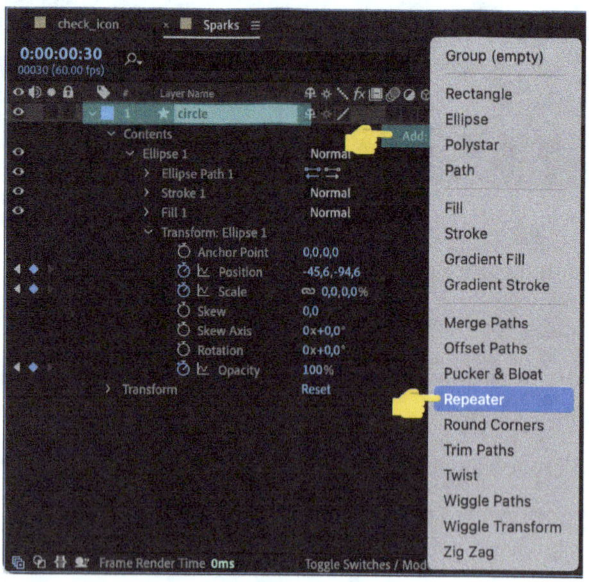

Figure 4.41 – Add menu view

4. The **Repeater 1** layer will show up in our **Layer** menu, as you can see in the following screenshot:

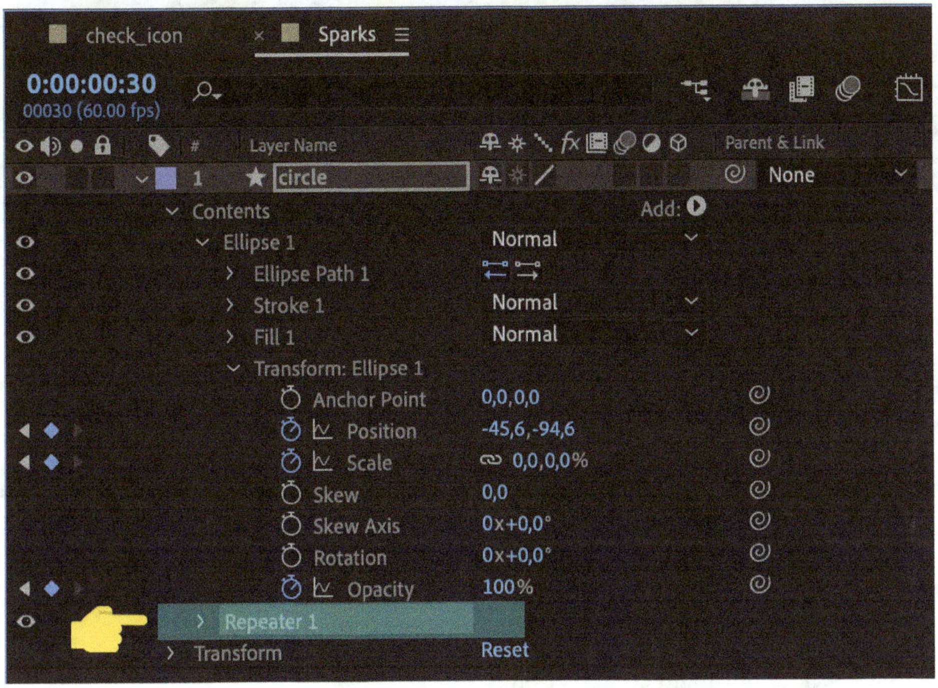

Figure 4.42 – Repeater 1 layer view in the Layer panel

Let's open it up and see what's in there. As you can see in the following screenshot, we find new properties and values. As always, I encourage you to play around with the values here:

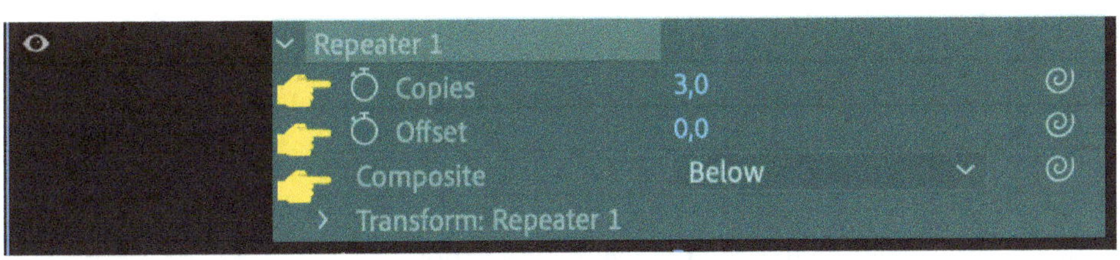

Figure 4.43 – The Repeater properties view

Let's continue. For our animation, I suggest you do the following:

1. Change the **Copies** value to **15**.
2. Open up **Transform: Repeater 1**.
3. Set **Position** to **0**.
4. Set **Rotation** to **24**.

And then, press play!

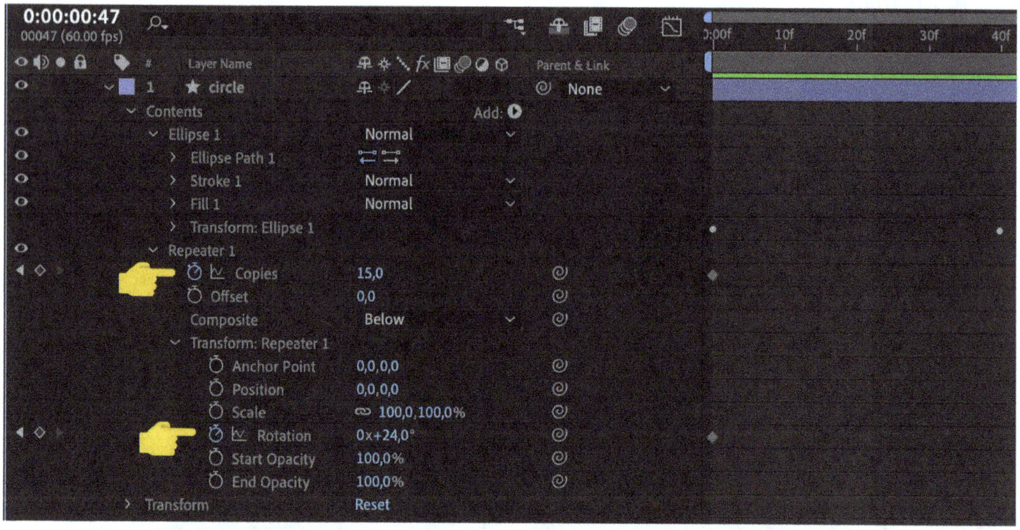

Figure 4.44 – Repeaters properties and transformations view

Isn't that cool? In just no time, we've created our version of sparks by just animating one circle. Imagine what we could do if we start adding some more elements!

Now, let's go back to our main composition:

1. Go to the **Project** panel.
2. Double-click on the **check** icon.

Let's finish our animation:

1. Drag the `Spark` composition from the **Project** panel to the **Layer** panel.
2. Go to the timeline.
3. Drag the `Spark` composition to the right, so that the animation starts at frame **21**. Our timeline will look like the following screenshot:

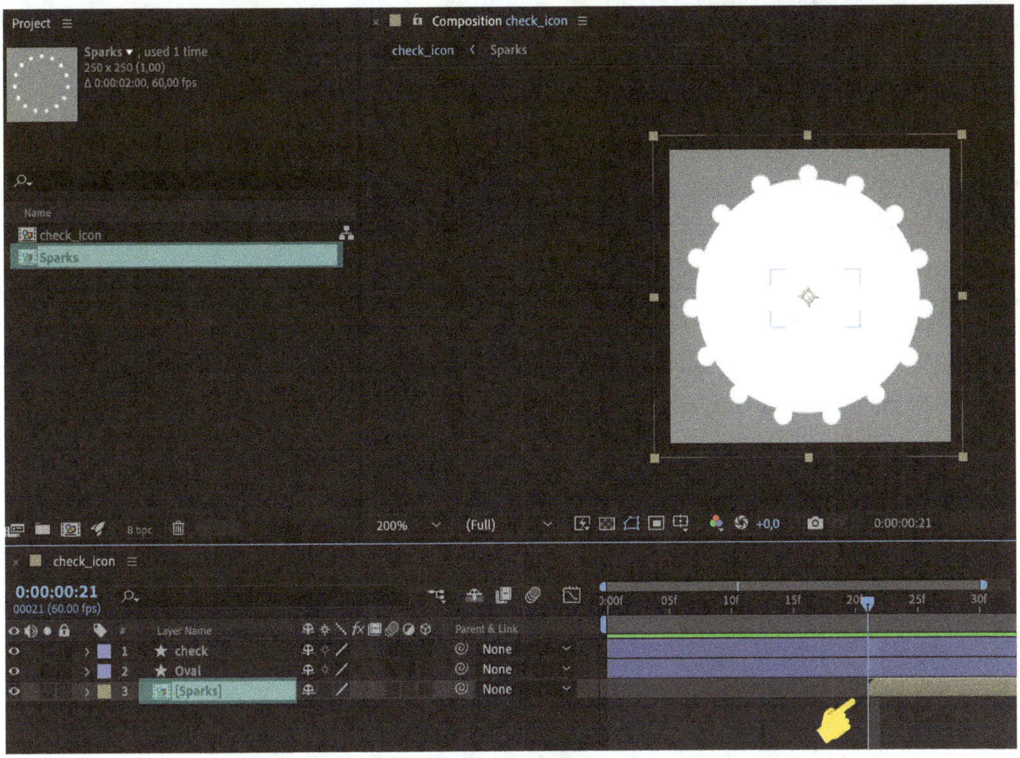

Figure 4.45 – View of the timeline of the Spark composition starting at frame 21

Now, let's play the animation! What do you think? I'm going to adjust **Scale** of `Sparks` a little bit; I'm going to change the value to `110`%. Let's do that and play it again. Nice! We are nearly done!

Figure 4.46 – Radial burst effect

Good job! We've come a long way! In this last section, we've learned about and practiced so many new things. We got hands-on with our first animated icon. We now know how to create keyframes and change the property values to create the illusion of motion and animation. We know that by changing the layer's scale, rotation, position, and transparency, we can achieve great effects.

We also learned two cool techniques that will save us a lot of effort when animating: Trim Paths and radial burst. We also applied some of the principles we learned in the first part of this book.

But, before we move to exporting and handing off our animations, I want to show you the Ease effect I've been talking about in the last two chapters. So, let's move forward; let's discover Ease!

Adding ease

Now that we've got our animation up and running, let's nail it by adding some **Ease**. Remember the **anticipation** principle we talked about back in *Creating the illusion: Get Rolling with the Basic Principles of 2D Classic Animation*? That's what we can achieve with Ease: the perception of acceleration and slowing down with just one click. And, this little tweak is going to make our animation look much nicer, smoother, and professional. Here's how to do it:

1. Open up the **Oval** layer to reveal its keyframes.
2. Go to the timeline, right-click on the **Scale** keyframe **0**, and select **Keyframe Assistant | Easy Ease Out**.

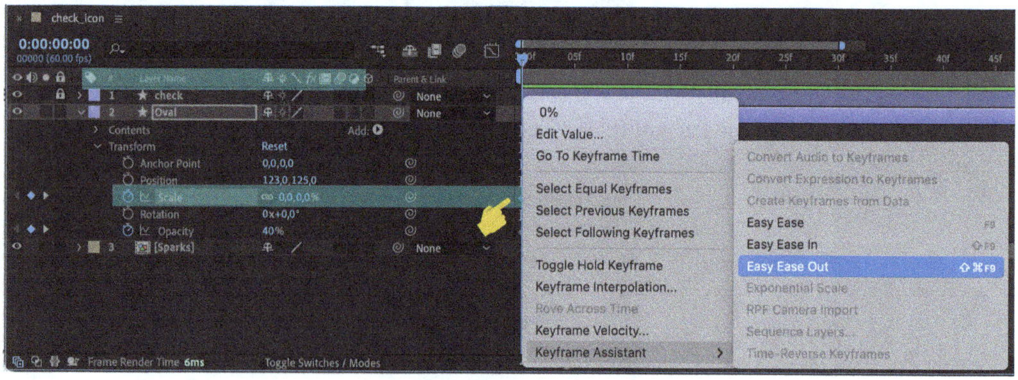

Figure 4.47 – Right-click on the Keyframe menu view

Now, let's do the same with the last keyframe, the one placed at frame **:1**.

1. Go to the timeline, right-click on the **Scale** keyframe **21**, and select **Keyframe Assistant | Easy Ease Out**.

2. For the second keyframe, the one placed at frame **18**, let's right-click on it and apply **Easy Ease In**, so your timeline should look as in *Figure 4.48*:

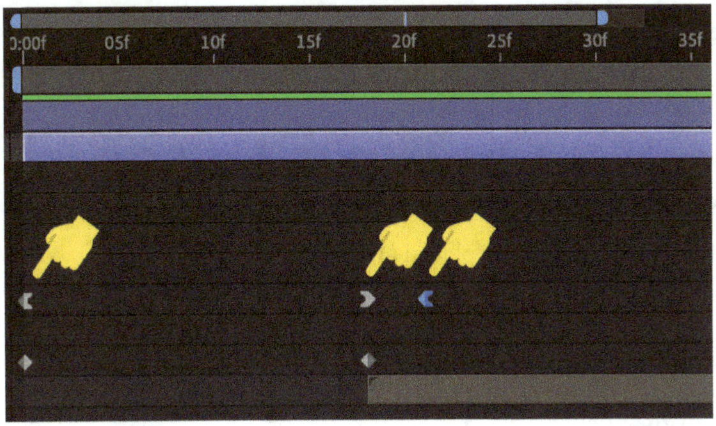

Figure 4.48 – Representation of Keyframes with Ease In and Out applied

Let's check the **Ease** panel. Click on the little icon from the timeline. From the graph, we can predict the velocity of the animation; it will accelerate exponentially at the beginning and slow down at the end.

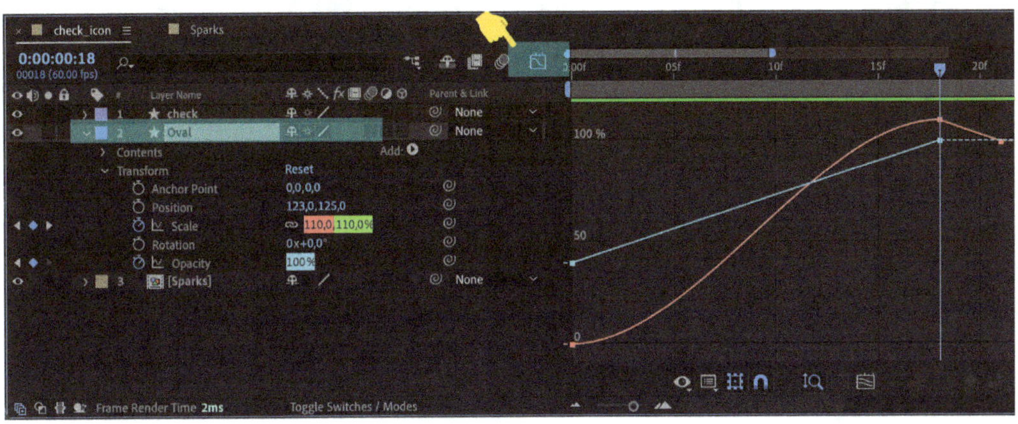

Figure 4.49 – The Ease panel view

Now, let's play our animation. What do you think? Can you tell the difference? I bet you can! Now, the animation looks smoother. But, before we move to do the same to the **check** layer, I suggest you play around with values and options. You know, learn by doing!

Great! We've got our **Oval** looking quite cool, so now let's do the same with **check**:

1. Open the **check** layer.
2. Open the **Contents** layer.
3. Open the **Trim Paths** layer.
4. Right-click on the keyframe placed at frame **21**, the first frame of our **check** animation.
5. Select **Keyframe Assistant | Easy Ease**.
6. Do the same for the keyframe placed at frame **35**.
7. Play the animation.

It's getting there! Now, to finalize it, I'm going to do that in the `spark` composition as well:

1. Go to the **Project** panel.
2. Double-click on the `spark` composition.
3. Select all keyframes.
4. Apply **Easy Ease**.
5. Go to the **Project** panel.
6. Double-click on the **check** icon composition.
7. Play it.

Our animation is done!

As you've just experienced, Ease is a really powerful tool that will make your animations look stunning in no time. Of course, there is a lot more to learn about it; we've just gone through a couple of aspects of it so that you have the basic skills to learn further on your own.

As we mentioned at the beginning of this book, we are not aiming to be an AE tutorial book; instead, we want to give you enough knowledge, background, and resources for you to start creating animations on your own, from concept to hand-off. So, I encourage you to explore and read more about Ease.

If you don't know where to start, you know we've got you sorted, so just keep reading as, in *Chapter 6, Don't Stop! Exploring Plugins and Resources That Will Keep You Going*, you'll find more resources about Ease and much more!

Summary

It wasn't that hard, was it? We've finished our first professional-looking animation in no time! Our customers won't feel confused after the purchase and our app will look much better. Win-win-win!

In this chapter, we've been through a real project and learned the UX animation AE workflow. We have now covered the whole process, from ideation to final animation. We know how to read and understand storyboards, we've learned how to import our assets to AE, set up a composition, create keyframes, and modify layer properties such as **Scale**, **Position**, **Rotation**, and **Opacity** to create our animation. We've also learned how to use Trim Paths and radial bursts to create special effects, how to adjust timing, and how to apply Ease to finalize our project.

Let's move on to the next chapter, where we will learn how to export our animation as a `.json` file and preview it on the LottieFiles platform. See you there!

5

Share It With the World: Working With LottieFiles

Here we are, ready to export our awesome first Lottie animation as a `.json` file to then add it to our app or website using **React Native**. Our app is minutes away from looking stunning and making a quality change. Follow me!

In this chapter, we are going to learn how to export our Lottie animation using both Bodymovin and LottieFiles plugins for Adobe **After Effects** (**AE**). We will guide you through creating a LottieFiles platform account so that we can preview our animations and hand them off to developers. We will also have a look at the LottieFiles mobile app for iOS so that we can effortlessly test our animations directly on mobile. We will also teach you how to create simple animations without even using AE and, finally, we will have some fun by converting animations into stickers for Telegram.

In this chapter, we are going to cover the following topics:

- Exporting our animations from AE to `.json` files
- Creating an account in LottieFiles
- Exploring the LottieFiles dashboard

- Importance of testing in desktop and mobile Lottie platforms
- Creating and editing Lottie animations without using AE
- Converting **Scalable Vector Graphics** (**SVG**) files to animated Lottie files
- Converting Lottie files to GIFs
- Creating Telegram stickers and sticker sets

Technical requirements

For this chapter, we are going to need some specific plugins that will help us export our animation as a `.json` file and preview them on both desktop and mobile devices. The tools that we require are as follows:

- Adobe AE
- Bodymovin for AE plugin
- LottieFiles for AE plugin
- LottieFiles for mobile
- Chrome, Safari, or a browser of your choice

Exporting our animation for handoff

To export our animation from AE to a `.json` file, we can use **Bodymovin** and **LottieFiles** plugins for AE. But, do we have to learn both? You are free to use any of them; they are available to download, are free to use, and are fully maintained and supported.

> **Downloading and Installing the Plugins**
>
> For downloading and a *how-to* installation guide, you can jump ahead to *Chapter 6, Don't Stop! Exploring Plugins and Resources That Will Keep You Going,* where we will guide you through the process.

So, just choose the one you feel more comfortable with or the one that best matches your workflow. Maybe working with Bodymovin is all you need, however, LottieFiles will give you additional testing and preview tools.

For me, I'm really used to working with Bodymovin, especially because, as you know by now, this was the first plugin ever to exist that would convert your animation into a `.json` file; it is simple and does the job. But, times change and new tools with new features appear.

There is a big team of professionals working behind the scenes of LottieFiles. I must say, these days, the LottieFiles plugin matches my workflow better. It allows me to easily preview my animations on both desktop and mobile devices and share them with stakeholders in the blink of an eye.

That said, I suggest you go through both plugins and then decide which one suits you best. Let's start by exploring Bodymovin.

Exporting our animation using Bodymovin

As we've seen in earlier chapters, Bodymovin was the first plugin ever released for AE that would allow us to export our animation as a `.json` file, and it works perfectly well. It is simple and gives some interesting exporting options, which we will see in a minute.

But, before we start, we are assuming you have already installed Bodymovin for AE, otherwise, you can jump ahead to *Chapter 6, Don't Stop! Exploring Plugins and Resources That Will Keep You Going*, and follow the steps to install it.

Right, let's say we've got everything ready to go (Adobe AE and the Bodymovin plugin installed), so let's open the Bodymovin plugin in AE:

1. Open Adobe After Effects.
2. Open our `check_icon.ae` project.
3. Go to the top navigation menu and click on **Window | Extensions | Bodymovin**:

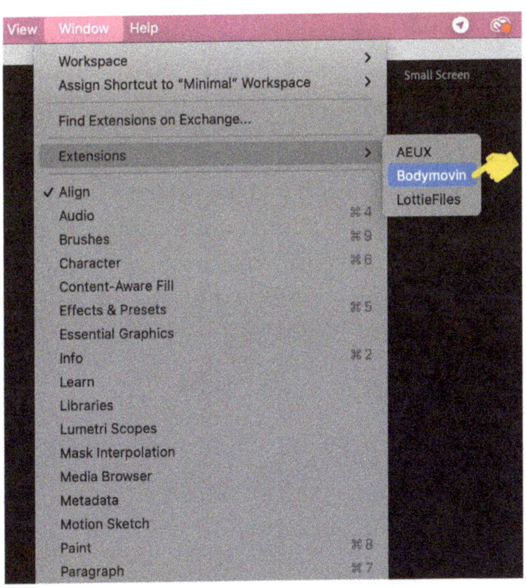

Figure 5.1 – Opening the Bodymovin panel in AE

Let's check the **Bodymovin** panel.

First, the panel opens up in the **Render** view. This is the view we are going to be focusing on as the other options are not relevant for us at this point. As we can see in *Figure 5.2*, the two compositions contained in our project are listed here as **check_icon** and **Sparks**:

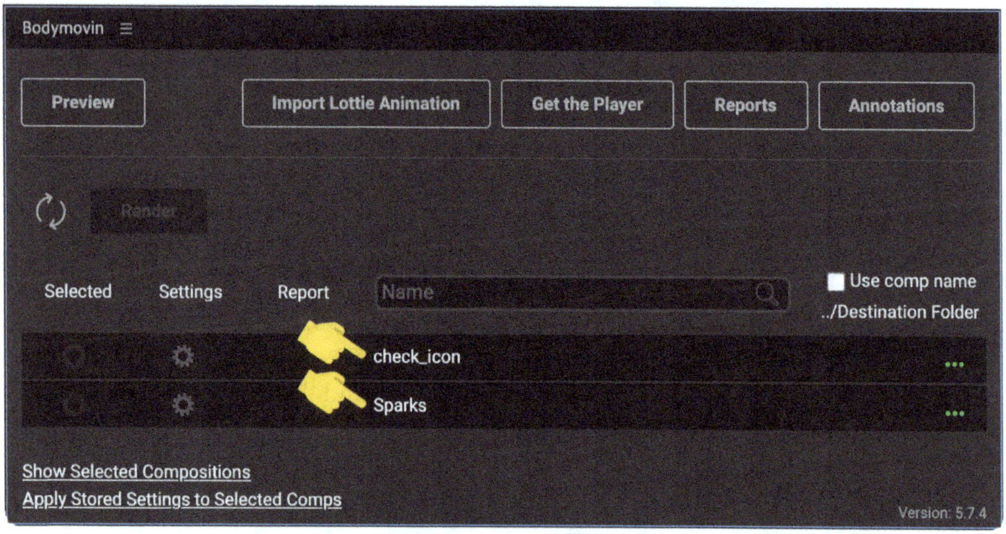

Figure 5.2 – Bodymovin composition view

We can export any of the compositions listed in the panel, but we want to export the whole animation. So, which of the compositions listed in the panel should we export? That's right, the main composition that contains the whole animation, which is the **check_icon** composition.

For each composition, there are a few settings we could adjust before exporting. That comes in handy in cases where we are using images, expressions, and live text, but as you know, I strongly recommend keeping our animations as simple as possible. If you want to get further information on that, you can check our discussion of supported Lottie features in *Chapter 6, Don't Stop! Exploring Plugins and Resources That Will Keep You Going.*

Now, let's export our animation:

1. Click on the little circle to the left of the **check_icon** composition, below the **Selected** column.
2. Click on the three green dots icon to the right to save your `.json` file and choose your folder destination. Notice the `.json` file is named as `data.json` by default, but you can give it any name you want. I'm going to call mine `check_icon.json`:

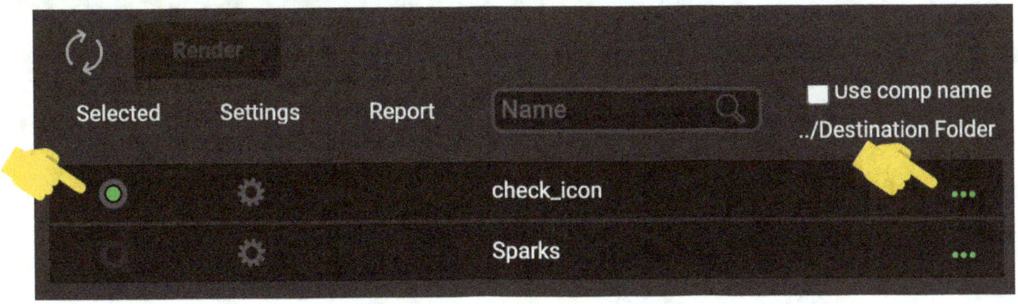

Figure 5.3 – check_icon selected

3. You can now see the **Render** button is highlighted and the destination folder is visible next to the **check_icon** name. Let's click the **Render** button:

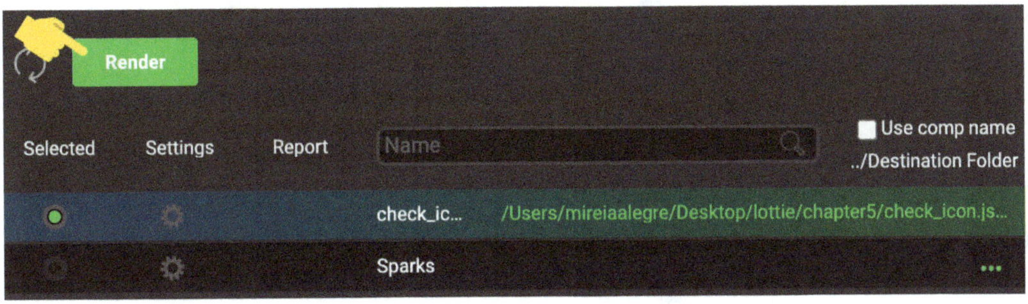

Figure 5.4 – Render button highlighted

4. Click the **Done** button:

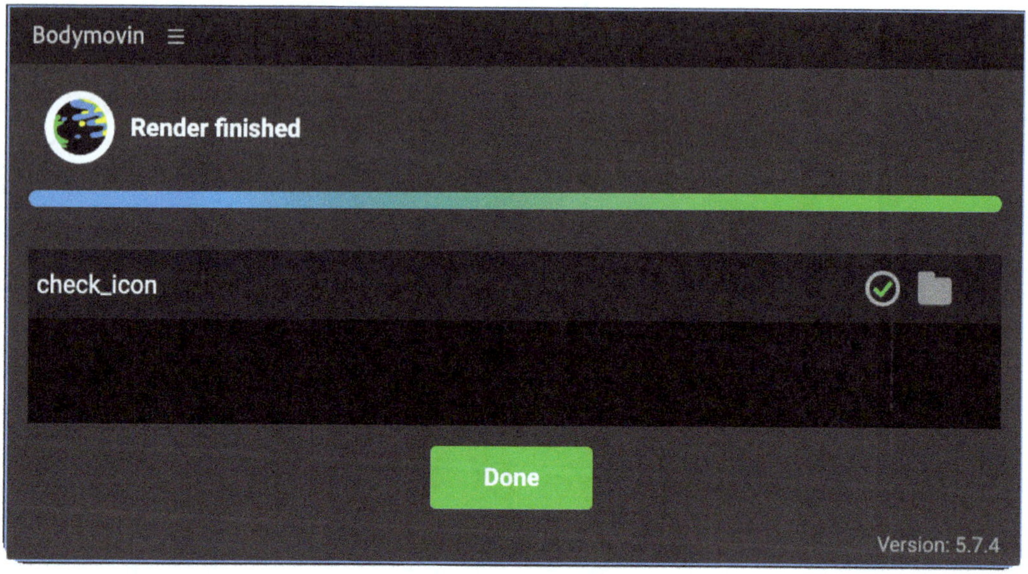

Figure 5.5 – Render successfully done

Great! Our animation is exported as a `.json` file and is ready for preview. But, before we do that, we are going to show you how to do the same using the LottieFiles plugin.

Exporting our animation using LottieFiles

People in the LottieFiles community have been very busy these last years and have come up with a new plugin for AE called **LottieFiles**.

The LottieFiles plugin is based on the actual Bodymovin open source but has some extra features that Bodymovin doesn't. That's why we are going to see how to export your animation using LottieFiles as well.

So, we are assuming you've got everything ready to go, otherwise, move ahead to the *Installing LottieFiles plugin* section in *Chapter 6, Don't Stop! Exploring Plugins and Resources That Will Keep You Going*, where we will show you the details on how to download and install the LottieFiles plugin.

Whenever you are ready, let's open the LottieFiles plugin in AE:

1. Open Adobe After Effects, in case you haven't done it yet.
2. Open our `check_icon.ae` project.
3. Go to the top navigation menu and click on **Window** | **Extensions** | **LottieFiles**:

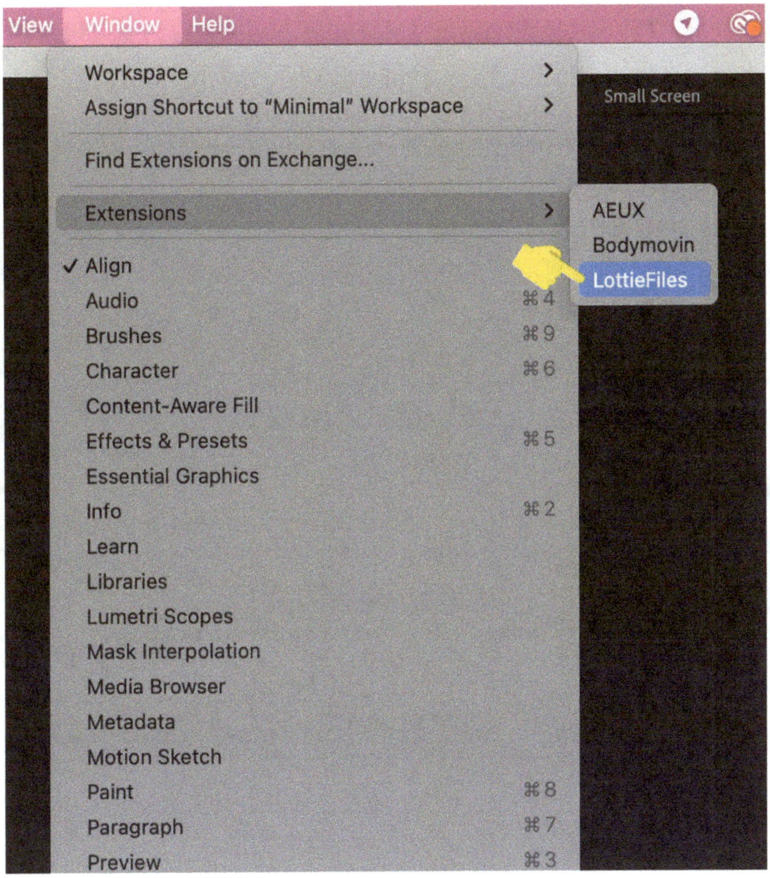

Figure 5.6 – Opening the LottieFiles panel in AE

> **Keep in Mind**
> To be able to access the LottieFiles plugin panel, you will need to create a LottieFiles platform account. We are covering that in the following section, so if you want to create your account now, just jump to the next section and then come back again. We will wait for you here.

Great! So, now that everything is sorted, let's check the LottieFiles plugin for AE panel.

At first sight, the LottieFiles panel is quite similar to Bodymovin. Both open up on the composition panel. We can also see a list of our compositions, the **Settings** tool icon next to each composition, and the **Exporting** arrow icon to export our animation, as shown in *Figure 5.7* for reference:

Figure 5.7 – LottieFiles panel composition view

Next to the **Composition** panel, we find some other icons such as an *eye* and a *compass*:

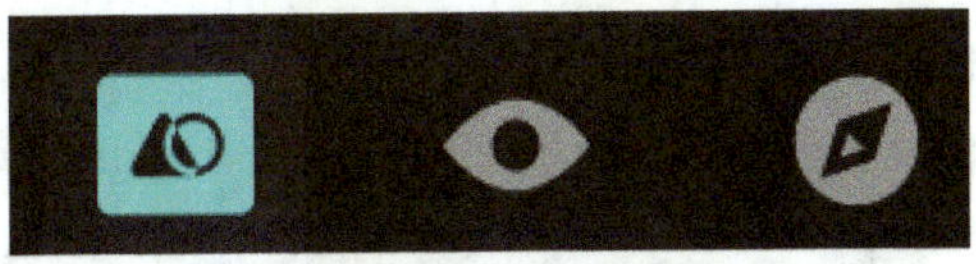

Figure 5.8 – LottieFiles panel top-bar icons

The *eye* represents the **Preview** panel. In this panel, we can find every previously rendered animation we've done so far, as shown in the following figure:

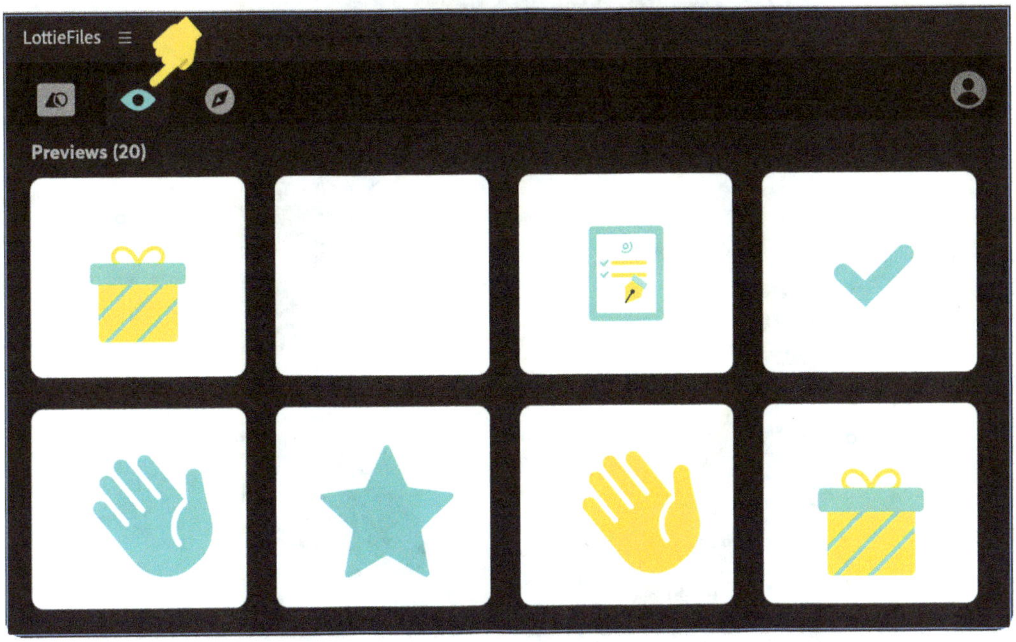

Figure 5.9 – LottieFiles panel Previews view

By selecting any of the shown animations, we will see its details such as the file size, frame rate, dimensions, and time of export. We can also change the background color to see how it looks in different scenarios or export it directly to our LottieFiles mobile app. We can save the file or share it with the community by clicking on the little *world* icon:

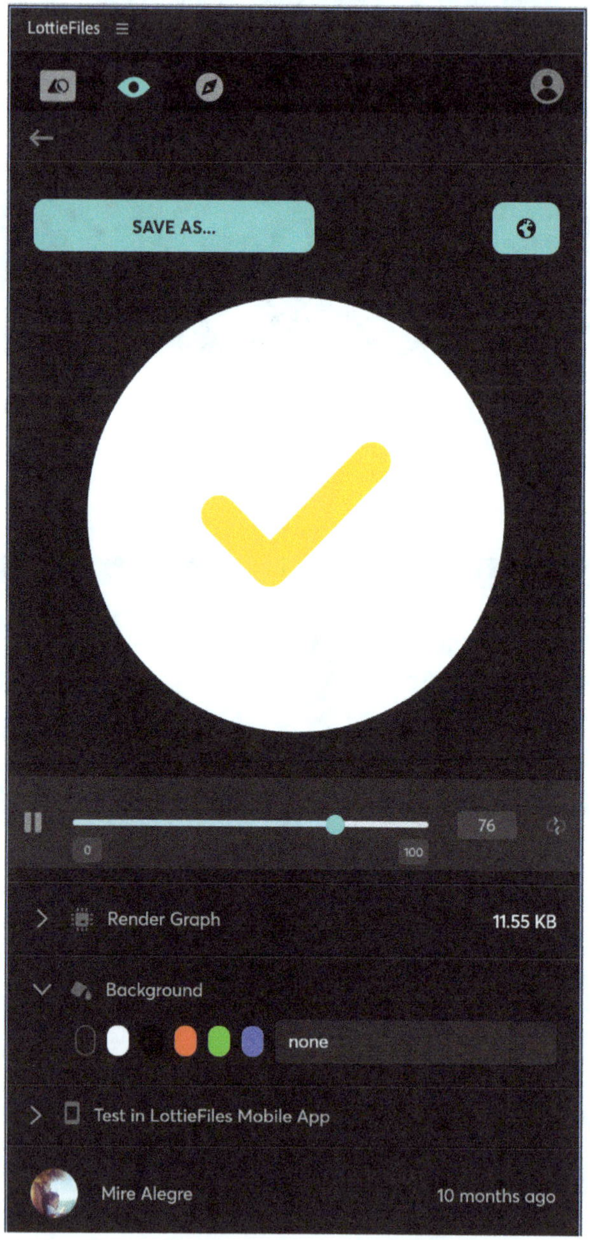

Figure 5.10 – LottieFiles panel preview details

The *compass* stands for the **Search** panel. In this panel, we can look into the LottieFiles library for free animations to use or get inspired. This becomes very handy when we don't need a totally personalized animation. Imagine we need a loading bar; we can search for one, load it into AE, and change whatever we need to, such as the color, the time, and so on.

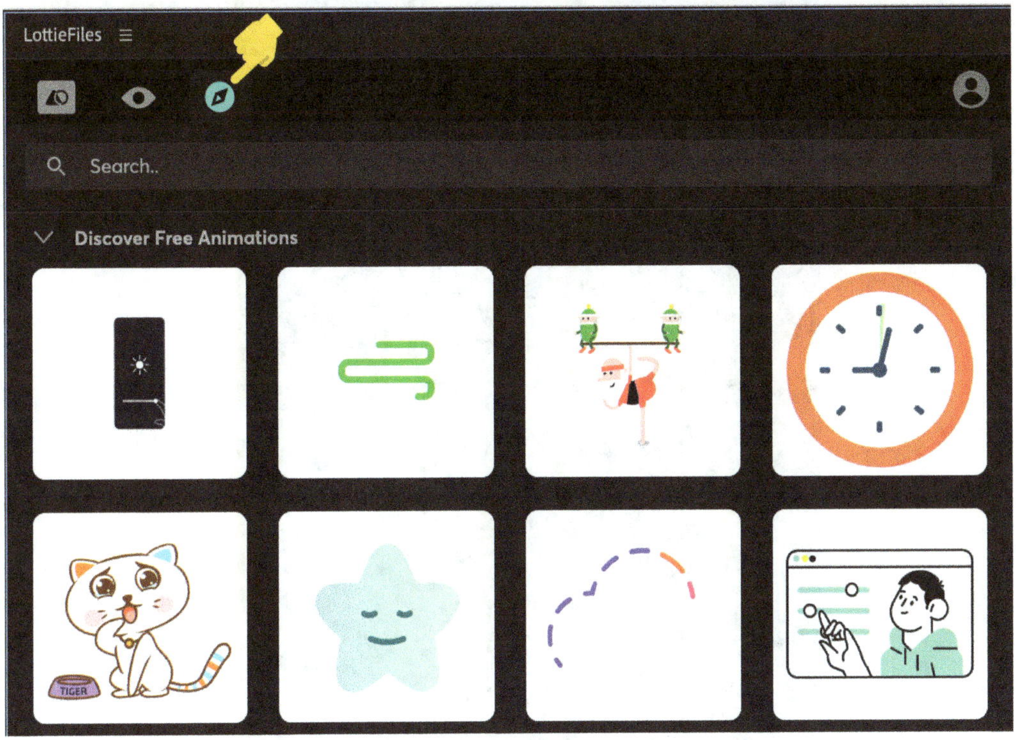

Figure 5.11 – LottieFiles panel – Discover Free Animations view

I sometimes look for an animation to use as a starting point of what I have in mind, to check how it was done, or just for style or timing inspiration.

Some of the animations in the LottieFiles library contain the `.json` file as well as the AE file, free to download and use. To know whether the animation can be downloaded as an AE file, you need to look for the ones that contain the **Download AEP File** button:

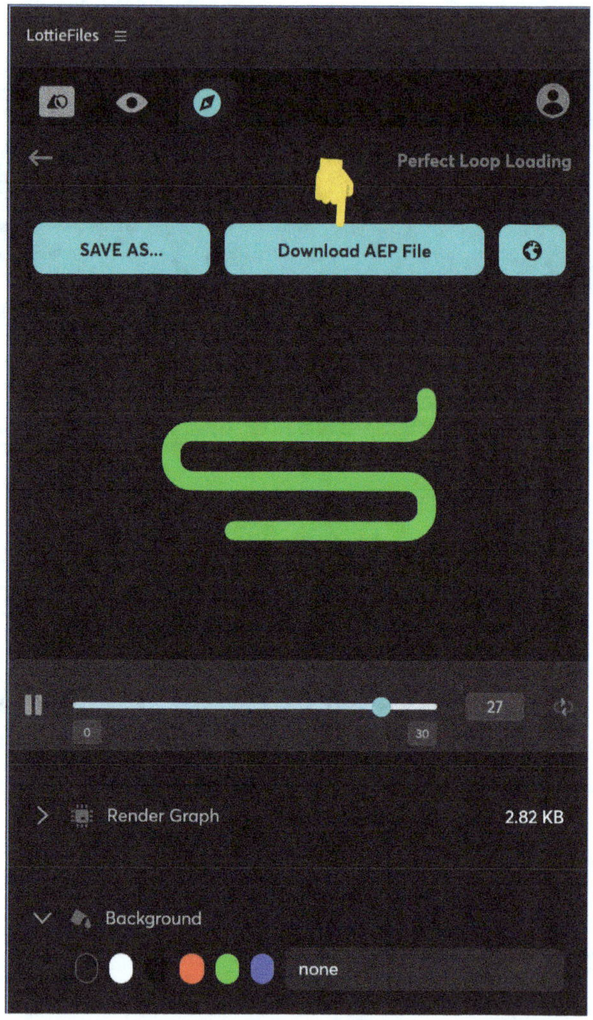

Figure 5.12 – LottieFiles panel – Discover Free Animations detail

Now that we've been through the different LottieFiles panel options, such as the **Composition**, **Preview**, and **Search** panels, let's focus on exporting our animation.

To do that, execute the following steps:

1. Let's click back on the **Compositions** panel view.

2. Click on the arrow next to **check_icon**:

Figure 5.13 – LottieFiles panel compositions view

Our **check_icon** animation shows up in the panel.

3. Now, we can save our file as a `.json` or `.lottie` file, which, as we mentioned earlier, is the same, or upload it to our previews:

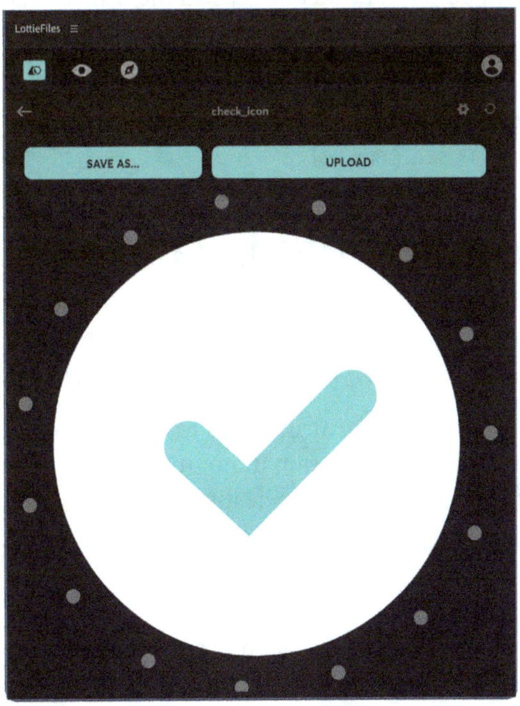

Figure 5.14 – LottieFiles panel – successfully exported Lottie

4. If we click the **Upload** button, the animation will appear in the **Previews** view. Yay!

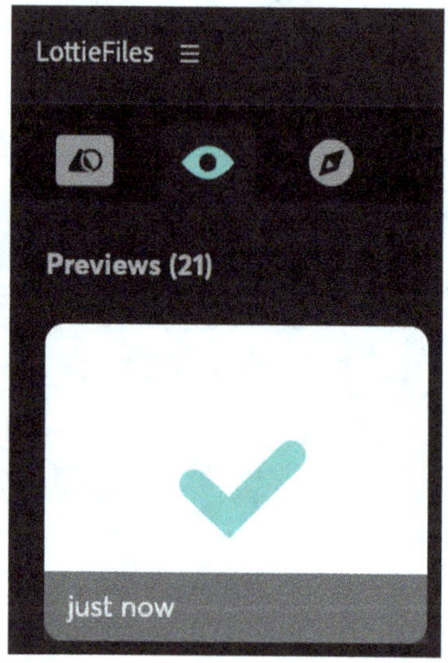

Figure 5.15 – LottieFiles panel – our new icon uploaded to the Previews view

Fantastic! We just exported our animation as a `.json` file, which means we have created our first ever Lottie!

Now that we know how to export our AE animated file to `.json` files either by using Bodymovin or LottieFiles plugins, let's move to get into the LottieFiles platform, and to do that, we are going to create a user. Let's go!

Creating a user account in LottieFiles

We've got our animation exported as a `.json` file and with that in hand, we could pass it over to the technical team or move ahead to the third part of this book, *Adding Your Lottie Animations Into Mobile Apps*, and learn how to implement our animation in our app.

But, let's not rush; the LottieFiles platform allows us to upload and test our animation before handing it off to the development team in no time, and that way, we ensure that everything is in place and we haven't used any feature that is not supported.

To do that, and as we've mentioned earlier, we need to sign up at the LottieFiles platform in order to be able to export our animations using the LottieFiles plugin for AE:

1. Go to `https://lottiefiles.com/` on your browser:

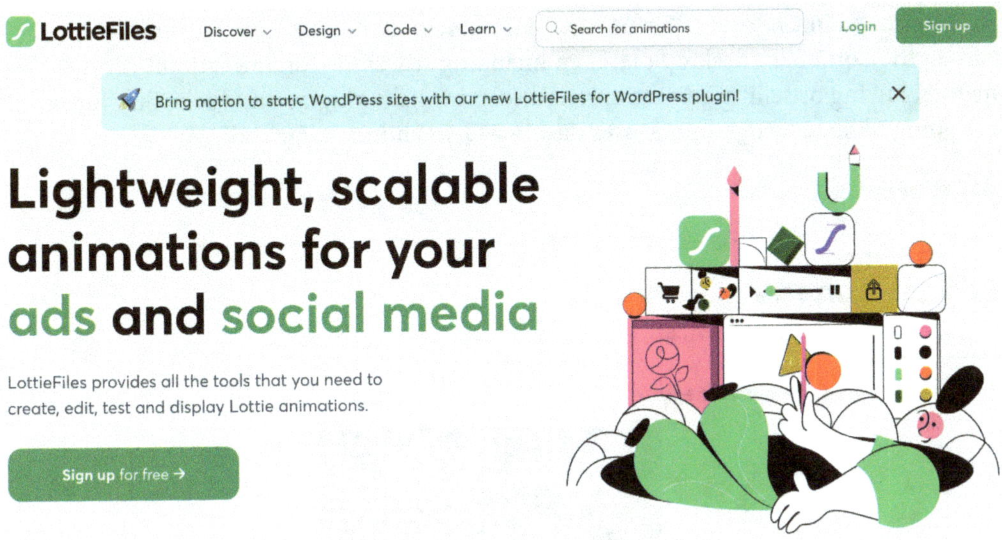

Figure 5.16 – lottiefiles.com desktop browser view

2. Click on the **Sign up for free** button.
3. Choose the option that best suits you to create your account, such as Facebook, Google, or email:

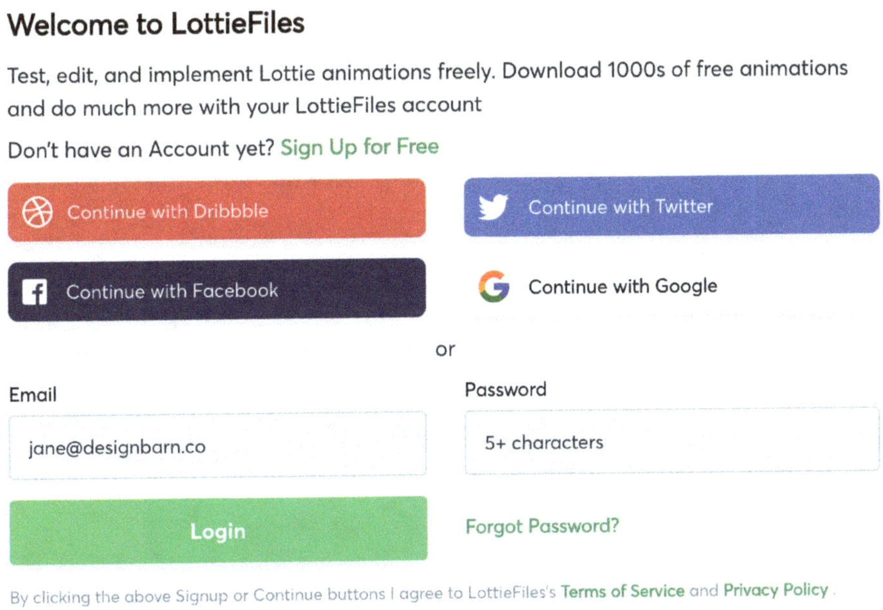

Figure 5.17 – LottieFiles login/sign up window

And, you are done!

As we mentioned in *Chapter 1*, *Get Started With Lottie*, there are plenty of things you can do on the LottieFiles desktop platform including searching for animations, hiring animators, buying or selling animations, and searching for plugins and tools. But, for now, we are going to be focusing on our user dashboard, as shown in *Figure 5.18*:

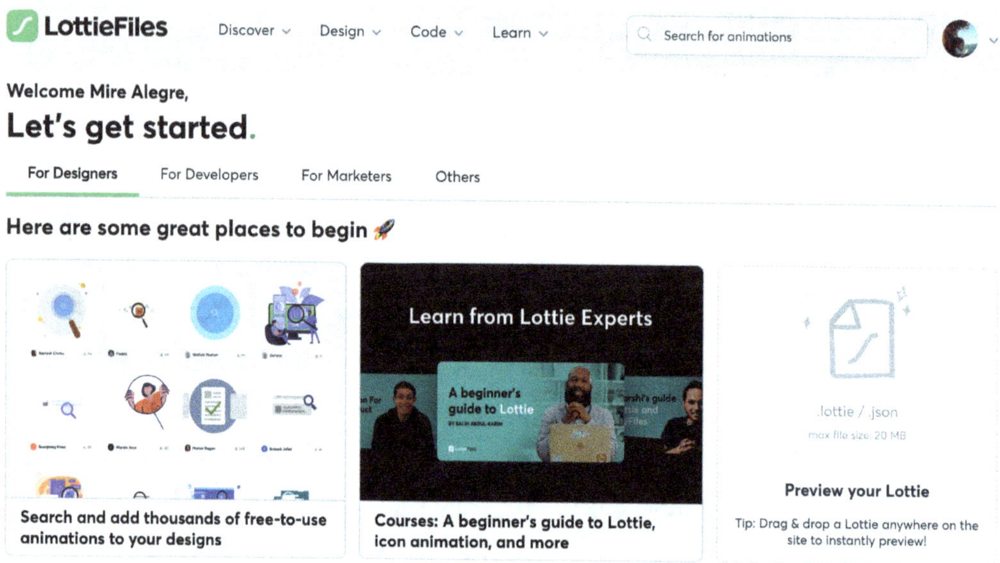

Figure 5.18 – LottieFiles platform home logged in view

Before we move to the next section to start exploring the LottieFiles platform, let me do a bit of a recap here. In this chapter, you just created your first LottieFiles account and exported the animation as a `.json` file using both Bodymovin and LottieFiles plugins for AE. There is just one step left for uploading and previewing our animated icon and sharing it with the world!

Exploring the LottieFiles dashboard

The LottieFiles platform allows us to upload, keep, and share our animations with developers, clients, and even with the world if we want to. And, not only that, but it also gives us the statistics about our public animations as well as information about likes, purchases, and more. How? Let's check it out. To do so, just hover over your avatar and select any of the options, such as, for example, the **My Public Animations** option:

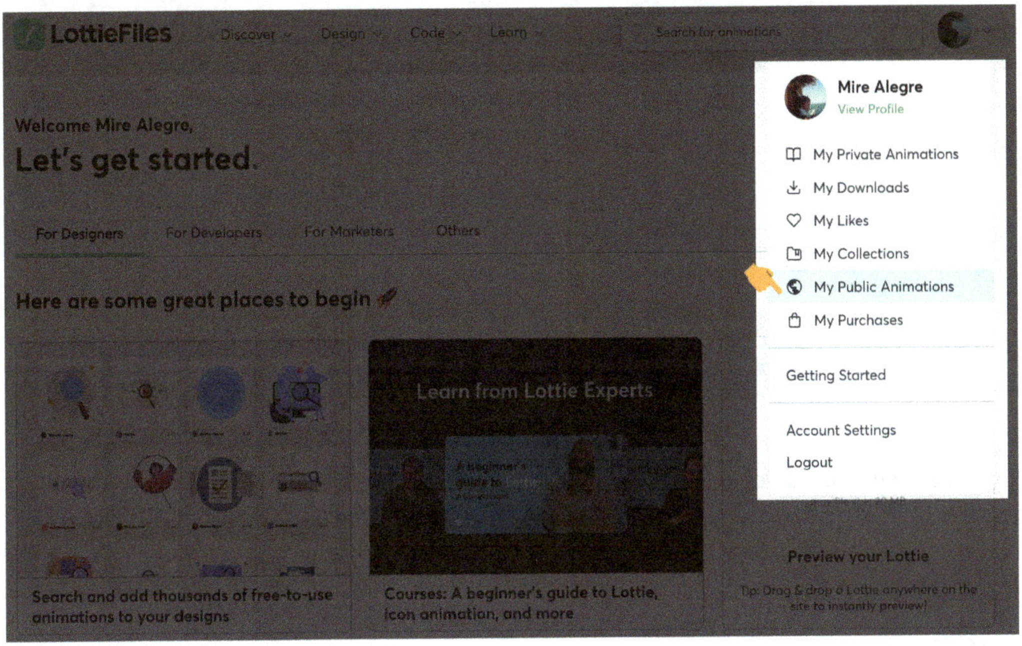

Figure 5.19 – The My Dashboard menu view

Once we open up our dashboard, we can see a few different options listed on the left-hand side of the screen. There is also an empty central section in which we see a message encouraging us to upload our first animation:

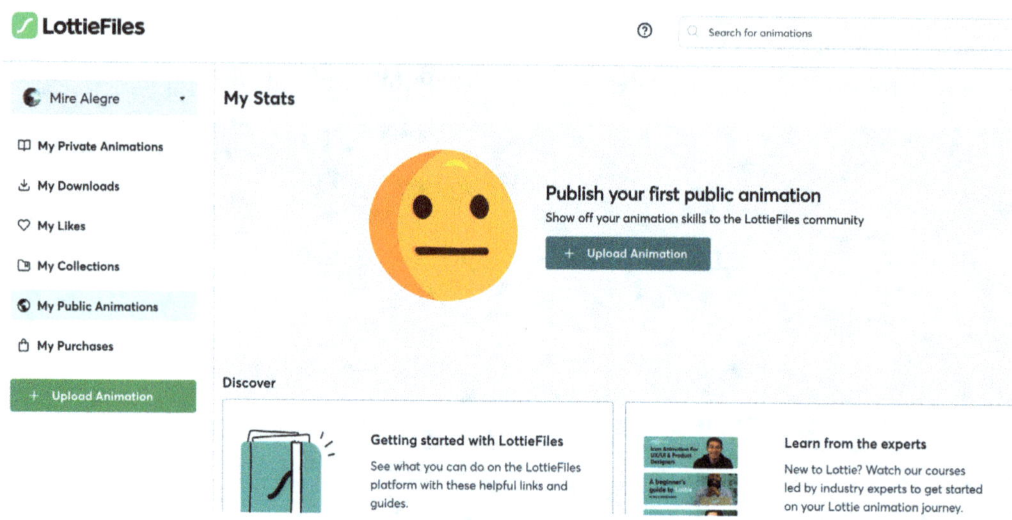

Figure 5.20 – The My Dashboard menu view

As you will see, LottieFiles is a very intuitive and easy tool to use. But, let's have a quick overview of the menu on the left. Here, we see a few sections, which we will look at next.

My Downloads

The My Downloads section is the place where we find a list by date of any animation that we have downloaded from the LottieFiles platform. Any `.json`, `.ae`, `.gif`, or any other file format you have downloaded will appear here:

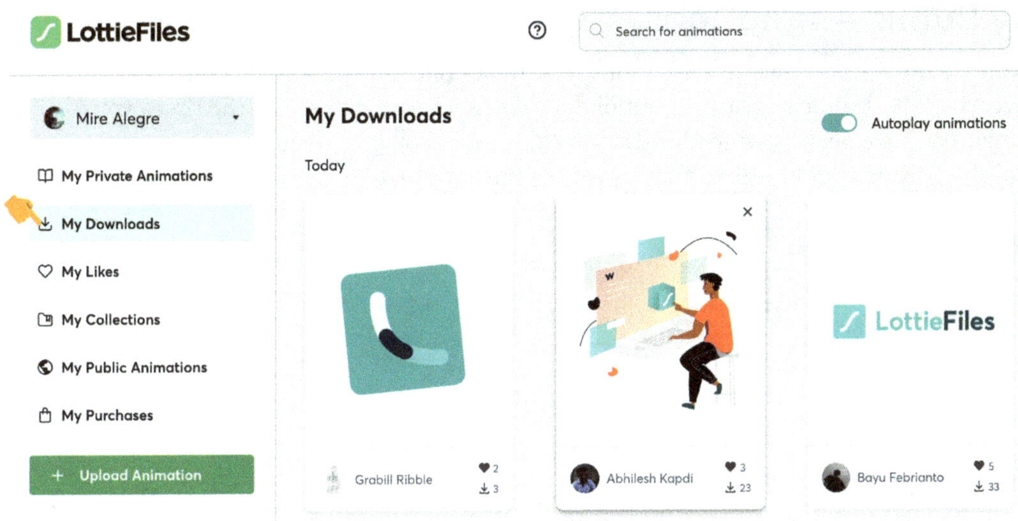

Figure 5.21 – My Downloads view

My Likes

In this section, we find a list of all the animations we have given likes to. I use it as a *save for later* kind of feature, so anytime I'm searching through LottieFiles and I see some animation that can work for me as a reference in the future, I give it a like so it gets saved in this section:

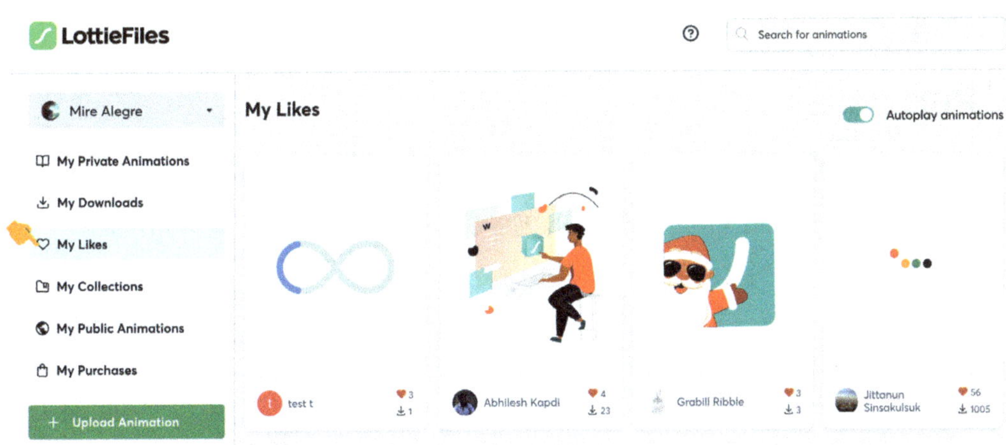

Figure 5.22 – My Likes view

My Public Animations

If you are up to sharing your animations with the public, this section is quite cool. Here, you'll find some statistics about likes other users have given you, the times your animations have been downloaded, and profile views. You'll also see a preview of all your published-to-the-public animations as well as the ones that are in review for sharing:

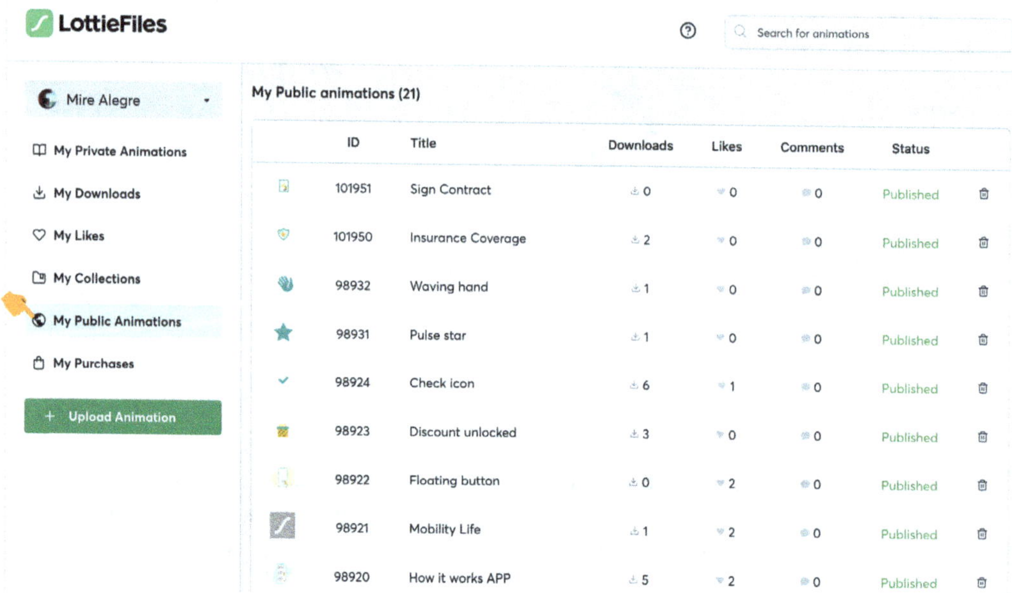

Figure 5.23 – My Public Animations view

My Purchases

Any time you purchase an animation, it will come up here. In my case, this area is empty, as I normally create my own animations, but I encourage you to have a quick look at the marketplace. It can provide inspiration as there are so many good animators out there:

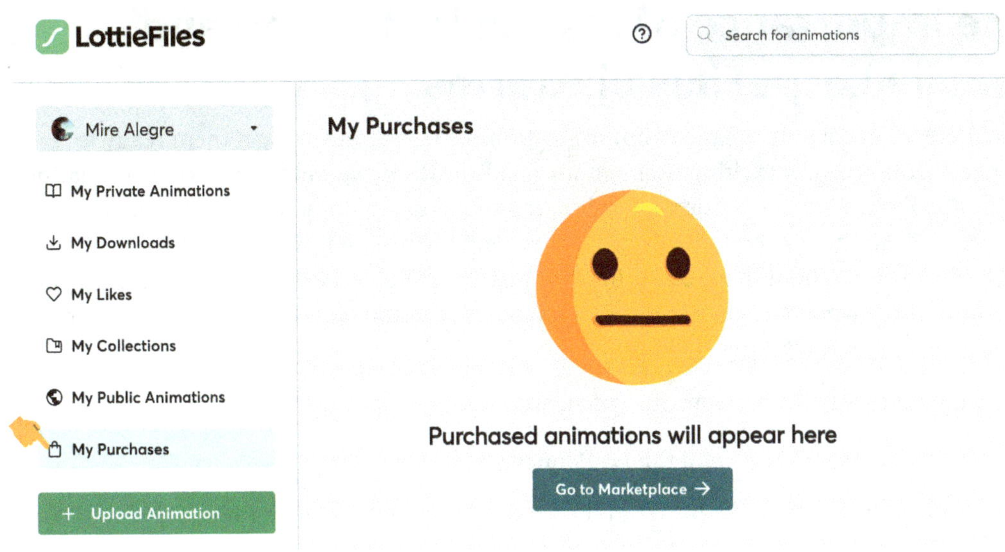

Figure 5.24 – My Purchases view

My Private Animations

And finally, and for me, the one I use the most, is the **My Private Animations** section. Here is where you'll find all the animations you have previewed in the LottieFiles AE plugin or the ones you have uploaded through the LottieFiles desktop and mobile platforms:

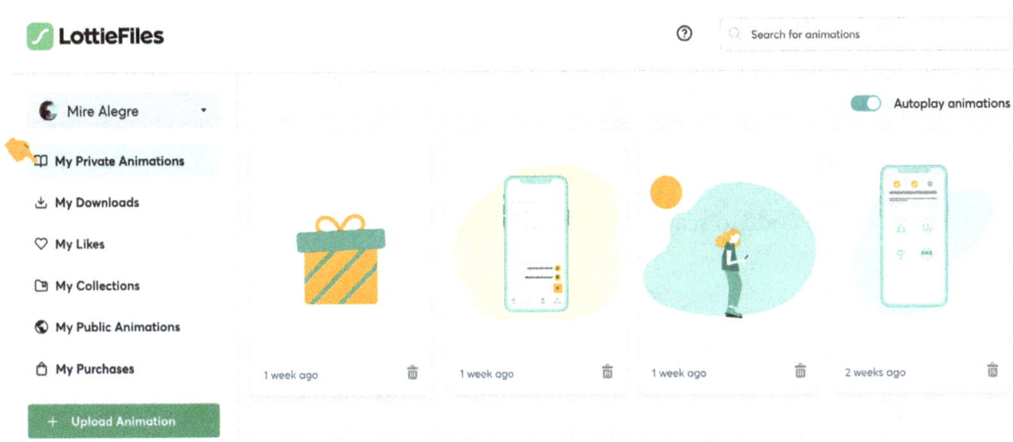

Figure 5.25 – My Private Animations view

Now that we are familiar with our LottieFiles dashboard, let's start uploading our animation; just follow me to the next section where we will learn all about it.

The importance of testing in desktop and mobile LottieFiles platforms

And, here we are, about to upload our animations to LottieFiles and get them ready to hand off. This is a very exciting moment for me. I see three big milestones when animating for Lottie. First, when we render our animation in AE using Bodymovin or LottieFiles plugins and we check everything works; the second big moment is this, right here, right now, when we are about to upload it into the platform to check everything works fine, and the third one is when our animation is live! But, let's not hurry; let's upload our icon and check everything is working nicely.

There are three ways to preview our `.json` animations:

- In the preview window of the LottieFiles plugin for AE.
- Upload, preview, and handoff in the LottieFiles browser platform.
- Preview in the LottieFiles apps for Android and iOS.

Previewing .json files using the LottieFiles plugin for AE

As we've already seen earlier in this chapter, once we render our animation in the LottieFiles plugin for AE, we can automatically see a preview of it in the same plugin panel, in the **Views** section. That's not the only thing we can do here. We can also do the following:

- View more information about the file size.
- Change the background color for the preview.
- Save it as a `.json` or `.lottie` file.
- Upload the file to **My Private Animations** in the LottieFiles dashboard.
- Generate a QR code to scan it from our mobile devices to preview it there.

So, as you can see, the LottieFiles plugin allows us to render, preview, upload, and hand off our animation all from the same place.

That said, I highly recommend uploading and previewing `.json` files wherever they are going to be shown (web, iOS, and/or Android), even if my animation looks perfect in the LottieFiles plugin. You'll experience why I say that soon.

Uploading and previewing .json files on the LottieFiles platform

Let's see how to get to the next step; let's see how to upload and preview our `.json` animation. We have already rendered and saved our `.json` animation with Bodymovin or LottieFiles plugins and now I want to test my animation and double-check everything works as expected. How? On **My Dashboard**.

Let's upload our animation. It is as easy as clicking on the **Upload Animation** button, which we can find in our LottieFiles browser dashboard, as shown in *Figure 5.26*:

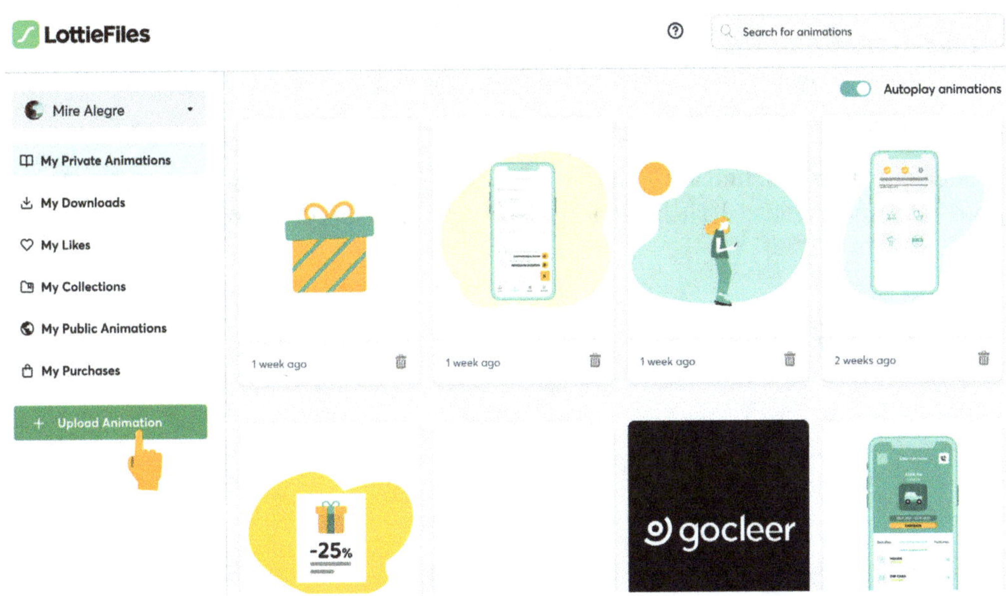

Figure 5.26 – Upload Animation button on the My Dashboards view

Once we click on the button to upload the file, a new window comes up. As you can see in the following screenshot, uploading our `.json` file is as easy as dragging it to the window:

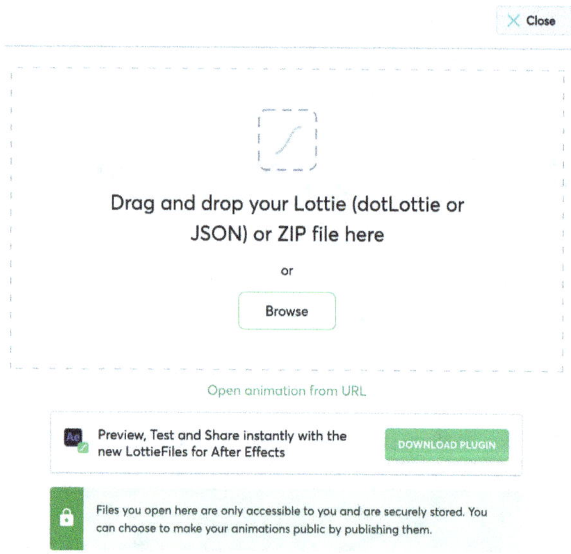

Figure 5.27 – Upload Animation drag and drop/browse screen

So, let's do that, let's drag our `icon_check.json` file here.

Once we do that, we will find a **Preview** window with our animation and also a few options that can be adjusted, such as background color and speed, for example:

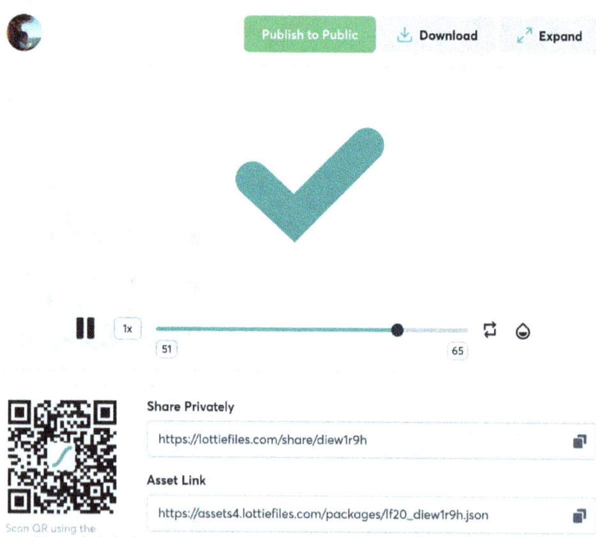

Figure 5.28 – Preview window

As you can see, previewing and testing `.json` files in the LottieFiles dashboard is very easy and straightforward. Let's move to the next section to learn to do the same from a mobile device.

Previewing our Lottie animations in the mobile LottieFiles app

Previewing our animations is a smart thing to do and will avoid us handing off LottieFiles that don't work properly. Remember we mentioned earlier, back in *Chapter 4, Move It! Animating Our First Lottie With After Effects*, there are some features not supported for specific devices. For example, **radial burst** is not supported on iOS.

> **Supported Features**
> You can learn more about supported features of LottieFiles in *Chapter 6, Don't Stop! Exploring Plugins and Resources That Will Keep You Going*, in the *Supported Lottie features for iOS, Android, and the web* section.

Let's see what happens when we preview the animation in our iOS mobile app:

1. Go back to AE.
2. Open the **LottieFiles** panel and scroll down to the bottom, where you'll see a list of your available devices:

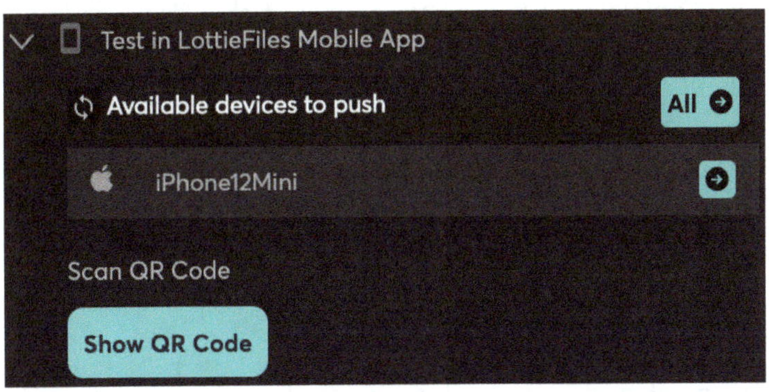

Figure 5.29 – Show QR Code button on the LottieFiles plugin for AE preview panel

3. Select the one you want to test. In my case, I'm going to choose **iPhone12Mini**.

4. Click on the **Show QR Code** button:

Figure 5.30 – Generated QR code on the LottieFiles plugin for AE preview panel

Now, let's grab your phone to finish the process:

5. Open up the LottieFiles app.
6. Click on **Scan** to scan the QR code and voilà, the animation shows up here!

If you are doing this from an iOS device, you'll notice something weird is happening, right? **Radial burst** is not showing correctly! Why? We've rendered our animations in AE using Bodymovin and LottieFiles plugins and it seemed to preview well. Also, when we uploaded it onto the LottieFiles dashboard, the animation showed properly, but not now, at least not on an iOS device (if you are checking this from an Android, you won't know what I'm talking about as it works perfectly well on Android, Windows, and the web).

But, why is that? Did we do something wrong? Well, not really, it's just because this feature is not supported on iOS. There, I've said it. Radial burst won't work on any iOS device. So, why have we done it in the first place? Of course, there is a list of supported features by device and platform, however, I wanted you to experience on your own how important it is to test things before handing them off. No matter how sure we are that something is going to work, sometimes, things just don't.

LottieFiles plugins and platforms are iterating constantly; one day things work, the next day, they don't, or vice versa. So, my suggestion here is to always *test*.

So, now what? Well, we can use our great animation with its radial burst effect for the web, Windows, and Android. But, what if we want to use it on iOS; do we have to go back to AE and redo things? Not really, LottieFiles allows us to tweak a few things in our animations without the need to go back to AE. So, stay with me, we are going to correct that in the blink of an eye.

Creating and editing a Lottie without using AE

That last section was a bit of a low kick; we were all really happy with our cool animation and now what? The nice effect won't show on iOS. Well, these things happen sometimes. We now have three choices:

- Complain about it.
- Go back to AE and add some little circles around our animation, one by one.
- Be lean and just remove the **radial burst** effect.

I'll go with the third option and you'll see how quick that is. We don't even need to go back to AE. Let's open **Lottie Editor**. To do that, follow these steps:

1. Go to the LottieFiles web dashboard.
2. Go to the left menu and select **My Private Animations**.
3. Click on the **check_icon** animation.
4. Click on the **Edit Animation** button, as highlighted in *Figure 5.31*:

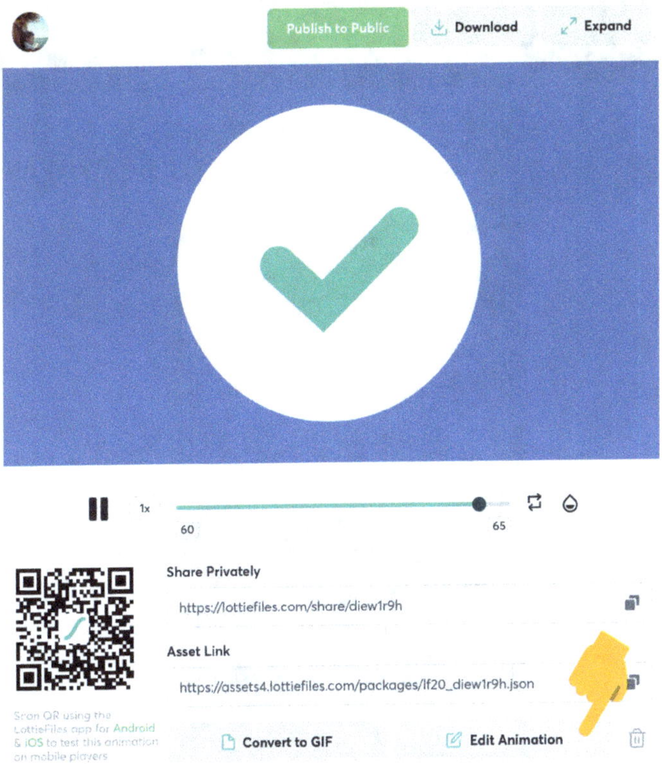

Figure 5.31 – Edit Animation button in LottieFiles desktop dashboard preview window

Lottie Editor appears and here is where we can also perform some magic. As we said, I'm going to keep my super cool sparkling icon for the web and Android and I'm going to adjust it for iOS.

Let's check the editor workspace view:

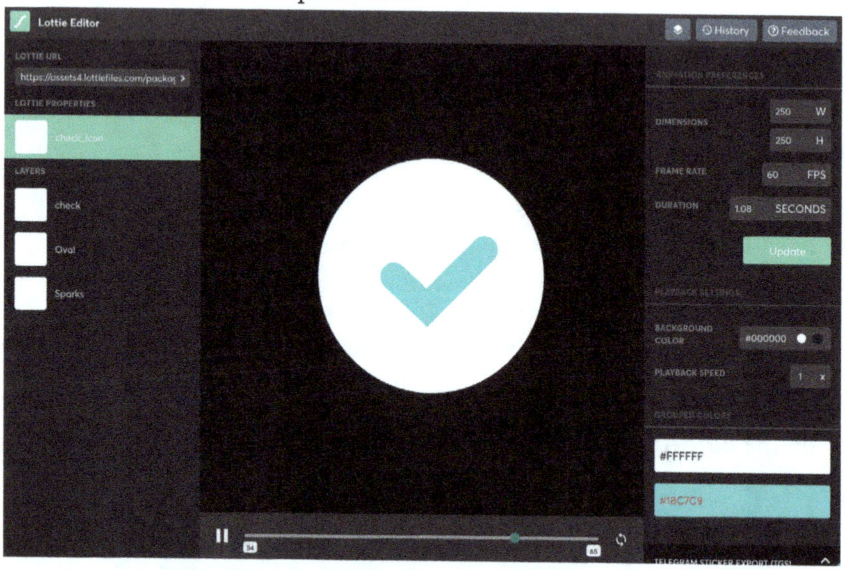

Figure 5.32 – Editor workspace view

On the left-hand side panel, we see **LOTTIE URL**, **LOTTIE PROPERTIES**, and **LAYERS**:

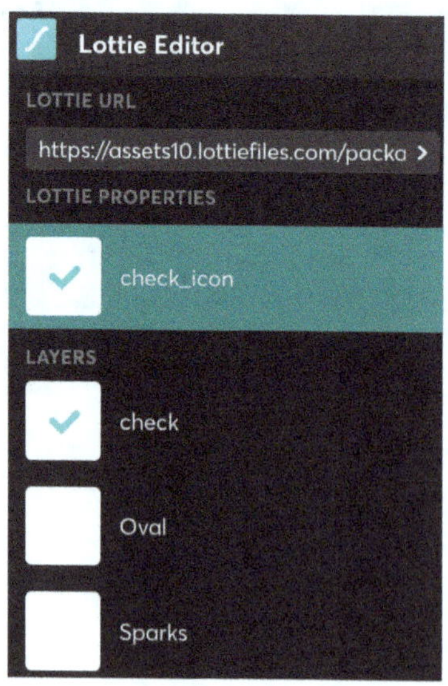

Figure 5.33 – Left-hand side editor panel

Lottie URL

The Lottie URL is the actual `.json` code itself. It contains all your animation's information and can be used to share your animation with the technical team. However, there are also some other more visual ways to share your animations, as we will soon see.

Lottie properties

When **LOTTIE PROPERTIES** is selected, a new panel opens up on the right-hand side of the screen, as shown in *Figure 5.34*. In this panel, we can change a few of our animation properties:

- **ANIMATION PREFERENCES**: This is the place where we can adjust **DIMENSIONS**, **FRAME RATE**, and **DURATION** of the animation.
- **PLAYBACK SETTINGS**: Lottie also allows us to change **BACKGROUND COLOR** but just for preview. So, since our animation is a white-over-white background, let's pick a different color. And, we can also adjust **PLAYBACK SPEED** to **1.5x**, **2x**, or **2.5x**.
- **GROUPED COLORS**: Here is where the magic happens. The colors we can see listed are the ones contained in the animation. We can change them by just clicking on one of them and selecting a new one. This will change the color everywhere in our animation but, if you stay with me for a moment, I'll show you how to change it bit by bit.
- **TELEGRAM STICKER EXPORT**: Here is where you can effortlessly convert your animation for Telegram, but we will see that in a minute. Let's focus on the editor for now.
- **EXPORT AS LOTTIE JSON**: Once you are happy with your animation, you can export it just by clicking the blue button. Easy-peasy, right?

- **UPLOAD TO LOTTIEFILES**: We've seen that you can export your new animation as a Telegram sticker and as a `.json` file, but you could also upload it back as a new animation into your dashboard **Previews** section:

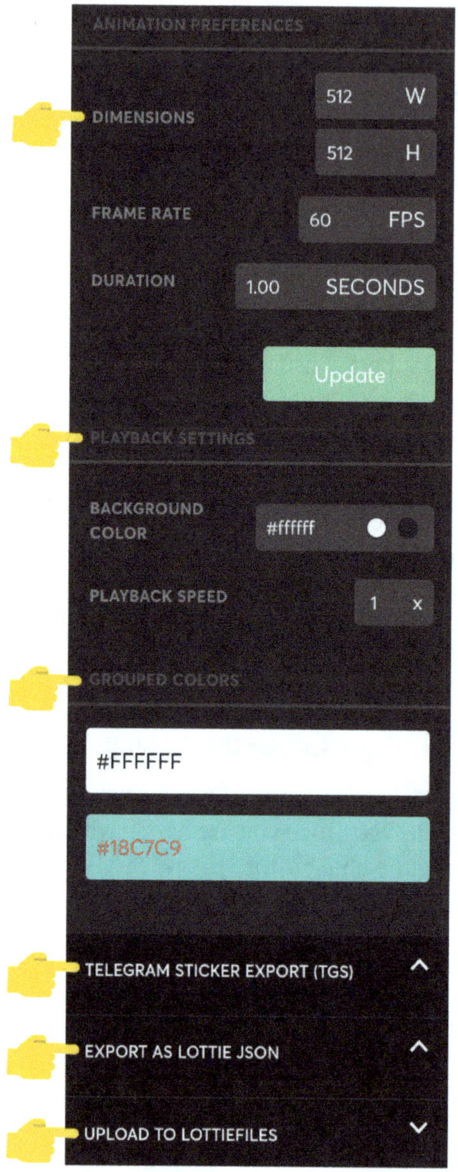

Figure 5.34 – Right-hand side editor panel

Now that we know how to change the main properties of our Lottie animation directly into **Lottie Editor**, let's see what else can be done.

Layers

We've just seen how to adjust some of the main properties of our animation, but **Lottie Editor** allows us to go a bit deeper into it thanks to layers.

As we can see on the left-hand side of the screen (*Figure 5.35*), there are three different layers contained in our animation, which are the same as we've got in our AE animation: **check**, **Oval**, and **Sparks**.

Now, let's select **Layers** | **check** and see what we can do with it:

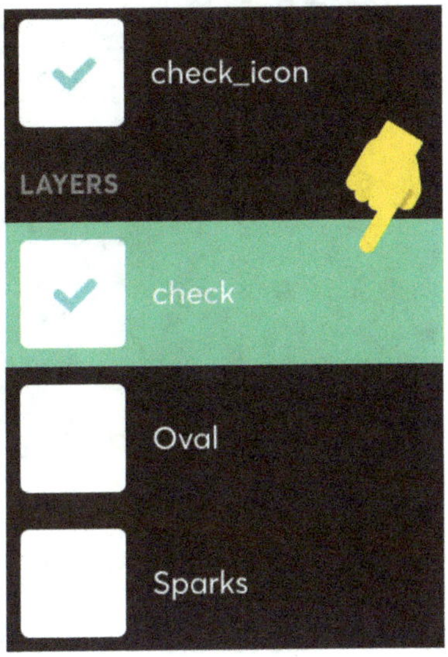

Figure 5.35 – Left-hand side panel, selected layer

When selecting the **check** layer, we notice on the right-hand side of the screen that the options change and new properties appear, such as the following:

- **LAYER VISIBILITY**: This property will allow us to hide the selected layer when clicking the little eye icon on the right. If a layer is hidden, it won't be exported in the `.json` file.
- **COLORS**: In here, we will find the colors used in each of the layers. In our case, we only see the blue color but if this layer had more colors, we would see them here and could change them by just clicking on the color and selecting a new one.

- **EXPORT LAYER**: With this option, we can just export the selected layer as a `.json` file without including anything else:

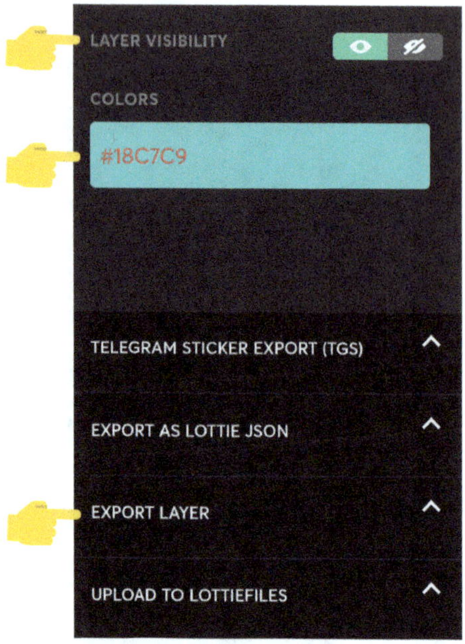

Figure 5.36 – Layer properties view

- **PROPERTIES FOR TEXT LAYER**: There is an extra option that we won't see in our icon example, which is **PROPERTIES FOR TEXT LAYER**. Although, if we had some text in our animation, we would see the text layer on the left-hand side of the screen, and when selecting it, we would see a different panel on the right-hand side of our working area, as shown in *Figure 5.37*. The property we can change here is the content itself, but apart from that, there is not much more we can do to it, at least not yet. Also, I wouldn't rely on it too much as sometimes updated content won't show up properly or even show up at all.

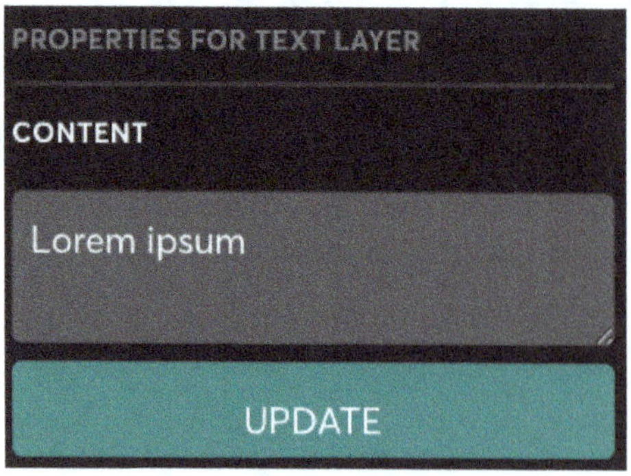

Figure 5.37 – Text properties view

So, having all that in mind, and depending on the project you are working on, it may come in handy to keep your layers as simple as possible in your AE project. Having a layer for each graphic may not be a bad idea as later on you can just come to **Lottie Editor** and adjust colors, show or hide them, or even change the content. Of course, that will depend on the project and the complexity of the animation, but it is always good to think in advance.

That said, let's go back to our icon. What do you think we need to do in order to have the icon working properly on iOS? Easy! Just hide the **Sparks** layer and export it again as a `.json` file under another name. Let's do it:

1. Select the **Sparks** layer on the left-hand side of the screen.
2. Click on the little eye icon that will appear on the right-hand side of the working area:

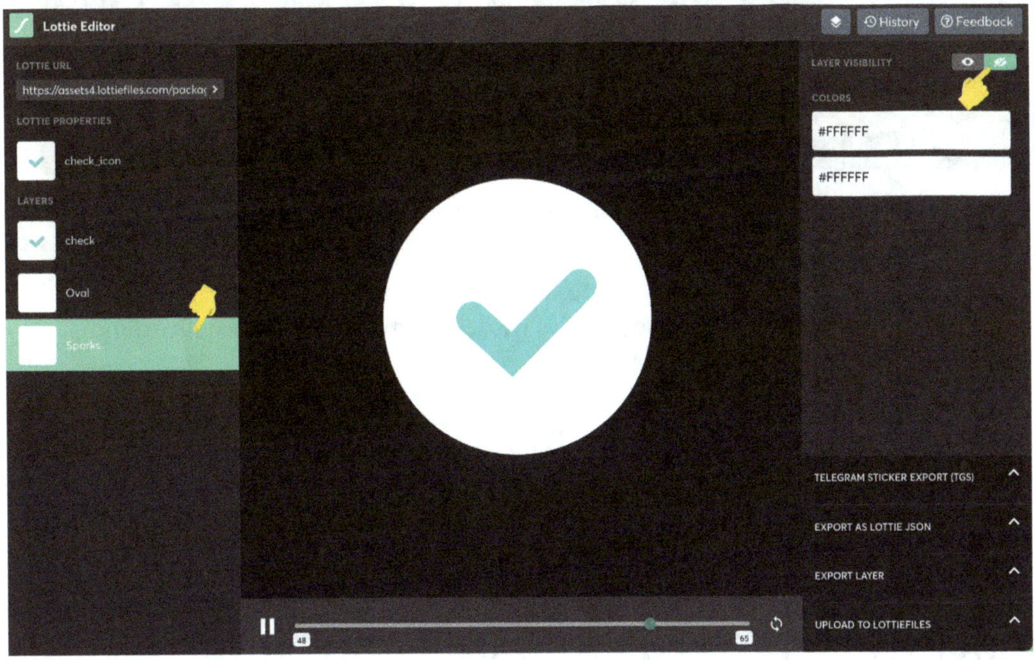

Figure 5.38 – Lottie Editor view – Sparks layer and hide icon highlighted

3. Move to **LOTTIE PROPERTIES** and select **check_icon**.
4. Export it again as a `.json` file.

5. Save it under a new name, for example, `check_icon_ios.json`:

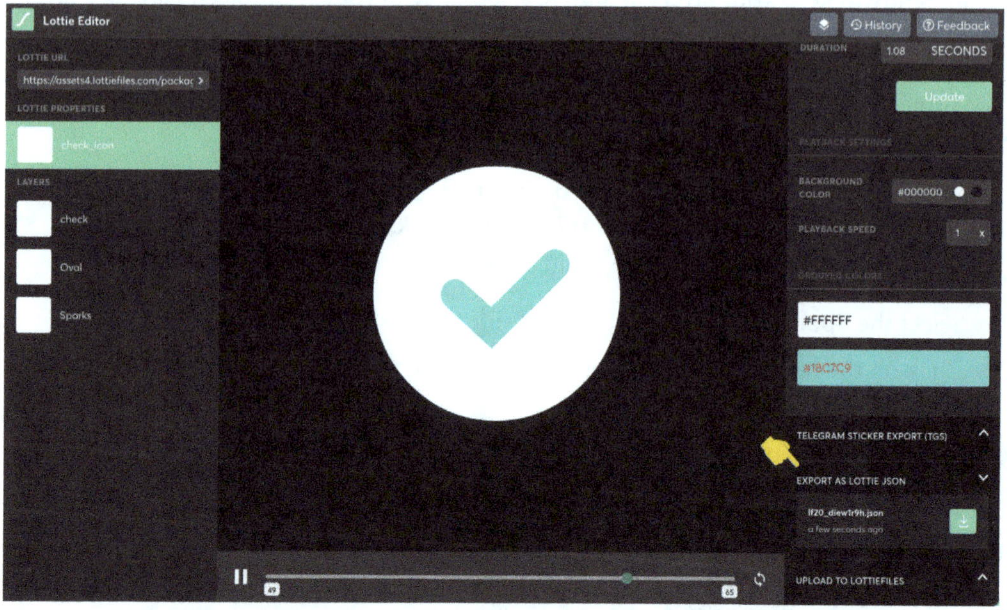

Figure 5.39 – Lottie Editor view with animation and Export as Lottie JSON button highlighted

And that's it! We have our specific icon ready to be implemented. One for Android and web, and the other for iOS. We are ready to hand it off to the developer's team and we can be sure our animation will look exactly as we designed it and animated it with no surprises.

Great! Now you know how to adjust the color, speed, and dimensions of a Lottie animation or its layers and are ready to move forward. But, don't go yet. There is still some stuff that can be done with LottieFiles that I'd like to show you. Let's move to the next section and learn how to build animations from a simple SVG without even using AE at all.

Converting SVGs to animated Lotties in seconds

Now that we've learned what we can achieve with Lottie Editor, such as changing colors, hiding or showing layers, exporting a single layer, and changing the content, dimensions, or speed of the animation, let's move to learn some other features the LottieFiles platform allows us to do with our animation in a single step. Let's forget about our **check_icon**, which is ready to be handed off to the development team. Let's see how easy and simple it is to animate an SVG file.

We talked about this feature back in *Chapter 1*, *Get Started With Lottie* but now we are going to show you how to convert your SVG files to Lottie:

1. Go to `https://lottiefiles.com/svg-to-lottie`:

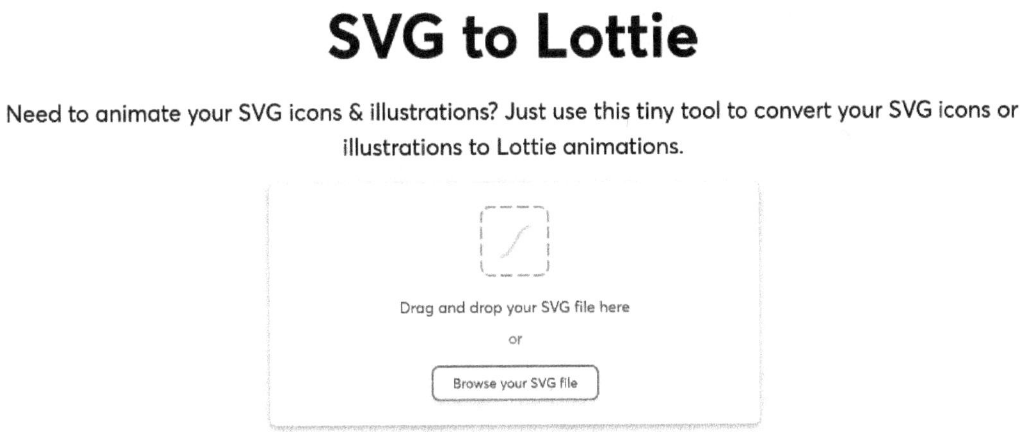

Figure 5.40 – SVG to Lottie feature view

2. Click on the **Browse your SVG file** button.
3. Browse for the `lottie/chapter05/SVGtoLottie.svg` file provided with this book.
4. Open the `SVGtoLottie.svg` file.

Well done! You'll notice the screen has changed, right? Let's see what's this all about.

In the center of the screen, we can see our static SVG, the star. This is the SVG file we've just uploaded. To the left of the star, there is a window named **Animations**, which contains a bunch of already made animations, and to the right, we find the exporting options.

So, this is it. Let's do an example:

1. Choose an animation you like from the animation window.
2. Check the results on the central view.
3. Do you like it? No? Try something else. Yes? Let's export it to `.json`.

4. Click on the **Download Lottie** button, and there you have it!

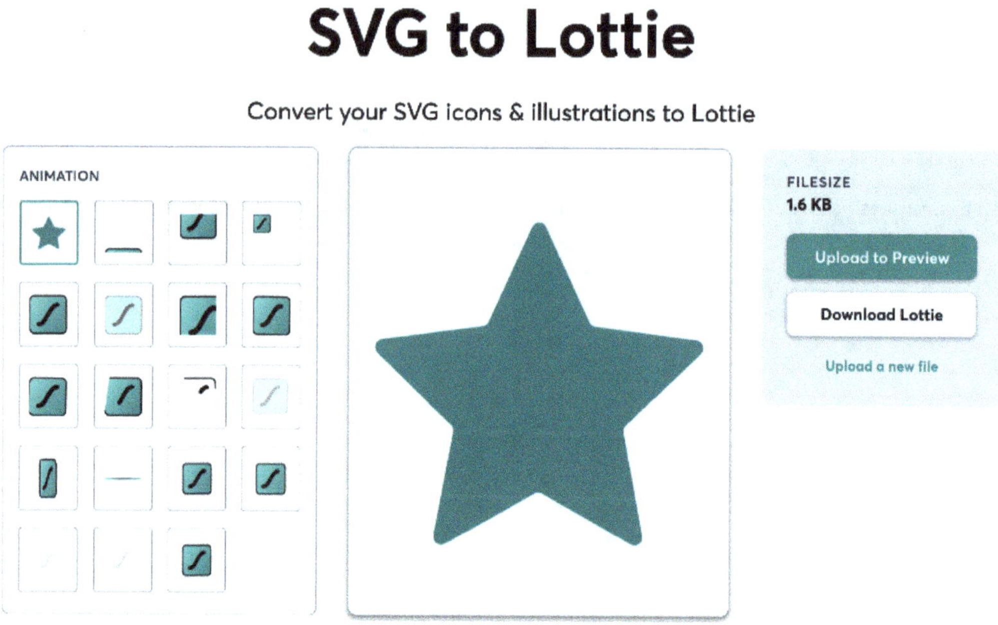

Figure 5.41 – SVG to Lottie main working area

As simple as that, you've just learned another way to create your own animations. Obviously, this is a very simple animation, but it can do the job sometimes.

So, now that you know how to animate an SVG, let's move on to converting Lottie to GIF.

Converting Lottie to GIF in just one click

If we are learning how to work with Lottie, it is because we want to avoid adding animated GIF files to our apps and websites as much as possible. As we said earlier in this book, GIF files can be very heavy file-size-wise, have low-quality images, and won't be responsive. However, sometimes, we may need this kind of format, for example, to use it for some social media posts.

LottieFiles gives us the option to convert the `.json` file to GIF in the blink of an eye, and here is how:

1. Go to `https://lottiefiles.com/lottie-to-gif`.
2. Browse for the `lottie/chapter05/LottietoGIF.json` file provided with this book (this is the Lottie we created in the *Converting SVGs to animated Lotties in seconds* section).

3. Open the `LottietoGIF.json` file:

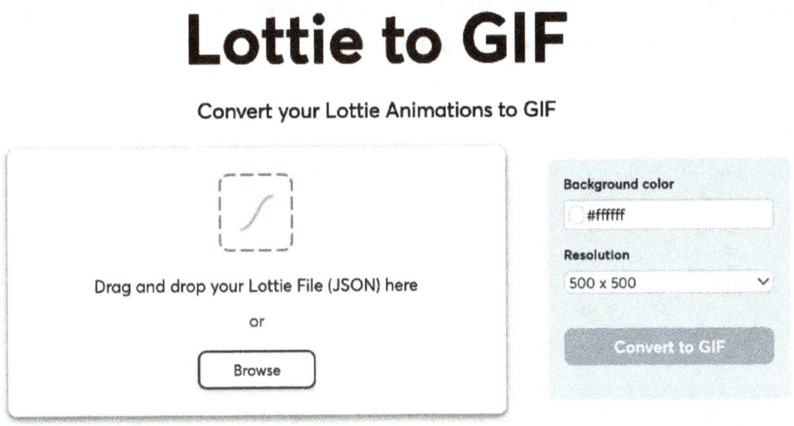

Figure 5.42 – Lottie to GIF feature view

Great! As you can see, it is pretty straightforward. We see our animated star in the center of the screen, and a couple of options such as **Background color** and **Resolution** on the right-hand side. So, this is it.

4. Choose a background color for your star; I'll just go with white.
5. Select a resolution; I think **500 x 500** works for me.
6. Click on the **Convert to GIF** button:

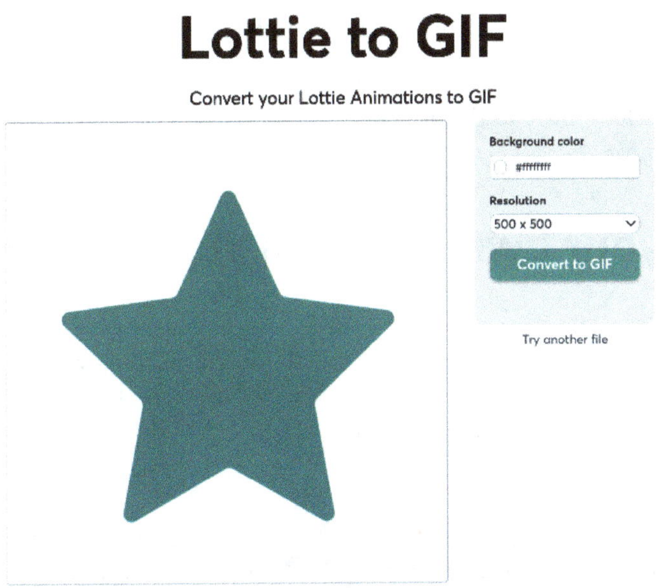

Figure 5.43 – Lottie to GIF main working area

You'll notice the animation may take some time to be converted, especially if we are working with complex ones. Just be patient. Also, notice as well that once the conversion is done, the **Convert to GIF** button is replaced by the **Download GIF** button:

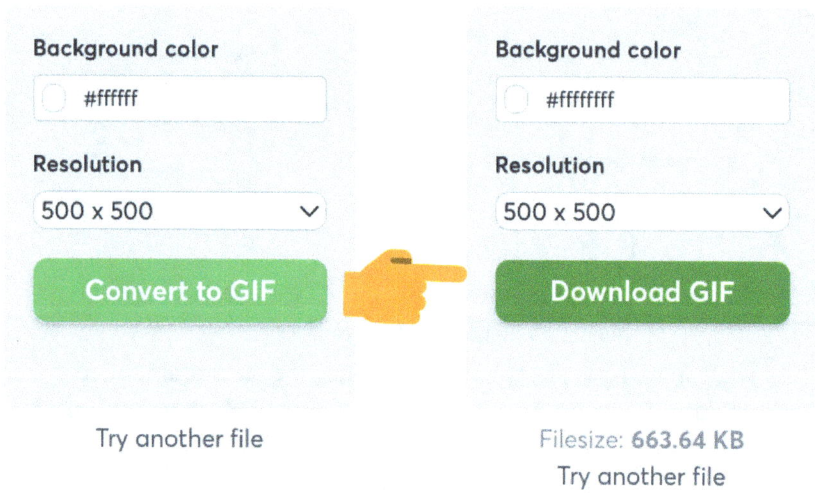

Figure 5.44 – Convert and Download GIF buttons view on GIF to Lottie working area

7. Click on the **Download GIF** button to download your animated GIF.

You have your `.json` animation converted into a GIF file ready to use anywhere.

So, now that you've learned how to convert your Lottie animation into a GIF file using LottieFiles features, let's move to the next section and see how to create Telegram stickers with LottieFiles Editor.

Creating your own personal stickers for Telegram

So, going back to Lottie Editor, remember we mentioned earlier that we can export our Lottie to be used as a Telegram sticker. Let's see how we do that. Don't be scared, it may look like a long process, but it is very straightforward:

1. Go to `https://lottiefiles.com/editor`.
2. Browse for the `lottie/chapter05/telegram_sticker.json` file provided with this book, which is a simple waving hand animation I did some time ago that I'm sharing here with you.

3. Open the `telegram_sticker.json` file.

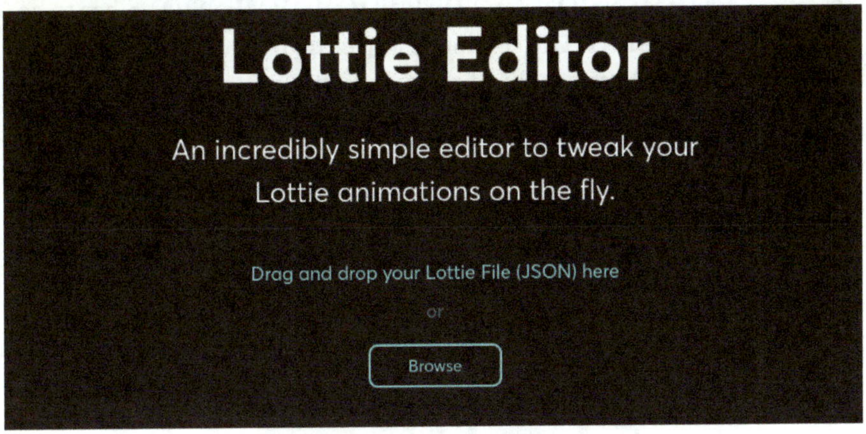

Figure 5.45 – Drag and drop or browse the Lottie Editor screen

Cool! Once the file is uploaded, you'll notice the view has changed and we are back to Lottie Editor, which we were working with earlier in this chapter. Notice the waving hand has loaded in the center of the screen, as shown in the following screenshot:

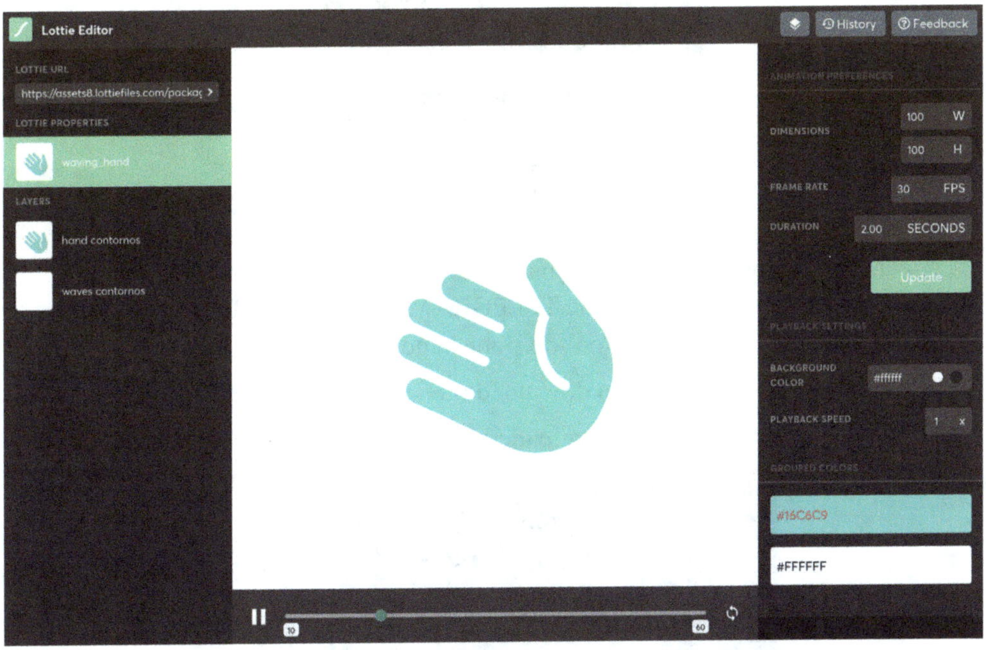

Figure 5.46 – Waving hand animation running in Lottie Editor

Now, let's continue to create the Telegram sticker.

There are two specs we have to review before exporting our animation as a Telegram sticker. These are **DIMENSIONS** and **DURATION**. **DIMENSIONS** has to be **512** by **512** exactly and **DURATION** cannot be longer than **3.00** seconds. However, remember we can always tweak this directly in **Lottie Editor**.

Since I'm reusing an old animation here, and by the time I made it, I wasn't thinking to use it for Telegram, we have to adjust the dimensions to `512`. So, let's change that in **Lottie Editor**.

4. Set **H** and **W** both to `512`.
5. Click the **Update** button.

The duration is okay, as it is just 3 seconds. The **ANIMATION PREFERENCES** panel is shown in the following screenshot:

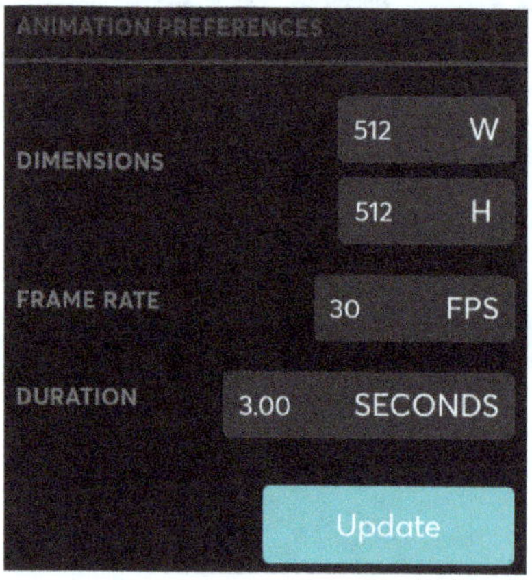

Figure 5.47 – Waving hand preferences

Perfect, now that we've got everything sorted, let's move a little bit down on the same panel. We are looking for the **TELEGRAM STICKER EXPORT** tool. You should see it by scrolling down on the right-hand side panel.

6. Click on the little blue button to download the waving hand as a Telegram sticker.
7. A `sticker.tgs` file will be downloaded.

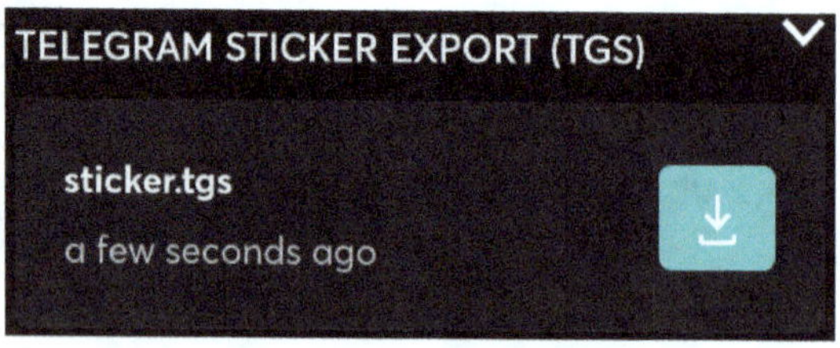

Figure 5.48 – Telegram sticker export panel view

8. Open **Telegram for desktop**.
9. In the search box, type `Stickers`.
10. Click on the **Stickers** verified contact:

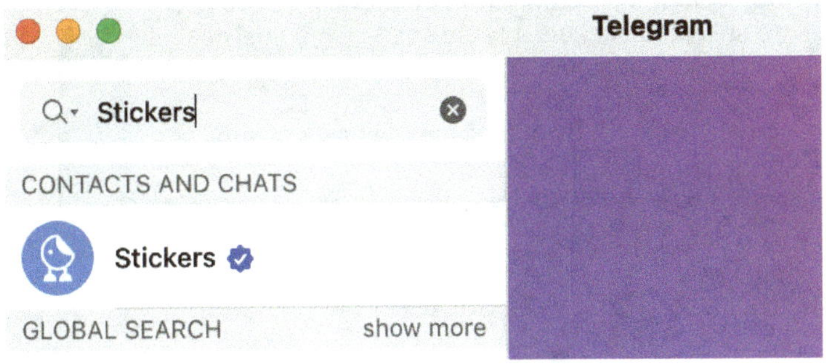

Figure 5.49 – Telegram for desktop searching for stickers bot chat

11. Click on **Start** to start a conversation with the **Stickers** bot:

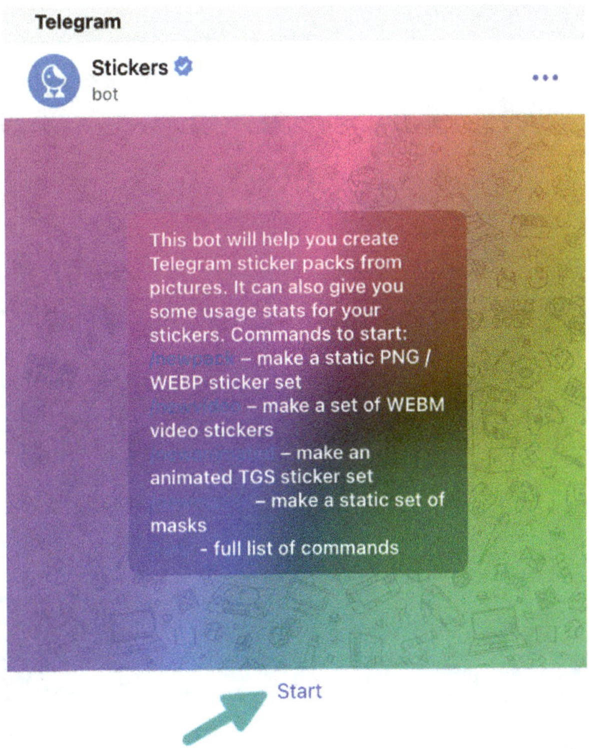

Figure 5.50 – The Stickers bot's Start a conversation button

12. Now, type `/newanimated` in the conversation window.

13. Send the message to the bot:

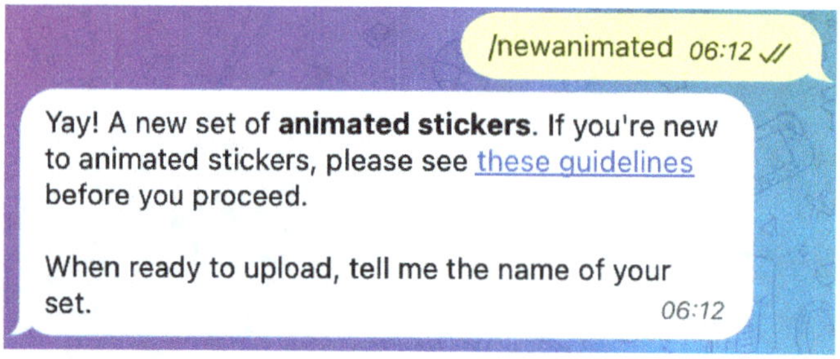

Figure 5.51 – Stickers bot conversation view

Let's follow the instructions given by the **Stickers** bot:

1. Let's give a name to our set of stickers (we have to do that even if we only have one sticker). I'll name mine `My First Lottie Stickers`.
2. Drag and drop the `sticker.tgs` file we've just downloaded from Lottie Editor to the chat:

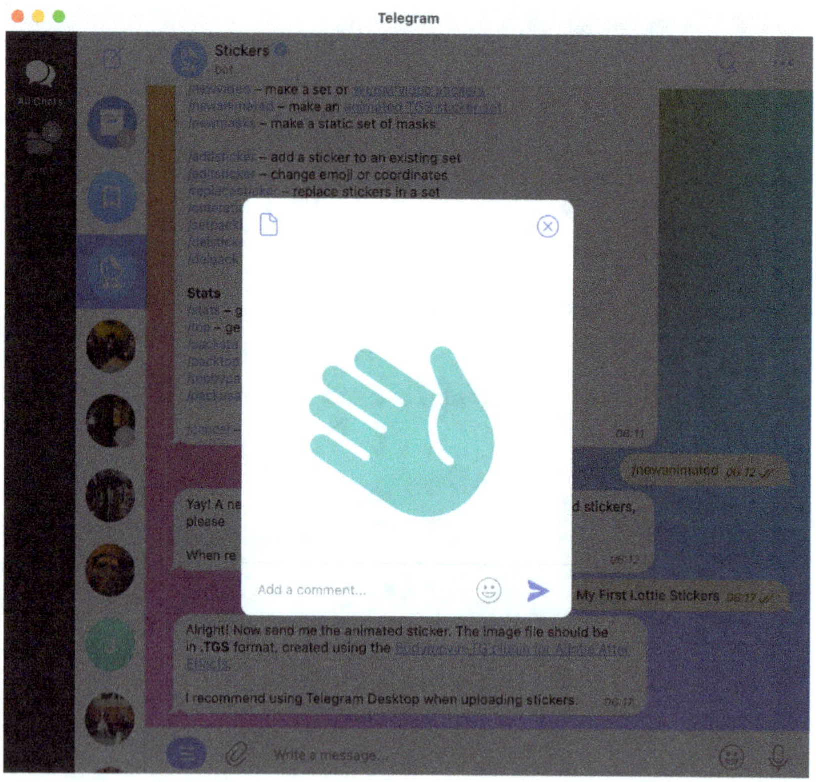

Figure 5.52 – Sending your sticker.tgs file

3. Send an emoji to the bot. This will be the emoji that the waving hand will be related to. We can send as many emojis as we want but I would recommend sticking to one or two. I'll relate mine with the existing waving hand emoji, 👋.
4. Type `/publish`.
5. Choose the **My First Lottie Stickers** sticker set:

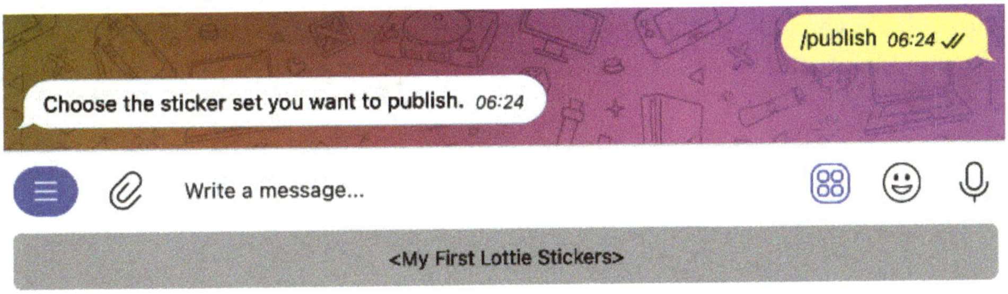

Figure 5.53 – Publish button on the Stickers bot

6. Type `/skip`.
7. Type a short name to create a URL to share. I've chosen `hellolottie`.
8. The URL is created as `https://t.me/addstickers/hellolottie`, which you can share with friends!

Isn't that cool? Now you know how to create an animation, import it to Lottie Editor, download it as a Telegram sticker, and create your own set of stickers in Telegram for you to share. Congratulations! We've gone a long way!

Summary

Wow! That's a lot of stuff we have done here; great job! And you know the best part? You are ready to have some fun and start creating your own animations from scratch to hand off! So far, we've learned how to export our animations from AE as `.json` files using the Bodymovin and LottieFiles plugins. We've gone through the process to test the exported `.json` files in AE, desktop, and mobile and realized the importance of testing it on every device before handing it off to the development team.

We've also created an account in the LottieFiles platform and learned all about the LottieFiles dashboard, where you can keep all your animations together. We've discovered Lottie Editor and how to quickly tweak any `.json` animation by changing the colors, dimensions, speed, and content.

We've also learned how to create very simple but straightforward animations by using static SVG files and also how to convert Lotties to GIFs for our social media or other related content.

And finally, the most fun part of it, we've exported a Lottie animation as a Telegram sticker and learned how to create a Telegram sticker set using the Stickers bot.

So, are you ready to fly the nest? I bet you are and that you've already started thinking about all the big things you can achieve and how cool, consistent, and user-friendly your apps will look from now on.

But, before I leave you to it, I'd like to share some references, tips, and tricks that may help you with the process. So, follow me to the next chapter, where I will tell you all about them.

6

Don't Stop! Exploring Plugins and Resources That Will Keep You Going

Looking back, I realize how many new things we've been through. At the beginning of this book, Lottie was something you may have heard about but maybe you weren't sure what it was or how it worked, and now, just five chapters later, I'm sure you feel confident enough when talking about Lottie's environment, animations and **After Effects** (**AE**). You've learned about and experienced the benefits of creating animations with AE and LottieFiles, you are now familiar with Adobe AE, and are capable of ideating, sketching, creating, and exporting your own unique animations, and have had the chance to learn and experience a real **user experience** (**UX**) animation workflow on your own.

That said, this chapter is a handy guide to keep closer when animating, a place you can come back to any time you need to find new resources for your animations. In the following sections, you'll find the links and instructions to download and install all the necessary tools and plugins we need to create our animations so you don't get lost.

We will cover a list of what features are or are not supported for each platform and device with tips and tricks on how to avoid them. Remember what happened to our icon back in *Chapter 5, Share It With the World: Working With LottieFiles*? The sparks didn't work, right? So, keep this table at hand, as it will be very useful when creating our animations in AE.

We will go through a list of shortcuts that will help speed up your work and save you tons of time. And finally, we will give you enough resources so that you can keep learning on your own.

Let's move forward to the next section to install all the tools and plugins we need.

I'd like to share some tips and tricks that will help speed up your work and save you time. Also, I'd like to share the resources I normally use when ideating, drawing, or animating, which I'm sure will help you out when you are about to create your animations.

In this chapter, we are going to cover the following topics:

- Downloading and installing the necessary tools and plugins you'll need to create your animations
- Supported Lottie features for iOS, Android, and web
- Main AE shortcuts for Windows and Mac
- Resources that will help with the animation process
- Tutorials to keep growing your animation skills

Technical requirements

For this chapter, we won't need anything except your preferred browser.

Downloading and installing the necessary plugins and tools

Before we start creating our animations, we need some specific tools and plugins that need to be installed on our computers and mobile devices first. These tools are going to help us import, create, edit, and export our files to create Lottie animations.

As you may remember, we've already talked about these tools and plugins back in *Chapter 1, Get Started With Lottie*. In this section, we will guide you through the process of downloading and installing them so you are all set up and ready to start animating. Let's go then.

Downloading and installing Adobe AE

As we mentioned earlier in this book, Adobe AE is not a free tool. It is subscription-based software, and you must purchase it as part of an Adobe Creative Cloud subscription. However, remember that Adobe offers a 7-day free trial period so you can *try before you buy*.

For complete instructions on installing the software and system requirements, visit `https://helpx.adobe.com/after-effects/using/setup-installation.html` and follow the instructions, as shown in the following screenshot:

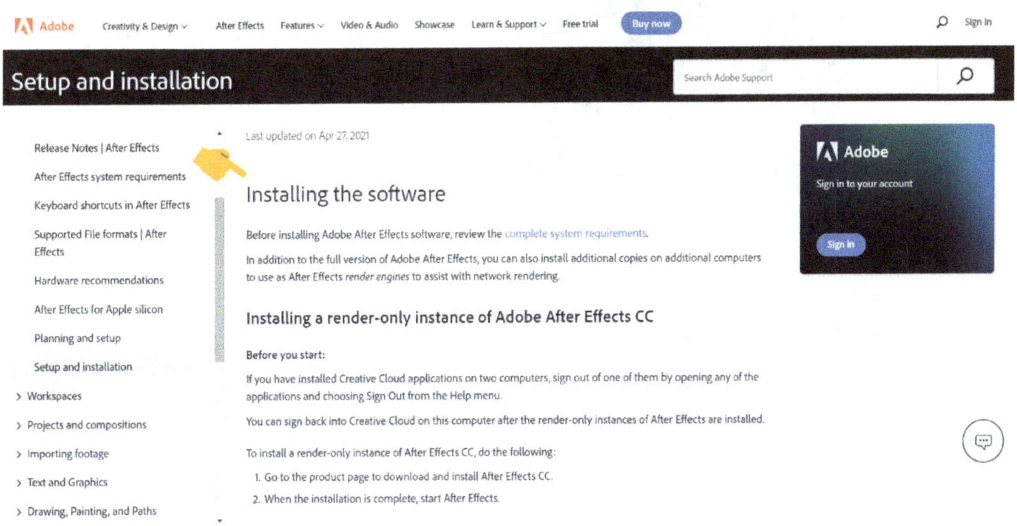

Figure 6.1 – Adobe AE user guide

Downloading and installing the Bodymovin plugin for AE

The Bodymovin plugin is very easy to install. Just follow these simple steps.

If you have a Creative Cloud subscription, follow these steps:

1. Go to `https://exchange.adobe.com/creativecloud.details.12557.bodymovin.html`.
2. Click on the **Install Now** button and follow the steps:

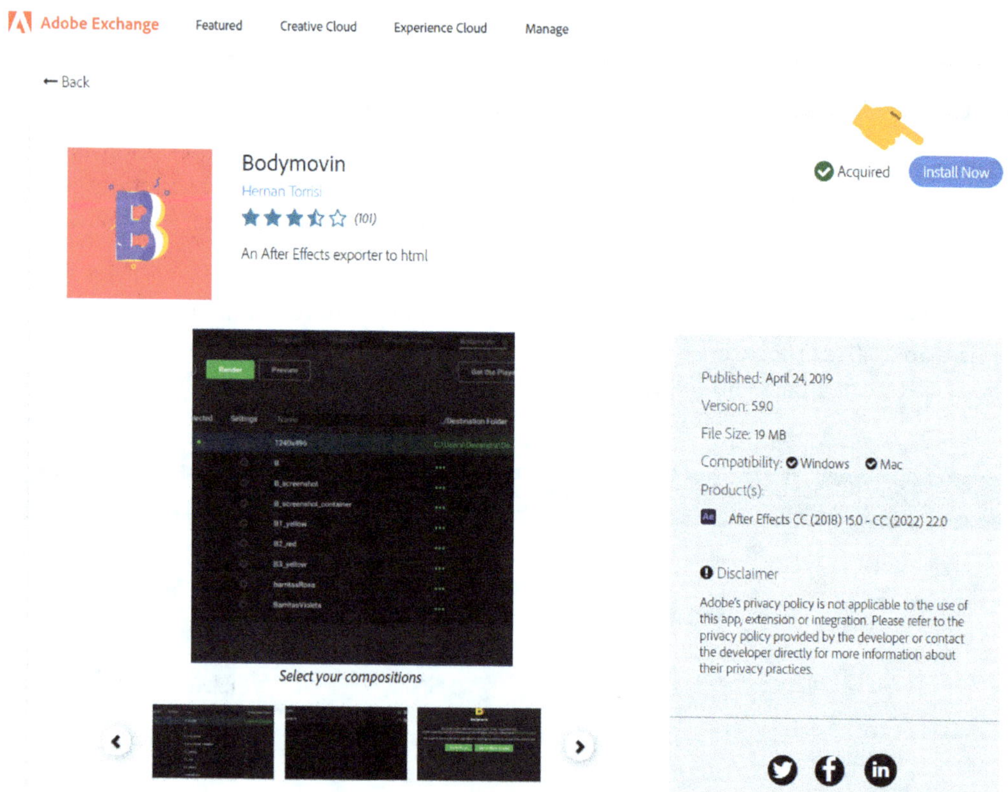

Figure 6.2 – Adobe Exchange platform – Bodymovin extension

If you don't have a Creative Cloud subscription, execute the following:

1. Download the Bodymovin extension from `https://aescripts.com/bodymovin/`. Bear in mind that you'll need to create an account to do that.

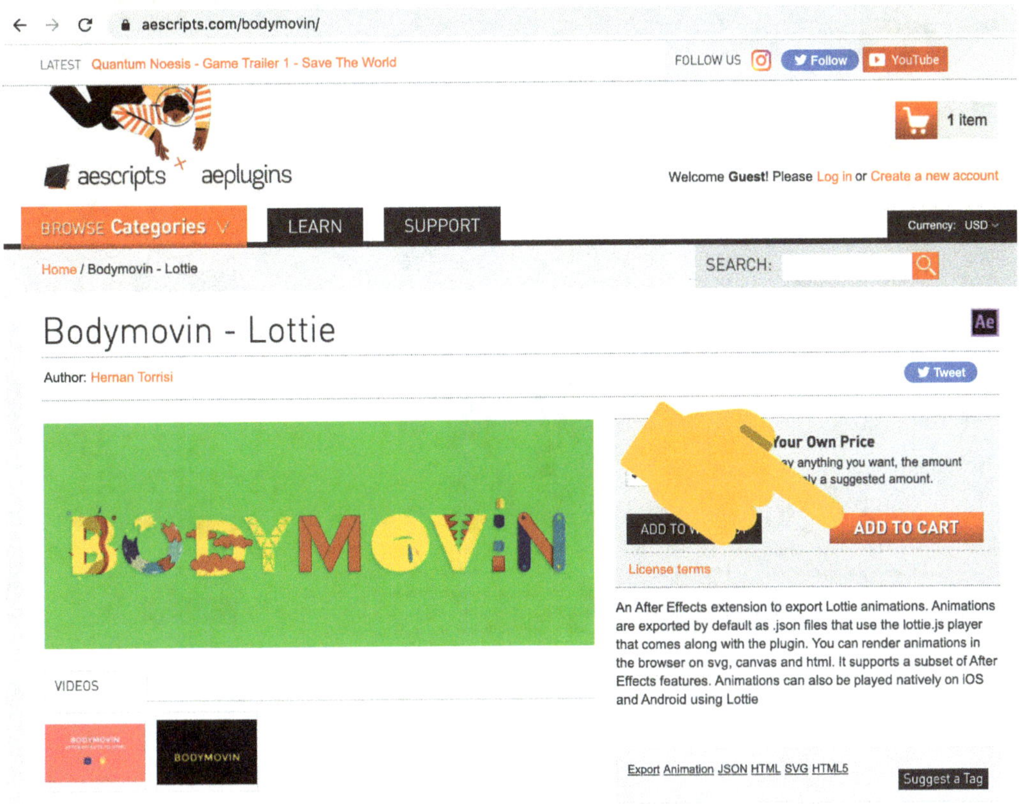

Figure 6.3 – Downloading Bodymovin

2. Download **ZXP Installer** (`https://aescripts.com/learn/zxp-installer/`) to install the plugin via Extension Manager:

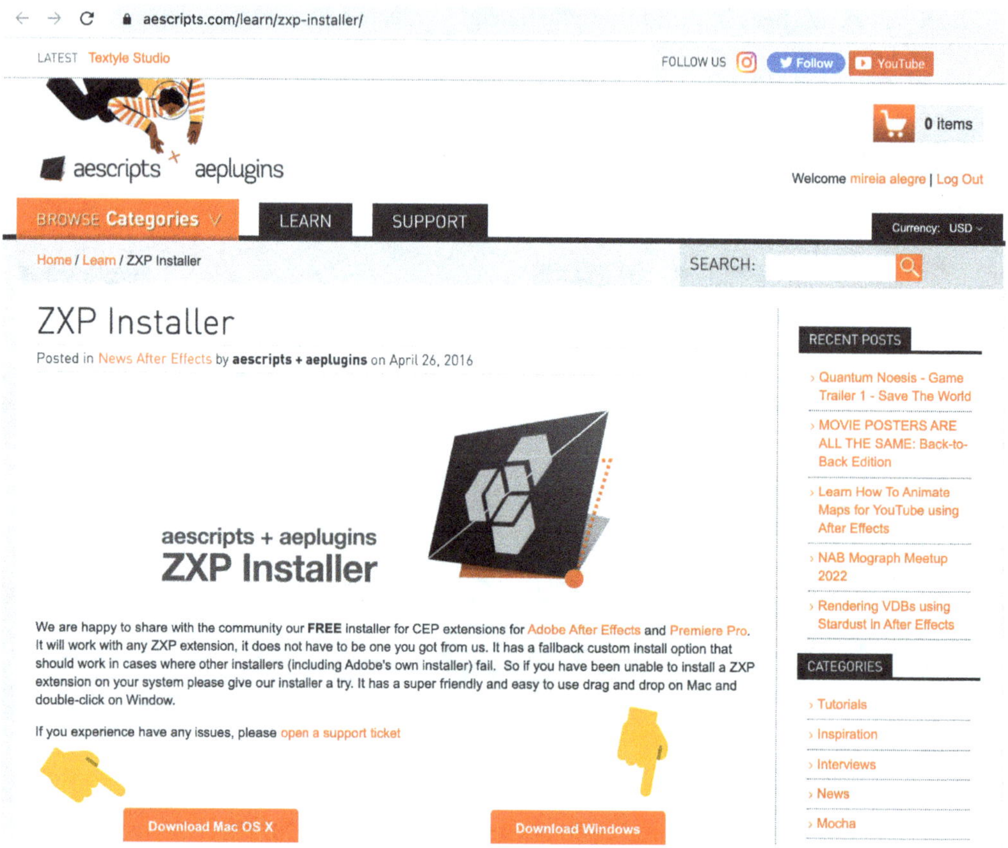

Figure 6.4 – Downloading ZXP Installer

3. Install and open **ZXP installer aescripts + aeplugins zxp installer (setup)** for macOS or Windows.
4. Drag and drop `bodymovin.zxp` into the ZXP Installer window.
5. Click **Ok** once the installation is successfully completed.
6. Open **Adobe After Effects**.
7. Go to the top navigation menu and click on **Window | Extensions**.

The recently installed Bodymovin extension should appear in the menu:

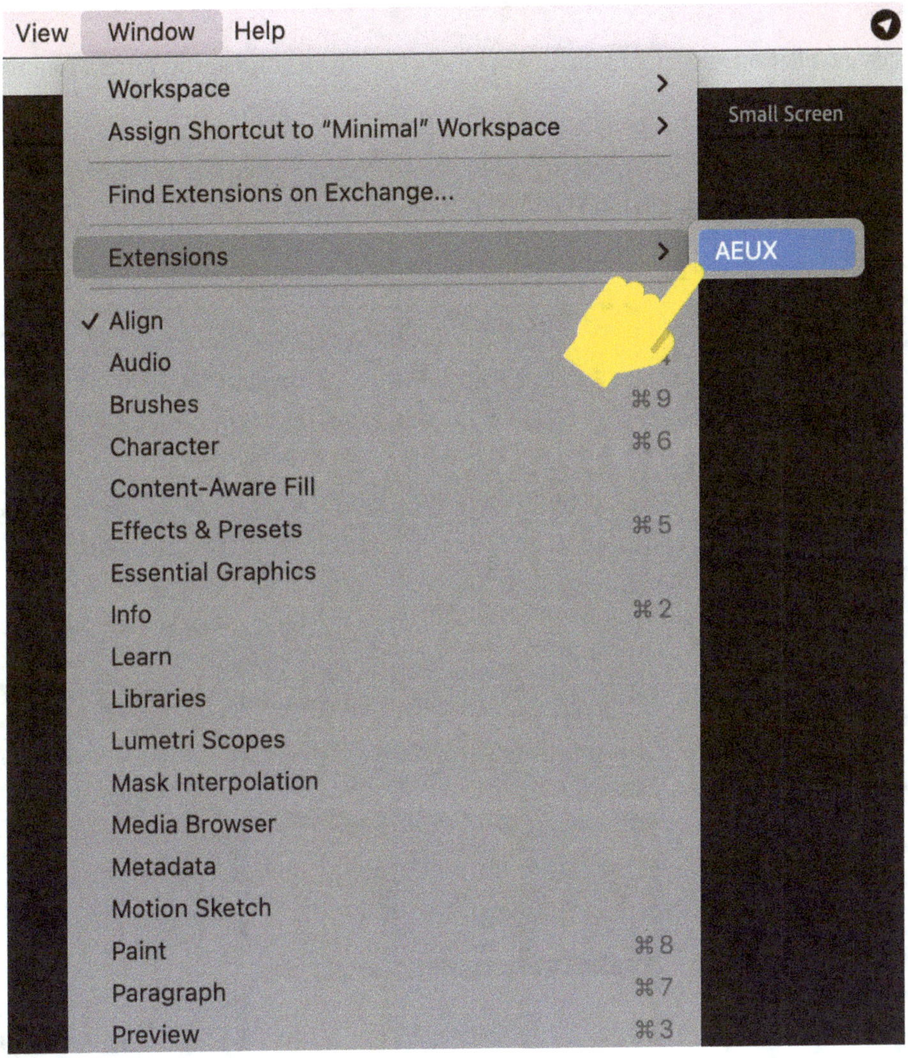

Figure 6.5 – Adobe AE Extensions window

Downloading and installing the LottieFiles plugin for AE

LottieFiles installation is very simple. If you have a Creative Cloud subscription, follow these steps:

1. Go to `https://lottiefiles.com/plugins/after-effects`.
2. Click on the **VIA ADOBE EXCHANGE** button:

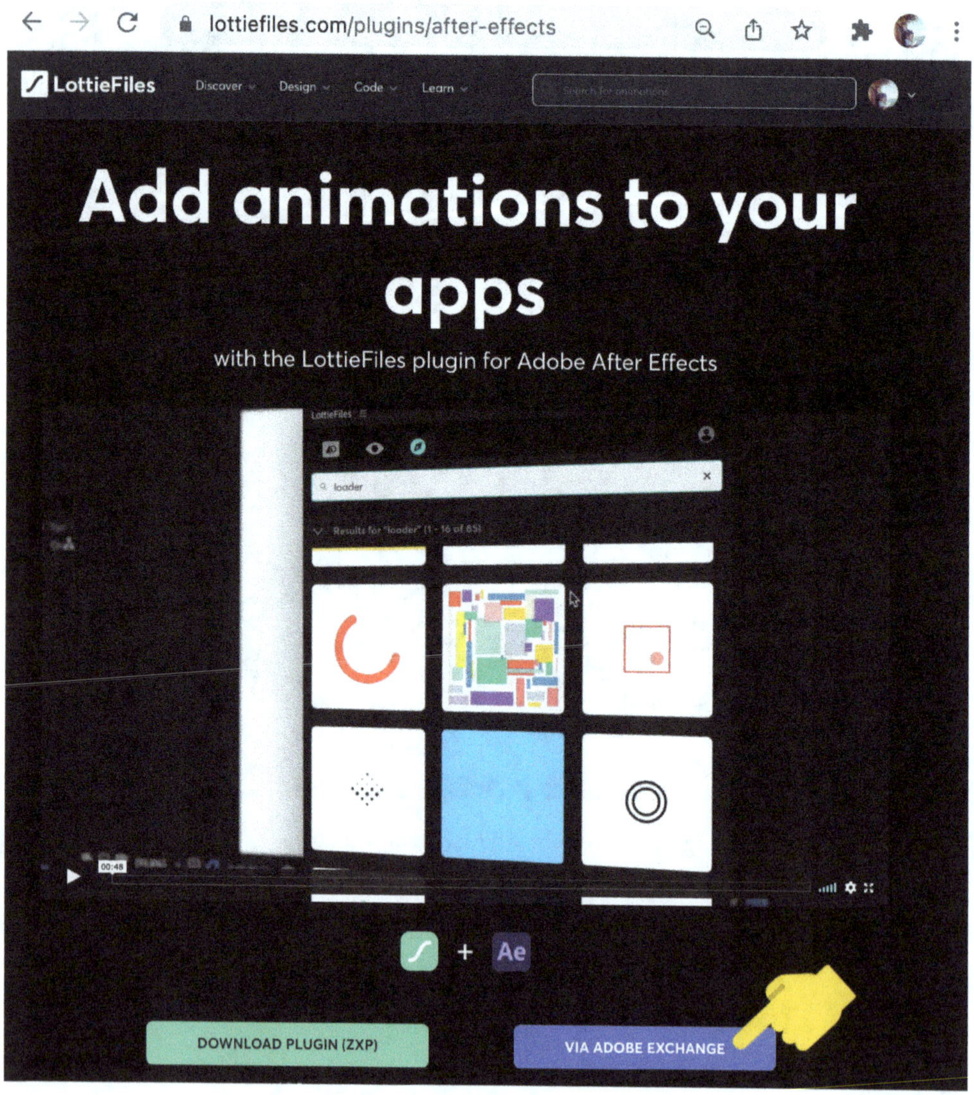

Figure 6.6 – LottieFiles plugin via Adobe Exchange

3. Click on the **Install Now** button and follow the instructions:

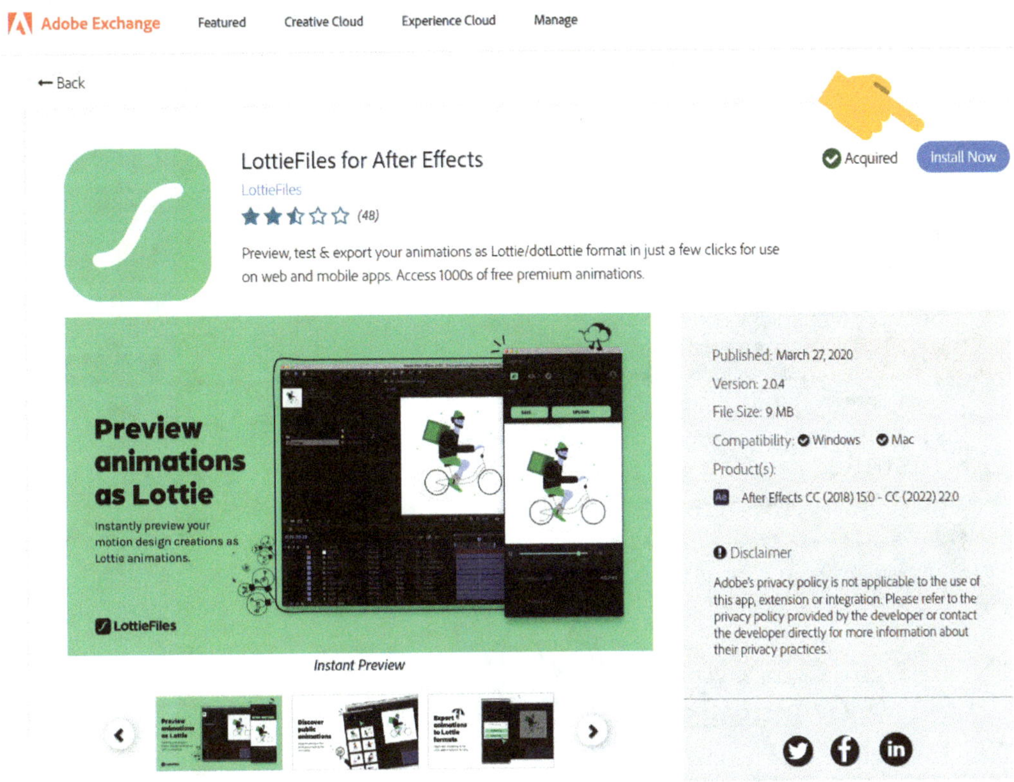

Figure 6.7 – Adobe Exchange platform – LottieFiles extension

If you don't have a Creative Cloud subscription, we will install the plugin using Extension Manager. To do that, execute the following steps:

1. Go to `https://aescripts.com/learn/zxp-installer/`.
2. Download **ZXP Installer**:

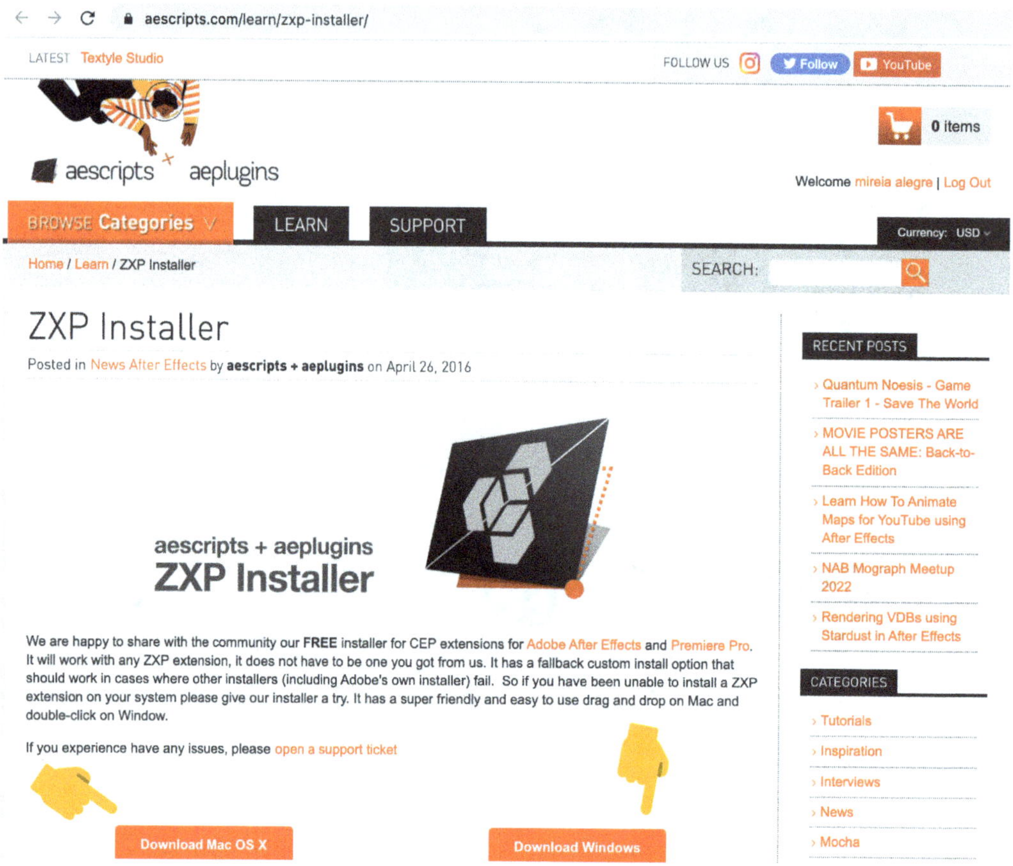

Figure 6.8 – ZXP Installer

3. Go to `https://lottiefiles.com/plugins/after-effects`.

4. Click on the **DOWNLOAD PLUGIN (ZXP)** button to install the plugin using Extension Manager:

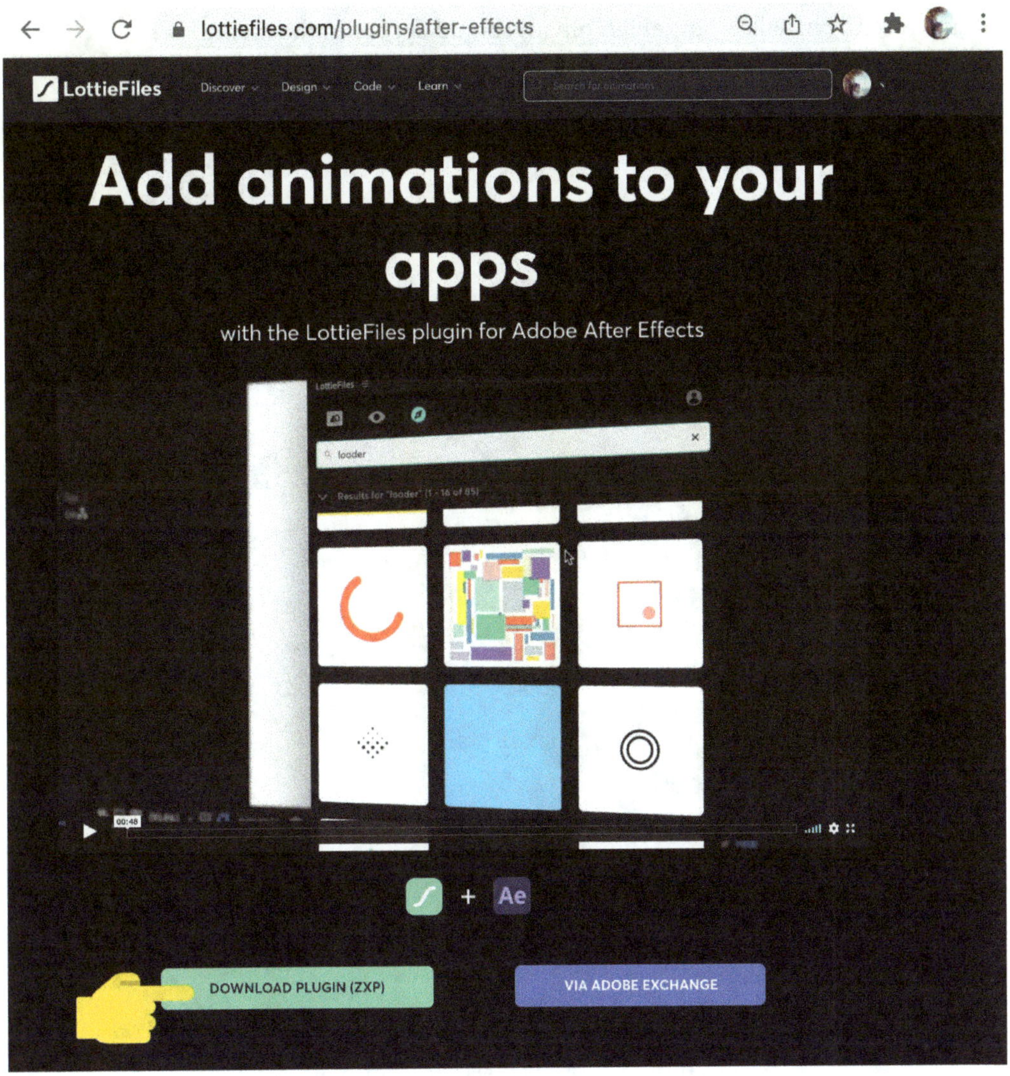

Figure 6.9 – LottieFiles plugin installing with ZXP Installer

5. Install and open **ZXP installer aescripts + aeplugins zxp installer (setup)** for macOS or Windows.
6. Drag and drop `ae-plugin-0.1.20.zxp` into the ZXP Installer window.
7. Click the **Ok** button once the installation is successfully completed.

8. Open **Adobe After Effects**.
9. Go to the top navigation menu and click on **Window | Extensions**.

   The recently installed LottieFiles plugin should appear in the menu:

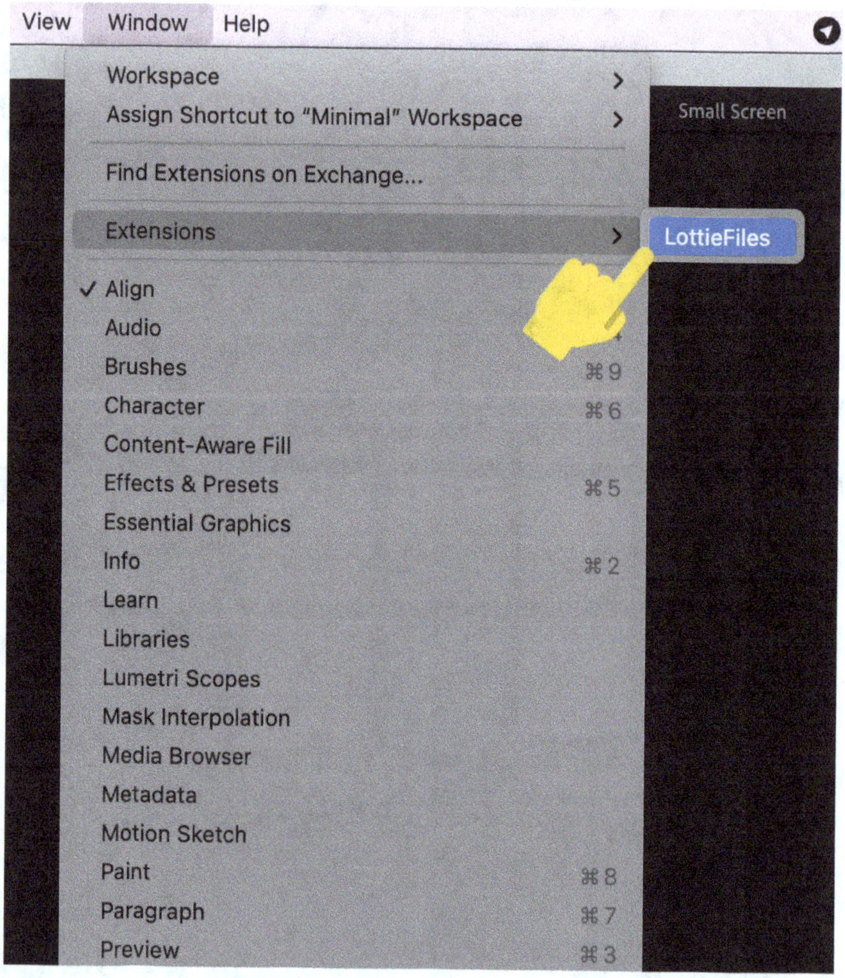

Figure 6.10 – Adobe AE LottieFiles extension menu

Downloading and installing the AEUX plugin for Sketch and Figma

If we are using Sketch or Figma for our illustrations and designs, this plugin will become very handy once we have to export the files from Sketch or Figma to AE. So, if that's the case, let's install our plugins:

Installing ZXP Extension Manager

To install any of the AEUX plugins for Figma, Sketch, or AE, we need to install the **ZXP Extension Manager** first. So, if you haven't done that yet in the previous sections, here's how you do it:

1. Go to `https://aescripts.com/learn/zxp-installer/`.
2. Download **ZXP Installer**:

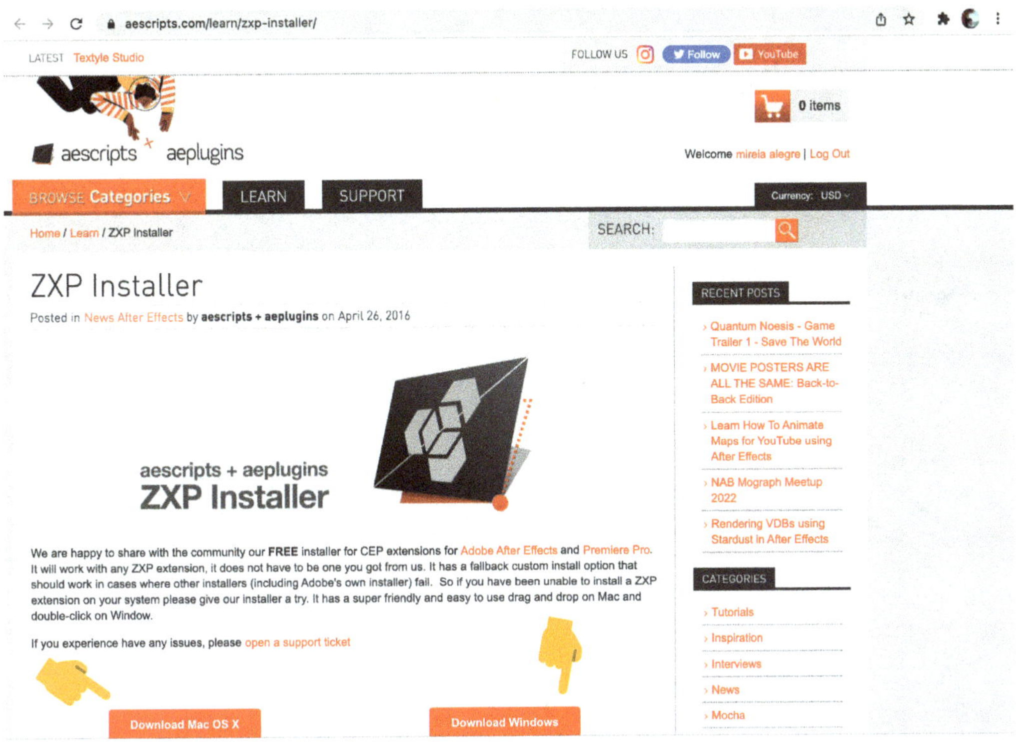

Figure 6.11 – ZXP Installer for macOS and Windows

3. Install and open **ZXP installer aescripts + aeplugins zxp installer (setup)** for macOS or Windows.

Installing AEUX for Figma

Now that we've got the ZXP Extension Manager up and running, let's install AEUX for Figma. Installing AEUX for Figma can be a bit tricky, so I recommend you follow the instructions described on their support website. To do that, follow these steps:

1. Download the AEUX for Figma plugin from `https://aeux.io/guide/download.html#sketch-57-figma`

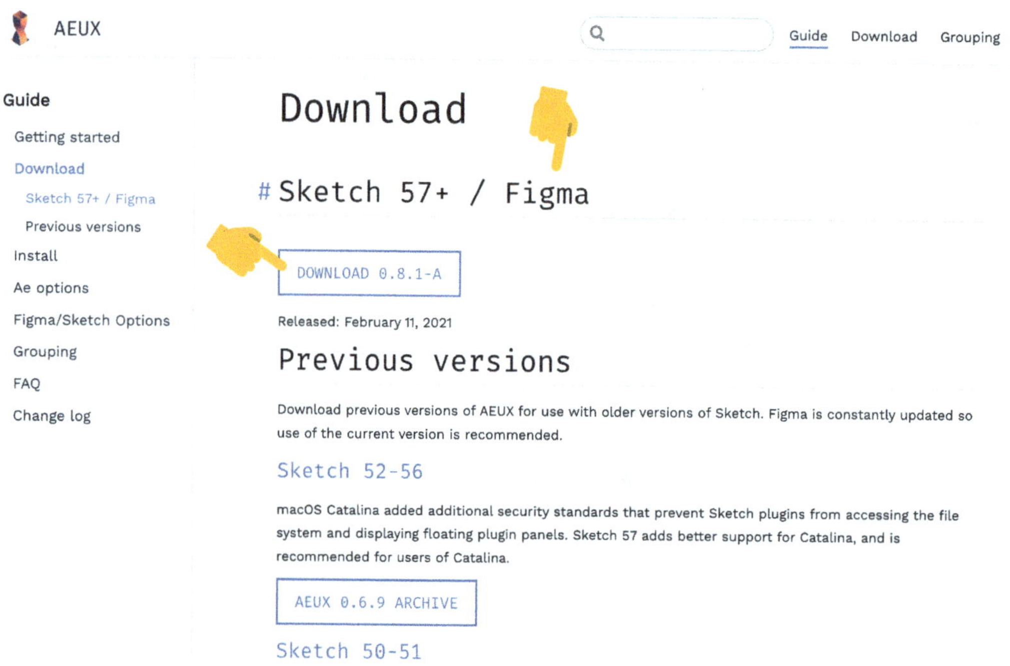

Figure 6.12 – AEUX download plugin for Figma and Sketch

2. Go to `https://aeux.io/guide/install.html#figma` and follow the instructions to install the plugin:

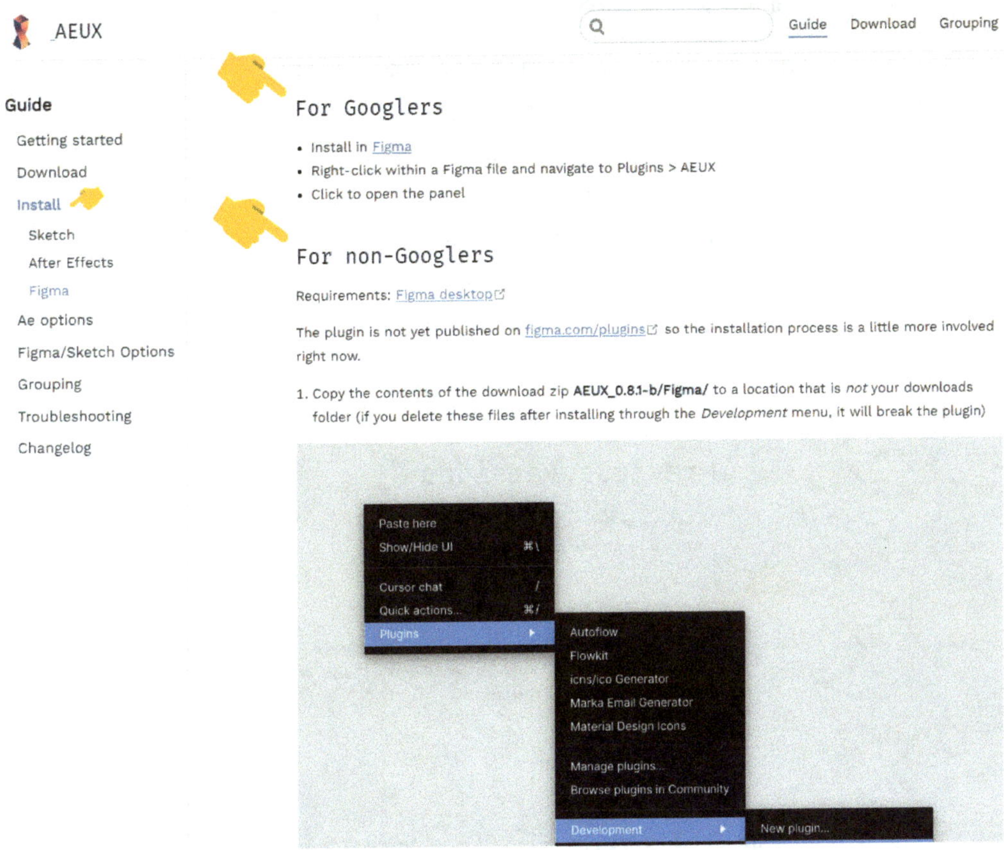

Figure 6.13 – How to install the AEUX for Figma plugin

Installing AEUX for Sketch

After we have installed the ZXP Extension Manager, we are going to download and install AEUX for Sketch. Installing AEUX for Sketch is very easy, and This is how it is done:

1. Download the AEUX for Sketch plugin from `https://aeux.io/guide/download.html#sketch-57-figma`:

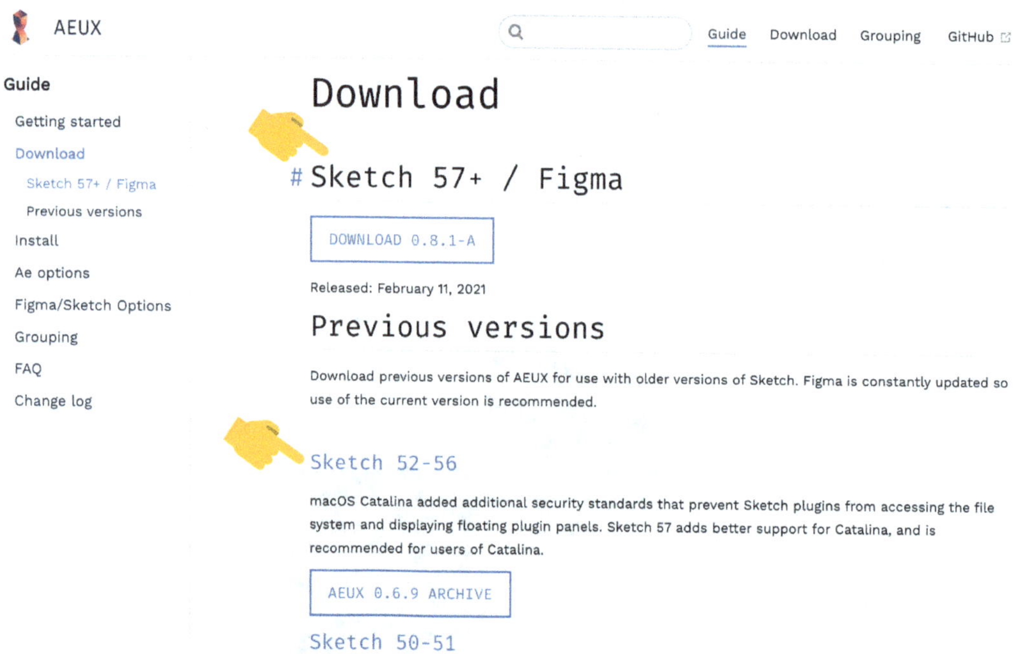

Figure 6.14 – How to install the AEUX for Sketch plugin

2. Unzip `AEUX_0.8.1-a.zip`.
3. Open the unzipped folder, `AEUX_0.8.1-a/Sketch`.

4. Double-click to open `AEUX.sketchplugin`:

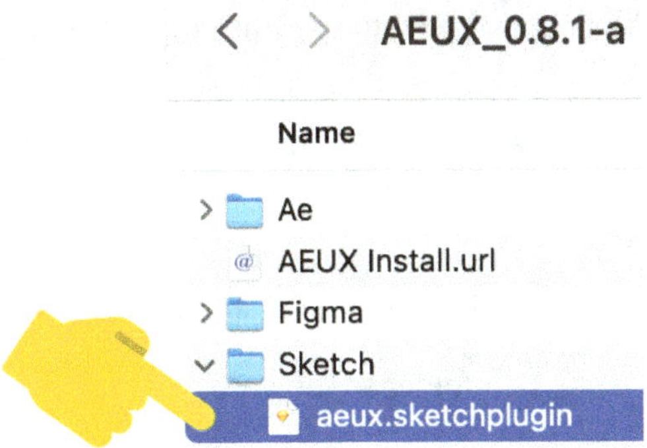

Figure 6.15 – AEUX Sketch plugin folder

Sketch will open and tell you once the plugin is installed:

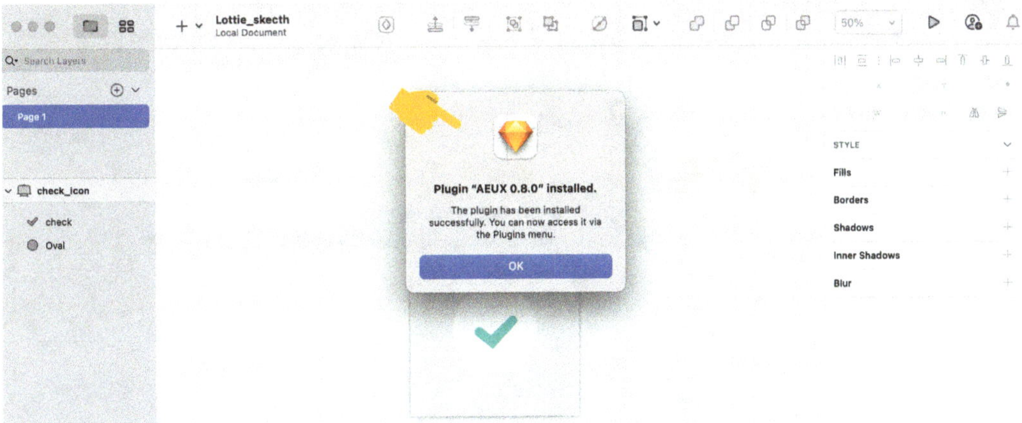

Figure 6.16 – The AEUX for Sketch plugin successfully installed

AEUX plugin for AE

We also need to install the AEUX plugin for Adobe AE if we want to import our designs from Figma or Sketch to AE. We are going to use this plugin to define how our layers are imported.

We are assuming you already installed the ZXP Extension Manager earlier in this section, otherwise, jump back to the *Installing the ZXP Extension Manager* section and follow the instructions described there.

Now, let's install AEUX for Adobe AE, and to do that, follow the next steps:

1. Look for the `AEUX_0.8.1-a` folder we downloaded when installing AEUX for Figma or Sketch.
2. Open **ZXP Extension Manager**.
3. Open `AEUX_0.8.1-a/Ae`:

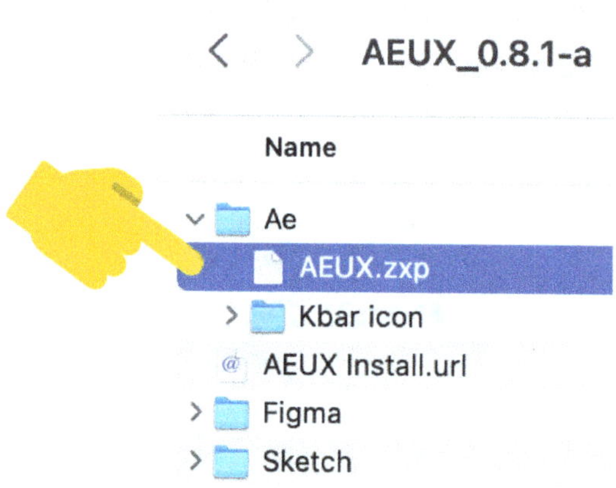

Figure 6.17 – AEUX for AE plugin folder

4. Drag and drop `AEUX.zxp` into the **ZXP Installer** window.
5. Close and reopen AE.
6. In AE, navigate to the top **Window** menu and select **Extension** | **AEUX**.

7. Click to open the panel:

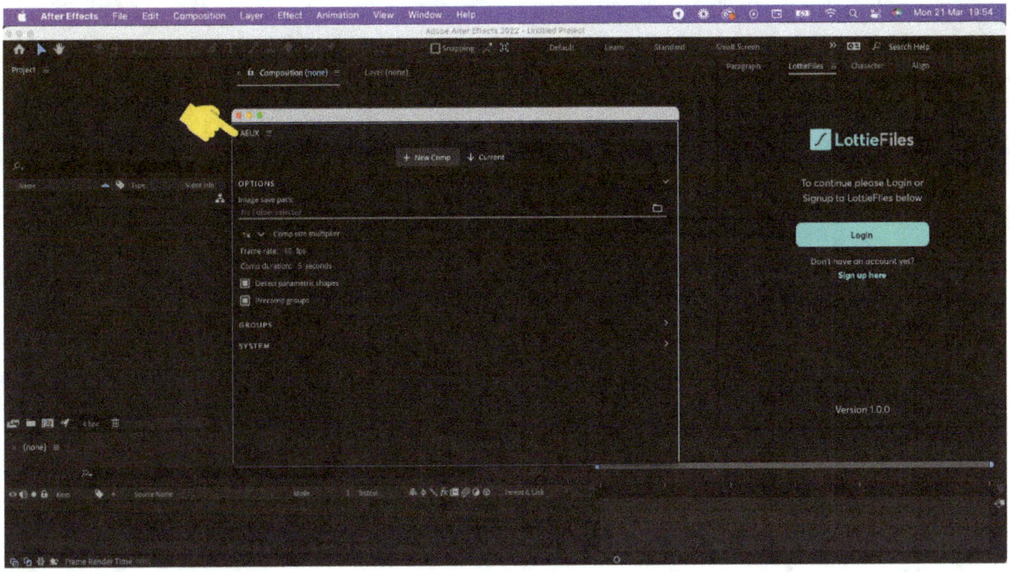

Figure 6.18 – AEUX for AE panel view

If this doesn't work, you can still try to install it manually. To do that, follow the instructions described at `https://aeux.io/guide/install.html#after-effects`.

> **Note – AEUX Plugin for AE**
> The main role of the AEUX plugin is to control how layers are built. We need to set the preferences and once that's done, there's no need to keep the panel open. So, our AE working area doesn't get too messy.

Before we start importing our files from Figma or Sketch, we can define some values here in the **AEUX** panel. As I mentioned earlier in this book, I normally work at 60 **frames per second (fps)** and turn the options in **Detect parametric shapes** and **Precomp groups** *on*. However, this is up to you and how you feel more comfortable working. If you want to get more information on this, just follow this link: `https://aeux.io/guide/ae-options.html`.

The LottieFiles platform

As you know by now, LottieFiles allows us to preview, test, and share our animations, among many other things such as edit animations, create stickers for Telegram, export our animations to GIF, or create animations from static SVGs, to mention a few.

If we want to test, edit, and share our animations on iOS, Android, and the web, we need to install a couple of tools. Just click on the following links to download the specific ones for each platform:

- **LottieFiles for Desktop**: `https://lottiefiles.com/desktop`
- **LottieFiles for Android**: `https://play.google.com/store/apps/details?id=com.lottiefiles.app&hl=en&gl=US`
- **LottieFiles for iOS**: `https://apps.apple.com/us/app/lottiefiles/id1231821260`

Supported Lottie features for iOS, Android, and the web

As we experienced a couple of chapters ago, Lottie does not support all features of Adobe AE. So, before we start creating our animations in AE, it is a good idea to have a look at the following tables if we want to avoid frustration and extra work. As we mentioned earlier, in this book, we are going to focus on iOS, Android, and web-supported features. However, you can check the following tables for supported features on Windows devices as well.

The simpler the better. It is good practice to keep our files tidy and create simple illustrations with single paths and fills. I recommend trying to avoid Boolean options directly in AE (we will see more about it in a minute), and the use of images, masks, and effects, as these features are not well supported on all devices. I also recommend creating animations that will work across all platforms and devices so that we don't need different `.json` files for each of them.

Shapes

Shapes are very well supported across all platforms. We can import our shapes from vector-based tools or create them directly in AE. We shouldn't have any problem when working with **Ellipse**, **Rectangle**, **Rounded Rectangle**, **Star**, **Polygon**, and **Trim Path**. However, remember back in *Chapter 4, Move It! Animating Our First Lottie With After Effects*, we had some trouble using the **Repeater** feature.

This won't show correctly when previewing our animation on iOS devices, so I recommend thinking about this feature as if it didn't exist and looking for another way around to achieve a similar effect:

Shapes	Android	iOS	Windows	Web (SVG)	Web (Canvas)	Web (HTML)
Shape	👍	👍	👍	👍	👍	👍
Ellipse	👍	👍	👍	👍	👍	👍
Rectangle	👍	👍	👍	👍	👍	👍
Rounded Rectangle	👍	👍	👍	👍	👍	👍
Polystar	👍	👍	⛔	👍	👍	👍
Group	👍	👍	👍	👍	👍	👍
Repeater	👍	⛔	👍	👍	👍	👍
Trim Path (individually)	👍	👍	⛔	👍	👍	👍
Trim Path (simultaneously)	👍	👍	👍	👍	👍	👍

Figure 6.19 – Shapes supported features

Fills

All **Fills** features are well supported for all platforms and devices, so there's no need to worry about working with fills at all. We can use plain colors, play around with opacity, and even use radial or linear gradients in our designs, as the use of these features won't affect our animation:

Fills	Android	iOS	Windows	Web (SVG)	Web (Canvas)	Web (HTML)
Color	👍	👍	👍	👍	👍	👍
Opacity	👍	👍	👍	👍	👍	👍
Fill Rule	👍	👍	👍	👍	👍	👍
Radial Gradient	👍	👍	👍	👍	👍	👍
Linear Gradient	👍	👍	👍	👍	👍	👍

Figure 6.20 – Fills supported features

Strokes

There is no need to worry when we work with **Strokes** either. We can use and apply any Strokes style or feature and we won't get into trouble. So, feel free to play around with **Color**, **Opacity**, **Width**, **Dashes**, **Gradient**, and so on:

Strokes	Android	iOS	Windows	Web (SVG)	Web (Canvas)	Web (HTML)
Color	👍	👍	👍	👍	👍	👍
Opacity	👍	👍	👍	👍	👍	👍
Width	👍	👍	👍	👍	👍	👍
Line Cap	👍	👍	👍	👍	👍	👍
Line Join	👍	👍	👍	👍	👍	👍
Miter Limit	👍	👍	👍	👍	👍	👍
Dashes	👍	👍	👍	👍	👍	👍
Gradient	👍	👍	👍	👍	👍	👍

Figure 6.21 – Strokes supported features

Transforms

When working with **Transforms**, there are a couple of options we want to avoid, such as **Auto Orient** and **Skew**:

Transforms	Android	iOS	Windows	Web (SVG)	Web (Canvas)	Web (HTML)
Position	👍	👍	👍	👍	👍	👍
Position (separated X/Y)	👍	👍	👍	👍	👍	👍
Scale	👍	👍	👍	👍	👍	👍
Rotation	👍	👍	👍	👍	👍	👍
Anchor Point	👍	👍	👍	👍	👍	👍
Opacity	👍	👍	👍	👍	👍	👍
Parenting	👍	👍	👍	👍	👍	👍
Auto Orient	⛔	⛔	⛔	👍	👍	👍
Skew	?	👍	?	👍	👍	👍

Figure 6.22 – Transforms supported features

Auto Orient is used when we are animating along paths. If we want to add this effect for our Lottie animations, we are going to have to do that manually by adjusting the rotation on each keyframe:

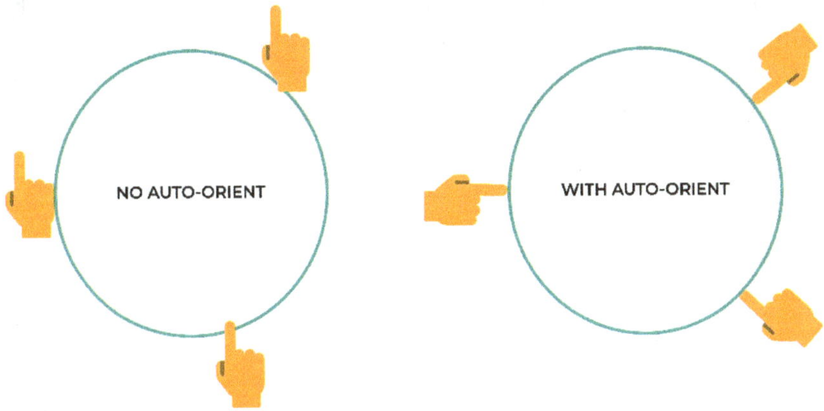

Figure 6.23 – Auto Orient feature

The second unsupported Transform option is **Skew**. This is not shown properly on Android devices, or at least we don't have enough information about it, as it sometimes works but sometimes doesn't. So, let's just stay away from it to avoid having any unpleasant surprises:

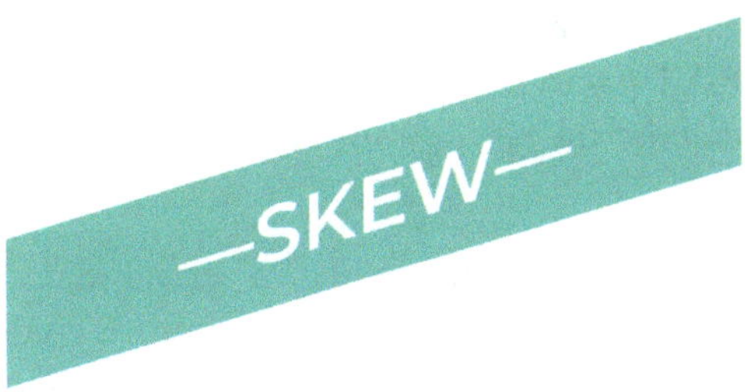

Figure 6.24 – Skew feature

Interpolation

Interpolation is another property we can play around with without causing any problems to our previews. And, now that we are talking about interpolations, I highly recommend reading more about **Rove Across Time** properties, as this is a cool feature that will help you smooth out your animation. You can find more information about the **Rove Across Time** feature at `https://helpx.adobe.com/after-effects/using/speed.html` and scroll down to **Create smooth motion with roving keyframes**.

Interpolation	Android	iOS	Windows	Web (SVG)	Web (Canvas)	Web (HTML)
Linear Interpolation	👍	👍	👍	👍	👍	👍
Bezier Interpolation	👍	👍	👍	👍	👍	👍
Hold Interpolation	👍	👍	👍	👍	👍	👍
Spatial Bezier Interpolation	👍	👍	👍	👍	👍	👍
Rove Across Time	👍	👍	👍	👍	👍	👍

Figure 6.25 – Interpolation supported features

Masks

In the early days, using **Masks** would get us into trouble when exporting our animations to Lottie, but times change and these days, there are a few **Masks** properties that are well supported. **Mask Path**, **Mask Opacity**, **Add**, **Subtract**, and **Intersect** can be used without getting into trouble. Forget about the rest as if they didn't exist, as we won't be using these at all.

Mastering masks is not hard to achieve and it will give you more resources when animating. As you know, this book doesn't pretend to be an AE guide (there are plenty of books out there that do that very well), although I'd recommend you read more about masks. You can check the Adobe help page for more information here: `https://helpx.adobe.com/after-effects/using/create-masks.html`.

Masks	Android	iOS	Windows	Web (SVG)	Web (Canvas)	Web (HTML)
Mask Path	👍	👍	👍	👍	👍	👍
Mask Opacity	👍	👍	👍	👍	👍	👍
Add	👍	👍	👍	👍	👍	👍
Subtract	👍	👍	👍	👍	👍	👍
Intersect	👍	👍	⛔	⛔	⛔	⛔
Lighten	⛔	⛔	⛔	⛔	⛔	⛔
Darken	⛔	⛔	⛔	⛔	⛔	⛔
Difference	⛔	⛔	⛔	⛔	⛔	⛔
Expansion	⛔	⛔	⛔	⛔	👍	👍
Feather	⛔	⛔	⛔	⛔	⛔	⛔

Figure 6.26 – Masks supported features

Mattes

We can use **Alpha Matte** for Lottie. Mattes work very similarly to masks; they show or hide a part of another layer. You can find more information about them at `https://helpx.adobe.com/after-effects/using/alpha-channels-masks-mattes.html`.

Mattes	Android	iOS	Windows	Web (SVG)	Web (Canvas)	Web (HTML)
Alpha Matte	👍	👍	👍	👍	⛔	👍
Alpha Inverted Matte	👍	👍	⛔	👍	👍	👍
Luma Matte	⛔	⛔	⛔	❔	❔	❔
Luma Inverted Matte	⛔	⛔	⛔	❔	❔	❔

Figure 6.27 – Mattes supported features

Merge paths

Houston, we have a problem! **Merge paths** won't work at all on iOS devices or the web. I would highly recommend forgetting about them and pretending these don't exist *only* if you want to use Boolean operations straight from AE. Otherwise, keep reading.

Merge Paths	Android	iOS	Windows	Web (SVG)	Web (Canvas)	Web (HTML)
Merge	👍 (KitKat+)	⛔	👍	⛔	⛔	⛔
Add	👍 (KitKat+)	⛔	👍	⛔	⛔	⛔
Subtract	👍 (KitKat+)	⛔	👍	⛔	⛔	⛔
Intersect	👍 (KitKat+)	⛔	👍	⛔	⛔	⛔
Exclude Intersection	👍 (KitKat+)	⛔	👍	⛔	⛔	⛔

Figure 6.28 – Merge paths supported features

As I said earlier, it is better to keep our illustrations as simple as possible, which means trying to avoid having multiple paths used in Boolean too. So, does that mean we have to stick to basic shapes? Not really. In XD, Figma, and Sketch, we can convert these multiple paths used in Boolean operations (such as **Add**, **Subtract**, **Intersect**, or **Exclude**) to a single one. Let's look at how to do that.

For **Adobe XD**, follow these steps:

1. Design using basic shapes.
2. Add the Boolean operation (**Add**, **Subtract**, **Intersect**, or **Exclude Overlap**).
3. Go to the top menu and select **Object | Path | Convert to Path**:

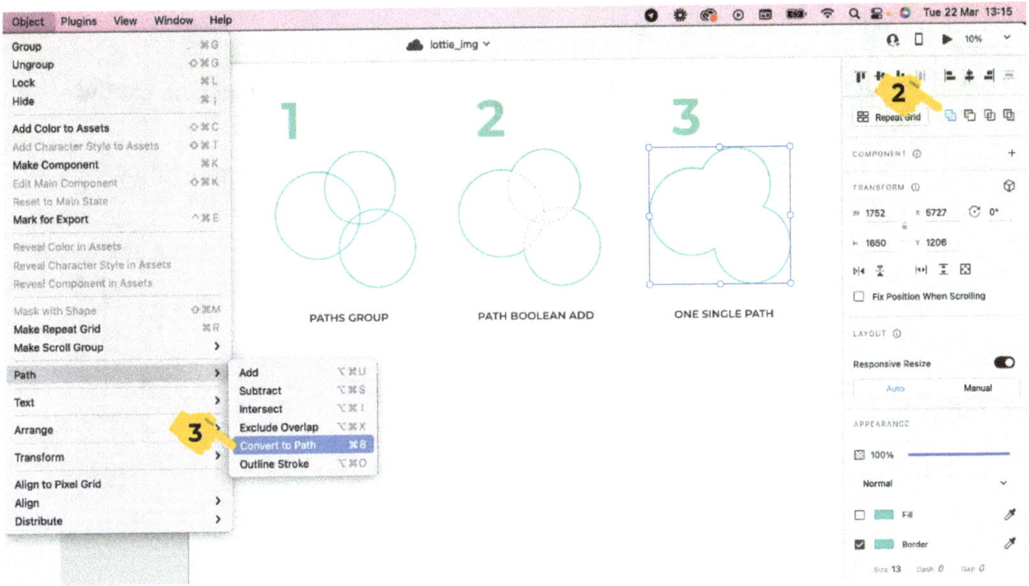

Figure 6.29 – Converting multiple paths to a single path in XD

If you work with **Figma**, follow these steps:

1. Do your drawing and add the Boolean operation (**Add**, **Subtract**, **Intersect**, or **Exclude Overlap**).
2. Select **Flatten Selection** from the top menu:

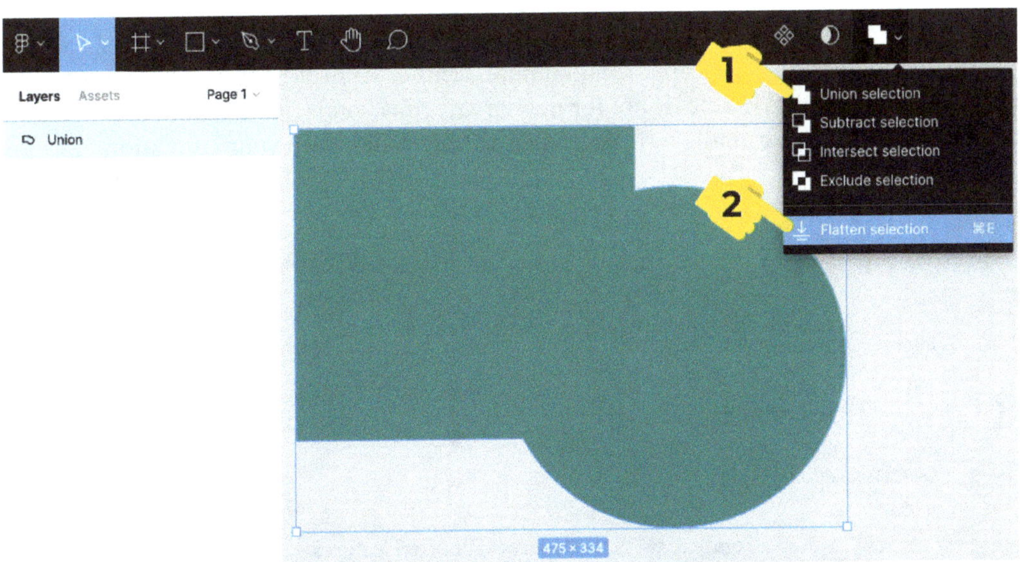

Figure 6.30 – Converting multiple paths to a single path in Figma

If you are on **Sketch**, follow these steps:

1. Add the Boolean operation to your shapes (**Add**, **Subtract**, **Intersect**, or **Exclude Overlap**).
2. Go to the top menu and select **Layer** | **Combine** | **Flatten** before exporting your work to AE:

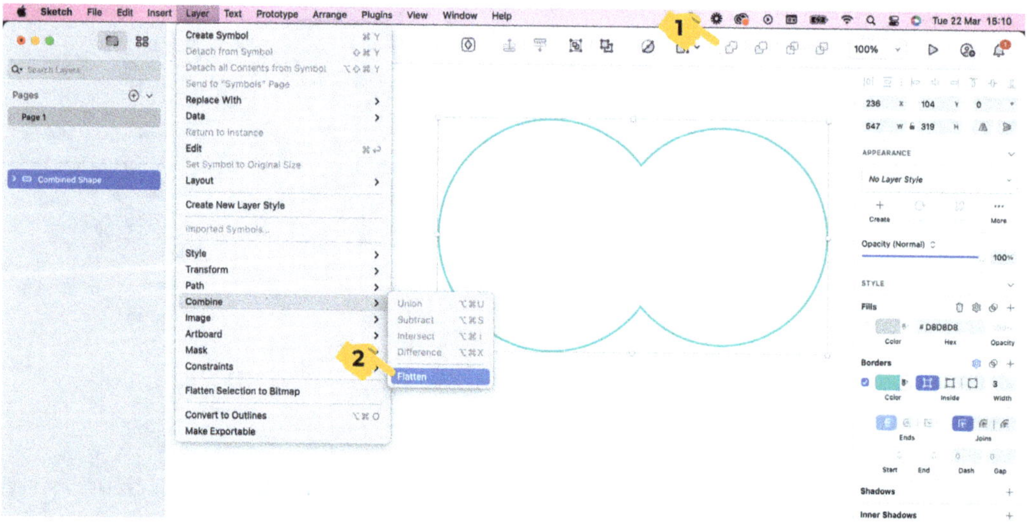

Figure 6.31 – Converting multiple paths to a single path in Sketch

Layer effects

Well, there's not too much we can talk about here. Neither Android nor iOS supports any **layer effects** created in AE, at least not for now or any time soon. However, if you want to use your animations *only* on the web, you could use layer effects on your animation.

Layer Effects	Android	iOS	Windows	Web (SVG)	Web (Canvas)	Web (HTML)
Fill	⛔	⛔	⛔	👍	👍	👍
Stroke	⛔	⛔	⛔	👍	👍	👍
Tint	⛔	⛔	⛔	👍	👍	👍
Tritone	⛔	⛔	⛔	👍	👍	👍
Levels Individual Controls	⛔	⛔	⛔	👍	👍	👍

Figure 6.32 – Layer effects supported features

Text

When we talk about fonts for Lottie, we see the basic stuff that can be done here. So, there's no problem with using **text** in AE, transforming it, or changing its fill and stroke.

That said, if you are thinking of including text in your animation so that it can be edited directly on the LottieFiles platform later on, well, I wouldn't recommend doing that. I've actually tried this myself: exported a `.json` file with text and edited it on the LottieFiles platform, but the text wouldn't show up right. Sometimes, the text wouldn't show up, or sometimes would just look weird. So, I just forgot about it for now, although, I'm sure this will be reviewed in future releases.

Text	Android	iOS	Windows	Web (SVG)	Web (Canvas)	Web (HTML)
Glyphs	👍	⛔	⛔	👍	👍	👍
Fonts	👍	👍	⛔	👍	👍	👍
Transform	👍	👍	⛔	👍	👍	👍
Fill	👍	👍	⛔	👍	👍	👍
Stroke	👍	👍	⛔	👍	👍	👍
Tracking	👍	👍	⛔	👍	👍	👍
Anchor point grouping	⛔	⛔	⛔	👍	👍	👍
Text Path	⛔	⛔	⛔	👍	👍	👍
Per-character 3D	⛔	⛔	⛔	👍	👍	👍
Range selector (Units)	⛔	⛔	⛔	👍	👍	👍
Range selector (Based on)	⛔	⛔	⛔	👍	👍	👍
Range selector (Amount)	⛔	⛔	⛔	👍	👍	👍
Range selector (Shape)	⛔	⛔	⛔	👍	👍	👍
Range selector (Ease High)	⛔	⛔	⛔	👍	👍	👍
Range selector (Ease Low)	⛔	⛔	⛔	👍	👍	👍
Range selector (Randomize order)	⛔	⛔	⛔	👍	👍	👍
expression selector	⛔	⛔	⛔	👍	👍	👍

Figure 6.33 – Text supported features

Other

You may have heard about AE **expressions**, but not in this book because they are not supported for Android or iOS. But if you were animating for the web, I'd highly recommend reading more about it, as it can be a big time and effort saver.

To introduce you to expressions, we could define them as a small piece of JavaScript code that you can plug in your layer's properties to add specific behavior to your animations. For more information, just go visit the following link: `https://helpx.adobe.com/after-effects/using/expression-basics.html`.

Now, let's talk about **images**. Images are supported for Android and iOS. But remember that if you use images in your animations, they will increase the file size and won't be responsive. So, it is up to you if you want to use images at all. In my case, I always try to avoid using them.

Other	Android	iOS	Windows	Web (SVG)	Web (Canvas)	Web (HTML)
Expressions	⛔	⛔	⛔	👍	👍	👍
Images	👍	👍	👍	👍	👍	👍
Precomps	👍	👍	👍	👍	👍	👍
Time Stretch	👍	👍	⛔	👍	👍	👍
Time remap	👍	👍	⛔	👍	👍	👍
Markers	👍	👍	👍	👍	👍	👍

Figure 6.34 – Other supported features

Now that we have an understanding of what can and cannot be done when animating for Lottie, Android, and iOS, let's move to the next section, which I'm sure will help you speed up your workflow.

Keyboard shortcuts that will make your life easier

You've seen that, at first, Adobe AE can be quite overwhelming. So many options, panels, and new keywords to learn about. However, once you get used to the shortcuts, it doesn't look that hard, does it? Especially when animating for Lottie, as we can just focus on some of the features and forget about most of the panels and tools.

To make it even easier, we can use some shortcuts to speed up our work and get our animations done quicker.

Here's a list of my time-saving shortcuts, although feel free to look around for more; the internet has plenty of websites with AE shortcut examples. Just get the ones you feel more comfortable with and start animating!

General shortcuts

Action	**macOS**	**Windows**
New Project	⌘ + ⌥ + *N*	*Ctrl* + *Alt* + *N*
New Composition	⌘ + *N*	*Ctrl* + *N*
Open Composition Settings	⌘ + *K*	*Ctrl* + *K*
Open Project	⌘ + *O*	*Ctrl* + *O*
Save	⌘ + *S*	*Ctrl* + *S*
Import File	⌘ + *I*	*Ctrl* + *I*
Undo	⌘ + *Z*	*Ctrl* + *Z*
Redo	⌘ + *Shift* + *Z*	*Ctrl* + *Shift* + *Z*
Select All	⌘ + *A*	*Ctrl* + *A*
Zoom in Time	= on main keyboard	= on main keyboard
Zoom out Time	- on main keyboard	- on main keyboard
Preview Composition	Spacebar	Spacebar
Activate Selection Tool	*V*	*V*
Activate Hand Tool	*H*	*H*
Temporarily Activate Hand Tool	Hold down spacebar	Hold down spacebar
Scroll to Current Time in Timeline Panel	*D*	*D*

Transform properties shortcuts

Action	**macOS**	**Windows**
Show only Anchor Point property	*A*	*A*
Show only Position property	*P*	*P*
Show only Scale property	*S*	*S*
Show only Rotation and Orientation property	*R*	*R*
Show only Opacity property	*T*	*T*
Show/hide Transform properties together	*Shift* + *A/P/S/R/T*	*Shift* + *A/P/S/R/T*

Frames and keyframes shortcuts

Action	macOS	Windows
Add or remove a keyframe at the current time	⌥ + *A/P/S/R/T*	*Alt + A/P/S/R/T*
Apply Ease In to current keyframe	*Shift + F9*	*Shift + F9*
Apply Ease Out to current keyframe	⌘ + *Shift + F9*	*Ctrl + Shift + F9*
Pull out all your keyframes	*U*	*U*
Jump back and forward between keyframes	*J* or *K*	*J* or *K*
Jump to the beginning of the layer	*I*	*I*
Jump to the end of the layer	*O*	*O*
Go forward one frame	⌘ + right arrow	*Ctrl* + right arrow
Go forward 10 frames	⌘ + *Shift* + right arrow	*Ctrl* + *Shift* + right arrow
Go backward one frame	⌘ + left arrow	*Ctrl* + left arrow
Go backward 10 frames	⌘ + *Shift* + left arrow	*Ctrl* + *Shift* + left arrow
Start or stop preview	Spacebar	Spacebar

Layers shortcuts

New solid layer	⌘ + *Y*	*Ctrl + Y*
Select next layer in stacking order	⌘ + down arrow	*Ctrl* + down arrow
Select previous layer in stacking order	⌘ + up arrow	*Ctrl* + up arrow
Precompose selected layers	⌘ + *Shift + C*	*Ctrl + Shift + C*
Lock selected layers	⌘ + *L*	*Ctrl + L*
Unlock all layers	⌘ + *Shift + L*	*Ctrl + Shift + L*

Free graphic resources and UX/UI inspiration

Last but not least, I'd like to share with you the resources I normally use when creating animations, which will help you out with your creative process.

Graphic resources

I am a digital designer with a graphic design background but I'm not an illustrator. Actually, my illustration skills are quite limited but not my illustration resources. What I mean by that is when I have to create an animation or an illustration, I normally search on the web for references to inspire me. Once I have a clear concept in mind, I look for a specific style, colors, or maybe a character illustration I can reuse and adjust to the look and feel I need. So, I don't go through the whole process of illustrating; I take some bits and pieces from here and there to create my own.

So, here's a list of free for personal use websites to search and download your graphic resources from.

Illustrations

My favorite one is **Freepik** (`https://www.freepik.com/`). You can search from thousands of different illustrations that cover all styles and concepts. You can download most of the files as vectors or pay a monthly subscription plan to access the premium files.

At **DrawKit** (`https://drawkit.com/`), you can search and download beautiful handmade illustration packs and icon collections for free.

Colors

With **Coolors** (`https://coolors.co/`), you can create your own unique color palettes as easily as pressing the spacebar. You can use it for inspiration to create your own or to search for color trends.

Icons

Flaticon (`https://www.flaticon.com/`) is probably the best icon website ever. Search through thousands of icon collections to download. And, if you have a premium subscription, you can download animated Lottie icons as `.ae` and `.json` files.

Download the **Font Awesome** (`https://fontawesome.com/`) icons kit and start using the icons for your designs as if they were a regular font.

Free stock images

There are a few stock image websites out there that offer really good quality images for free. My favorite ones are **Unsplash** (`https://unsplash.com/`) and **Pexels** (`https://www.pexels.com/`).

Fonts

When using fonts, I always try to stick to **Google fonts** (`https://fonts.google.com/`) as they are multiplatform and can be used on your websites.

If I'm doing some off-line project or when I need to be more creative, I look for some specific fonts at **Free Fonts** (`https://www.freefonts.io/`).

Animations

For me, the best place to look for inspiration to create my own Lottie animations can only be **LottieFiles** (`https://lottiefiles.com/`).

UX/UI inspiration

You know, inspiration is not something you can just sit down and come up with, but sometimes, you need to get inspiration at a specific time of the day so you can get your job done. Here's a list of websites that will help you out with this:

- **Behance** (`https://www.behance.net/`) is the Adobe online community platform to showcase and discover creative work.
- **Dribbble** (`https://dribbble.com/`) is a great place to get inspiration from.
- **UX Movement** (`https://uxmovement.com/`) teaches you how to improve the UX of your apps and websites through tips, techniques, and best practices.
- **Collect UI** (`https://collectui.com/`) is a platform for your daily inspiration, based on handpicked Dribbble.
- Visit **UI Garage** (`https://uigarage.net/`) to find specific design inspiration for web, mobile, and tablet.
- **User Interface Design patterns** (`https://ui-patterns.com/`) "*are recurring solutions that solve common design problems. Design patterns are standard reference points for the experienced user interface designer.*"
- **Mobbin** (`https://mobbin.design/`) saves you hours of UI and UX research thanks to its thousands of mobile app screenshots.

Summary

Looking back now, in this second part of the book, we've been going through so many new concepts, keywords, tools, and plugins. We've learned how to create an animation from scratch to finally export it and hand it off to the dev team, covering the whole UX animation workflow. We've also seen how to download and install all the necessary tools, extensions, and plugins we need to get our animation done.

We've checked the list of what can or cannot be done in AE when creating animations for Lottie so that our work is going to be previewed properly. We've gone through a list of shortcuts to speed up our work and, finally, you've ended up with my list of resources, which I hope will inspire you and give you enough resources to create your animations.

Now, let's jump to the third part of this book, *Adding Your Lottie Animations Into Mobile Apps*, where we will learn how to implement our animation into a mobile app and web with React Native.

Part 3 - Adding Your Lottie Animations Into Mobile Apps

At this point we already have some Lottie animations ready to be integrated into our apps. In this part, we will learn how to unleash the full potential of `lottie-react-native`, the React Native package which renders and plays Lottie animations into our iOS and Android apps.

We will cover the following chapters in this section:

- *Chapter 7, An Introduction to lottie-react-native*
- *Chapter 8, Installing lottie-react-native*
- *Chapter 9, Let's Do Some Magic: Integrating Your First Lottie Animation*
- *Chapter 10, How To Nail It: Controlling Your Animation*
- *Chapter 11, Any Questions? lottie-react-native FAQs*

7
An Introduction to lottie-react-native

In this chapter, we will be introduced to `lottie-react-native`, a library that allows us to render Lottie animations in our React Native apps. We will learn about its history, current state, and documentation to make sure we get the most out of the library. It is an open source library that's distributed as an `npm` package and can be found at the following links:

- **GitHub**: `https://GitHub.com/lottie-react-native/lottie-react-native`
- **NPM**: `https://www.npmjs.com/package/lottie-react-native`

In this chapter, we will cover the following topics:

- How did `lottie-react-native` come into being?
- What is `lottie-react-native`?
- Why are we not using Animated or Reanimated?
- The basics of `lottie-react-native`

How did lottie-react-native come into being?

React Native was released in 2015 due to Facebook's need to speed up their mobile development teams, with the vision of releasing dozens of new apps and improving their current apps in shorter and more effective development cycles. Some may say React Native's number one strength is its multiplatform development capabilities (*learn once, write anywhere*), but there are also other benefits, such as reusing proven libraries and tools that have been living in the web development world for a long time – longer than iOS and Android have been around.

Attracted by this promise, Airbnb spun up a team to investigate whether they could copy Facebook based on their multiplatform reuse strategy using React Native. Their conclusion was not only that the Airbnb mobile team could benefit from this strategy, but that they could reuse their vast knowledge of the web and create multi-disciplinary teams to build new features on the web, Android, and iOS immediately by reusing a large portion of code.

The result of their investigation included large architectural decisions, such as how React Native should be integrated into existing apps, how to keep the performance standards they had, and how to integrate their tooling into the new framework they would be deploying into their native apps. One such tool was their beloved animation library: Lottie.

Airbnb already had web, Android, and iOS open source libraries for Lottie (lottie):

- **Web**: `https://GitHub.com/airbnb/lottie-web`
- **Android**: `https://GitHub.com/airbnb/lottie-android`
- **iOS**: `https://GitHub.com/airbnb/lottie-ios`

All of them were well maintained and served Airbnb's needs, but adding React Native into the mix meant they would need a specific library that could be used not only by them but also by the thousands of developers who were already building the Lottie community.

The requirements were clear: they needed a tool that could render Lottie animations in React Native code in the same manner they were being rendered in iOS or Android apps. This endeavor included performance and feature requirements. The outcome was a fully-featured open source library that could easily be integrated into all sorts of apps built on React Native.

For this task, a small team of iOS, Android, and web developers were put together to successfully release `lottie-react-native` on their public GitHub repository in early 2017: `https://GitHub.com/lottie-react-native/lottie-react-native`.

In 2018, Airbnb reevaluated its investment in React Native and decided they would be stopping their involvement with Facebook's project and withdrawing all their React Native code from their apps. This decision was explained in a series of blog posts revolving around issues related to the complexity of maintaining three large code bases (iOS, Android, and React Native) that needed hard coordination for a team that was not proficient in React Native.

React Native has come a long way since that day but this meant that Airbnb, a large promotor, stopped contributing to this technology, including their involvement with `lottie-react-native`. The library was not left on its own, though. Some of the owners of `lottie-react-native` looked for maintainers within the community and finally transferred the project to the top active contributors at that time (`emilioicai` and `lelandrichardson` at GitHub).

What is lottie-react-native?

`lottie-react-native` is a project that's composed of two main parts:

- The open source project, which is hosted on GitHub. All development, improvement requests, issue reporting, and code hosting happens here. It's the center of the development community and helps update and improve the library as a whole.
- The `npm` package, where all the new downloadable versions of the library are hosted. Usually, developers would use this npm repository to include `lottie-react-native` in their React Native projects.

`lottie-react-native` has a hard dependency on `lottie-ios` and `lottie-android` and serves as a wrapper for those two libraries, in which heavy load happens. In fact, in most of React Native's native packages, `lottie-react-native` works by receiving data from the JavaScript side and then transforming and sending that data to the native libraries (`lottie-ios` and `lottie-android`).

In 2021, `lottie-react-native` became one of the most popular libraries in the React Native ecosystem. It has more than 14,500 stars on GitHub and, even without Airbnb's involvement, keeps receiving several releases per year.

`lottie-react-native` has become the go-to library when it comes to rendering complex animations in React Native by keeping up with new releases of `lottie-ios` and `lottie-android`, all while following changes in React Native closely so that it can easily be integrated with new versions of `lottie-ios` and `lottie-android`.

Now that we know what `lottie-react-native` is and what its dependencies are, let's learn why we should use it for our React Native apps.

Why are we not using Animated or Reanimated?

A common question for React Native beginners is which library they should use for displaying animations on their apps. After a quick search, three different ways of doing so arise: the Animated API, Reanimated, or `lottie-react-native`.

Animated and Reanimated are not technologies that compete `lottie-react-native` as they serve different purposes. Both Animated and Reanimated excel in animating React and native components on iOS and Android, but they are based on transforming mobile UI components (for example, Text, Containers, Views, or Lists). This means they are not designed to create complex animations or visual icons, which designers can do with Adobe After Effects.

Let's look at an example of what Animated/Reanimated can do versus what Lottie is capable of:

What Lottie does easily:

Figure 7.1 – Typical lottie-react-native animation

What Animated and Reanimated do well:

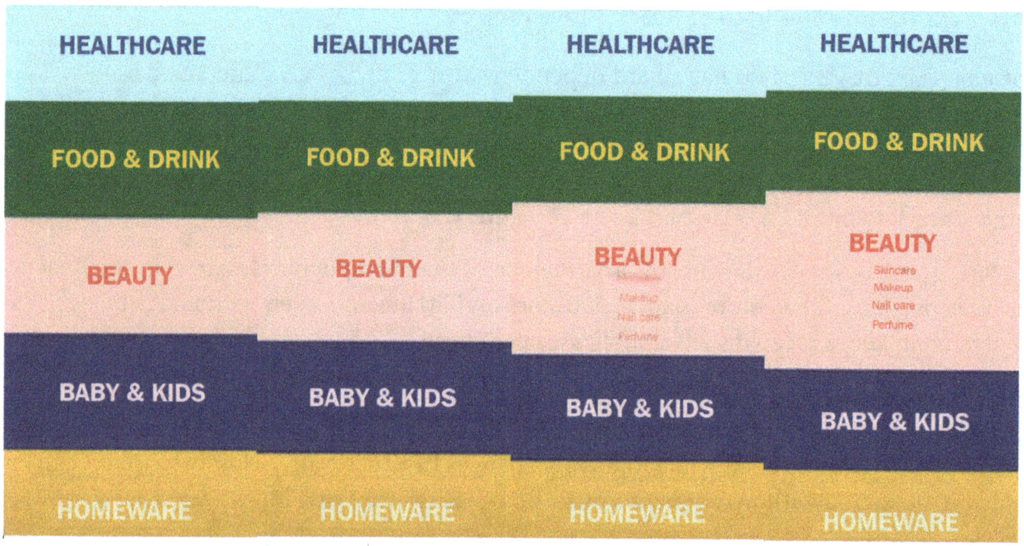

Figure 7.2 – Typical Animated/Reanimated animation

It may be complex to understand the difference, but as a general idea, developers should note that Lottie is useful for displaying complex animations in which different shapes are in play. These kinds of animations are usually created by designers and frames, timing, and UI layers are important parts of them.

Animated and Reanimated should be used for animating views, containers, or platform-specific components, as shown in the preceding diagram.

So far, we've learned when and why to use `lottie-react-native` in our apps. Now, let's learn the ins and outs of the `lottie-react-native` project itself.

The basics of lottie-react-native

In this section, we'll learn how `lottie-react-native` is structured as a project. This will give us the full picture and allow us to get the most out of the resources that are available for developers so that we can integrate Lottie animations into our React Native projects.

The open source project

The easiest way to become acquainted with `lottie-react-native` is by going to its GitHub repository (`https://github.com/lottie-react-native/lottie-react-native`). There, developers can read about its API, request fixes for specific issues, send pieces of code to be incorporated into the code base via **Pull Requests** (**PRs**), or just browse the code to understand how the library works.

Since 2018, this project is maintained by a sole maintainer, but new releases come out regularly to incorporate bug fixes, changes in React Native, and changes in `lottie-ios` or `lottie-android`.

In the `README.md` file, developers can find a basic explanation of how to integrate and use the library. Besides this explanation, a couple of code samples (`https://github.com/lottie-react-native/lottie-react-native/tree/master/example`) are provided to help developers understand how `lottie-react-native` can or should be used with ease.

Alongside those samples, there is a small API reference that shows the most common properties and methods that are used for displaying Lottie animations on React Native apps. Finally, the `README.md` file also shows a couple of examples of Lottie animations, which can be downloaded from LottieFiles, and a couple of lines about how to get more information.

An important point to keep in mind when using `lottie-react-native` is versioning, since different versions of React Native only work with specific versions of `lottie-react-native` (the different versions will be shown shortly). The main reason for this is how the build system works.

Besides the `README.md` file, other pieces of documentation can be found in the repository:

- The API documentation
- The TypeScript disclaimer
- A list of supported After Effects features on every supported platform
- The `examples` folder

Besides this documentation, the **Issues** page is commonly used as a source of help when it comes to understanding errors, features, or logs. So, it's recommended to search on that page when the documentation is not helpful enough, which may be the case when some issues arise when new versions of React Native, `lottie-ios`, or `lottie-android` come out.

The `lottie-react-native` community is very active in terms of submitting PRs, and new functionality or bug fixes can usually be found there before they are officially released on the npm repository through a new version of `lottie-react-native`. Here, you can also find interesting conversations revolving around specific features or problems that would not fit as well in the `lottie-react-native` project's documentation.

New users can create new PRs from their own forks. The following requirements are what all users can expect if they wish their PRs to be merged into the master branch:

- Documentation must be provided
- An example must be added to the `examples` folder
- The PR template must be fulfilled properly
- All issues and comments must be addressed in the PR thread

Once a PR has been merged into the master branch, the maintainers will prepare a release, depending on the urgency and the timings of the repository. Users can expect their changes to be released as a patch – either a minor or major version.

The repository changelog (`https://github.com/lottie-react-native/lottie-react-native/blob/master/CHANGELOG.md`) is the best place to learn about what features are released in every version. There's also a releases page (`https://github.com/lottie-react-native/lottie-react-native/releases`) that users can check out to understand how the library is evolving.

On average, new releases of `lottie-react-native` are being made available every 2 and a half months.

Platforms

React Native was designed to be multiplatform and not limited to iOS and Android only, which projects such as `react-native-web` and `react-native-windows` prove. `lottie-react-native` follows the same principles and is designed to be run on any platform React Native runs on. However, as of 2021, only two platforms are fully supported: iOS and Android. Windows support is slowly being added thanks to the efforts of a team from Microsoft and Flirc TV that is pushing commits to the project to make sure the library catches up.

In the case of iOS and macOS, `lottie-react-native` needs `lottie-ios` to run. This dependency is explicit and `lottie-ios` needs to be installed separately due to a legacy issue from when an Airbnb team (mostly composed of native iOS developers) decided to use this kind of dependency instead of doing it implicitly. In any case, this doesn't affect `lottie-react-native` in any way other than developers having to install `lottie-ios` separately and making sure the right version of this library is installed.

Since this is a library that runs native code, `lottie-ios` is installed as a pod and requires developers to run `pod install` the first time `lottie-react-native` and `lottie-ios` are installed.

On the other hand, `lottie-android` is automatically managed by Gradle, who detects it is a dependency of `lottie-react-native`. Then, the right version is always installed automatically.

Both platforms use the same API but there are minor differences between the platforms:

- `lottie-ios` is written in Swift and a bridging header might be needed for it to work properly on iOS (`https://github.com/lottie-react-native/lottie-react-native/issues/739#issuecomment-883591123`).
- If you need external assets for your animations, Android requires them to be put in a folder. Your Lottie component should include the `imageAssetsFolder` prop, which allows you to specify the URL where that folder can be found.

- Developers can specify whether they want hardware acceleration on Android by using the `renderMode` prop.
- Caching can be activated on Android through the `cacheComposition` prop.

Windows support was added with version 4.0.0 of `lottie-react-native` but it is still under experimentation and should be used with caution.

Versions

`lottie-react-native` has largely evolved to accommodate new versions of React Native, `lottie-ios`, and `lottie-android`. All these versions are available through the npm repository.

Developers should consider that newer versions include performance improvements and bug fixes, so it is always recommended to use the latest version that's available in the npm repository. However, working on specific versions of React Native may require developers to install a specific version of `lottie-react-native`. The following table shows the compatibility list:

App Built-In React Native Version	Requires lottie-react-native Version	Requires lottie-ios Version
From 0.1 to 0.17	N/A	N/A
From 0.18 to 0.40	1.2.0	1.2.0
From 0.41 to 0.58	2.5.11	2.5.3
0.59	3.0.2	3.0.3
From 0.60 onwards	4.0.2	3.2.3

The npm package

This library can be found in the npm repository as `lottie-react-native` (`https://www.npmjs.com/package/lottie-react-native`), and all its versions and documentation can be downloaded from `https://www.npmjs.com/`. Here, users can also find the package's dependencies (the **Dependencies** tab) or which packages have `lottie-react-native` as a dependency (the **Dependants** tab).

Both Yarn and npm can be used to install the package, as we will learn in the next chapter.

Summary

In this chapter, we learned that `lottie-react-native` is a great alternative for displaying complex animations in our React Native apps. Serving as a wrapper for `lottie-ios` and `lottie-android`, `lottie-react-native` can easily be found as an npm package, as well as an open source repository on GitHub. Its documentation can be edited and accessed through regular GitHub PR mechanisms.

Now that we have a better understanding of the theory surrounding the library, it's time to move toward a more practical approach. In the next chapter, we will install and use the `lottie-react-native` library to start rendering our Lottie animations in our Android or iOS applications, which have been built on React Native.

8
Installing lottie-react-native

Before using `lottie-react-native`, we need to install the library into our React Native project as a node module so we can import it inside the code base of our app. To perform this installation, we have two different options:

- npm
- Yarn

Both tools will result in the same output (`lottie-react-native`) and its dependencies will be installed inside the `node_modules` folder inside our React Native project folder. Using one tool or another will be up to each developer and should not influence the resulting product in any way.

The topics we will cover in this chapter are as follows:

- Basic installation (using npm or Yarn)
- Dependencies of `lottie-react-native`
- iOS requirements when installing `lottie-react-native`

- Android requirements
- Installing previous versions of `lottie-react-native`

Basic installation

Installing `lottie-react-native` follows a similar process as any other npm library, taking into account that it's a library that depends on native libraries written in Swift and Java. Taking this into account, developers can always read about the installation process in the GitHub repository URL: `https://github.com/lottie-react-native/lottie-react-native`.

When installing `lottie-react-native`, developers should know that, because of the way it is built, the iOS native library for Lottie should also be installed to enable `lottie-react-native` to render Lottie animations in iOS apps.

Let's take a look at the steps we need to follow in order to complete a successful installation.

Using npm

Follow these steps to install the `lottie-react-native` library using npm:

1. Navigate to our terminal in the React Native project root folder. Once we are there, we should run the following command:

   ```
   npm i --save lottie-react-native
   ```

   This command will follow four different steps:

   I. Download the source files for the library from the npm repository.

   II. Create the container folder inside the `node_modules` folder.

   III. Install the source files in the created container folder.

   IV. Update the `package.json` and `package.json.lock` files to mark the library as a dependency of the React Native project.

   npm detects and installs the latest version of the library from the npm public repository, but we could force a specific version of the library by specifying it after an `@` sign followed by the version number we would like to install.

2. Once npm is finished installing the library, we need to install its iOS dependency if we are going to require our Lottie animations to be rendered on iOS devices:

   ```
   npm i --save lottie-ios@3.2.3
   ```

Running this command will trigger the installation of `lottie-ios` on a very specific version, 3.2.3, which is the compatible version for `lottie-react-native` to work properly on iOS devices.

3. Once npm finishes installing `lottie-ios`, we need to install its pod dependencies. We will do so by going into the `ios` folder inside our React Native project and running the following:

   ```
   pod install
   ```

   This action will trigger CocoaPods, a dependency management tool for iOS and macOS projects that will download and install all the dependencies required by `lottie-ios` to function.

Once all these dependencies are installed, we can start using the `lottie-react-native` library inside our React Native app.

Using Yarn

Using Yarn for installing `lottie-react-native` is similar to using npm.

Let's see how to do so:

1. Navigate from our terminal into our React Native project root folder. Once in that folder, we will run the following command:

   ```
   yarn add lottie-react-native
   ```

   This command will follow four different steps:

   - Download the source files for the library from the npm public repository.
   - Create the container folder inside the `node_modules` folder.
   - Install the source files in the created container folder.
   - Update the `package.json` and `yarn.lock` files to mark the library as a dependency of the React Native project.

   Yarn always looks for the latest version of the library in the npm public repository, but we could force a specific version of the library by specifying it after an @ sign followed by the version number we would like to install.

2. Once Yarn has finished installing the library, we need to install its iOS dependency if we are going to need our Lottie animations to be rendered on iOS devices. We can install it by running the following command in our project's root folder:

   ```
   yarn add lottie-ios@3.2.3
   ```

Running this command will install `lottie-ios` on its version number 3.2.3, which is the compatible version for `lottie-react-native` to work properly on iOS devices.

3. Once Yarn finishes installing `lottie-ios`, we need to install its pod dependencies. We will do so by going into the `ios` folder inside our React Native project and running the following:

   ```
   pod install
   ```

   This action will trigger CocoaPods, a dependency management tool for iOS and macOS projects that will download and install all the dependencies required by `lottie-ios` to function.

Once all these dependencies are installed, we can start using the `lottie-react-native` library inside our React Native app. This library depends on other packages in order to deploy all its functionality. Let's take a look now at these packages.

Other dependencies of lottie-react-native

As with many other libraries, `lottie-react-native` depends on a number of libraries that will be automatically installed when running npm or Yarn installations, as we did in the previous section of this chapter. The full list of dependencies is as follows:

```
"peerDependencies": {
    "lottie-ios": "^3.2.3",
    "react": "*",
    "react-native": "|=0.46"
  },
  "dependencies": {
    "invariant": "^2.2.2",
    "prop-types": "^15.5.10",
    "react-native-safe-modules": "^1.0.3"
  }
```

As we can see, `lottie-react-native` needs to run on a project that contains at least three dependent libraries: `lottie-ios` (which should be installed using npm or Yarn, as we saw in the previous section of this chapter), `react`, and `react-native` (version 0.46 or higher).

On top of those peer dependencies, lottie-react-native also requires three regular dependencies: invariant, prop-types, and react-native-safe-modules. All of them will be installed automatically by npm or Yarn so developers do not need to take any manual action to install them.

Let's take a look now at the platform-specific requirements that lottie-react-native has.

Installation requirements

Both platforms have specific requirements for lottie-react-native to be installed properly. Let's take a look now at what those differences are and how we can complete the installation in iOS and Android.

iOS devices

For its iOS version, lottie-react-native depends on lottie-ios, which is a library built by Airbnb in Swift. This means we need to enable our React Native app to read and execute Swift code. In order to do so, we need to create a bridging header (if we haven't done it yet) so the Objective-C part of our app can communicate with the Swift part and therefore, send and receive messages to lottie-ios.

If we don't have a bridging header in our project, we can create one by following these steps:

1. Open your <project_name|/ios/<project_name|.xcworkspace file in Xcode and go to **File** | **New** | **File...**:

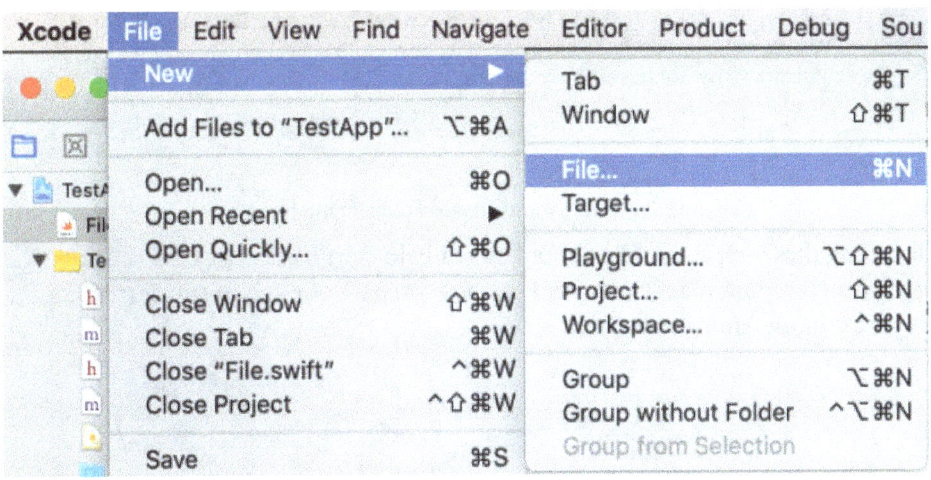

Figure 8.1 – Creating a new file in your Xcode project

2. Select **Swift File** as the file type:

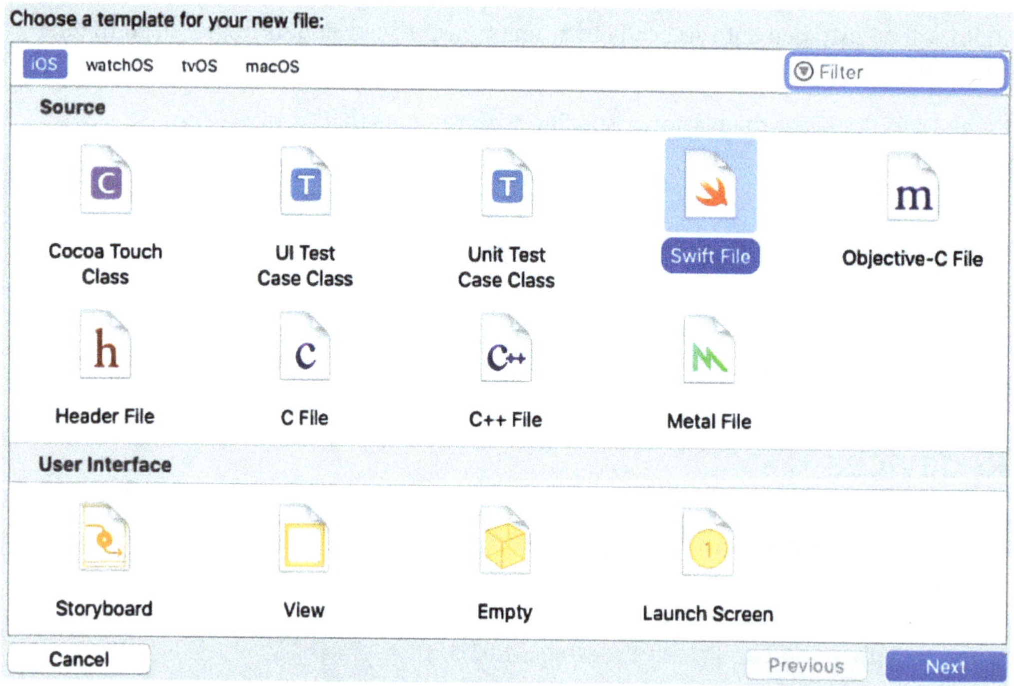

Figure 8.2 – Selecting Swift as file type

3. Confirm the creation of a bridging header:

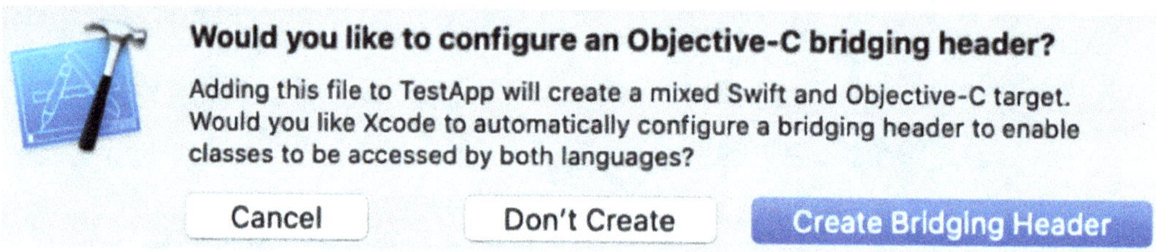

Figure 8.3 – Confirming creation of bridging header

Upon finishing these steps, our app should be ready to start using `lottie-react-native` on any iOS and macOS device. Let's now prepare our app to run `lottie-react-native` on Android devices.

Android devices

On some rare occasions, auto-linking may not work properly when installing lottie-react-native on Android devices. This will result in the app crashing when trying to build it. In this case, you would need to follow these steps to fix the issue:

1. Make the following changes in android/app/src/main/java/<project_name|/MainApplication.java:

    I. Add import com.airbnb.android.react.lottie.LottiePackage; in the import section.

    II. Add packages.add(new LottiePackage()); in List<ReactPackage| getPackages();.

2. Make the following change in android/app/build.gradle:

    I. Add implementation project(':lottie-react-native') in the dependencies block.

3. Add the following lines in android/settings.gradle:

```
include ':lottie-react-native'
project(':lottie-react-native').projectDir = new
File(rootProject.projectDir, '../node_modules/lottie-
react-native/src/android')
```

When all these changes are done, rebuild the app for Android devices and check whether the crash is fixed. As we have our installation finished, let's move on now to see the limitations and possibilities of using the most well-known Lottie features.

Limited features of the lottie-react-native library

Not all Adobe **After Effects** (**AE**) features are supported by lottie-react-native. In fact, Airbnb maintains a list of non-supported features on their website: https://github.com/airbnb/lottie/blob/master/supported-features.md.

The support list for the most common features at the time of writing is as follows:

- Lottie support for basic geometric shapes in AE:

Shapes	Android	iOS	Windows	Web (SVG)	Web (Canvas)	Web (HTML)
Shape	✓	✓	✓	✓	✓	✓
Ellipse	✓	✓	✓	✓	✓	✓
Rectangle	✓	✓	✓	✓	✓	✓
Rounded Rectangle	✓	✓	✓	✓	✓	✓
Polystar	✓	✓	✗	✓	✓	✓
Group	✓	✓	✓	✓	✓	✓
Repeater	✓	✗	✓	✓	✓	✓
Trim Path (individually)	✓	✓	✗	✓	✓	✓
Trim Path (simultaneously)	✓	✓	✓	✓	✓	✓

Figure 8.4 – Support for shapes features

- Lottie support for basic text effects and formats in AE:

Text	Android	iOS	Windows	Web (SVG)	Web (Canvas)	Web (HTML)
Glyphs	✓	✗	✗	✓	✓	✓
Fonts	✓	✓	✗	✓	✓	✓
Transform	✓	✓	✗	✓	✓	✓
Fill	✓	✓	✗	✓	✓	✓
Stroke	✓	✓	✗	✓	✓	✓
Tracking	✓	✓	✗	✓	✓	✓
Anchor point grouping	✗	✗	✗	✓	✓	✓
Text Path	✗	✗	✗	✓	✓	✓
Per-character 3D	✗	✗	✗	✓	✓	✓
Range selector (Units)	✗	✗	✗	✓	✓	✓
Range selector (Based on)	✗	✗	✗	✓	✓	✓
Range selector (Amount)	✗	✗	✗	✓	✓	✓
Range selector (Shape)	✗	✗	✗	✓	✓	✓
Range selector (Ease High)	✗	✗	✗	✓	✓	✓
Range selector (Ease Low)	✗	✗	✗	✓	✓	✓
Range selector (Randomize order)	✗	✗	✗	✓	✓	✓
expression selector	✗	✗	✗	✓	✓	✓

Figure 8.5 – Support for text features

- Lottie support for masking effects in AE:

Masks	Android	iOS	Windows	Web (SVG)	Web (Canvas)	Web (HTML)
Mask Path	✓	✓	✓	✓	✓	✓
Mask Opacity	✓	✓	✓	✓	✓	✓
Add	✓	✓	✓	✓	✓	✓
Subtract	✓	✓	✓	✓	✓	✓
Intersect	✓	✓	✗	✗	✗	✗
Lighten	✗	✗	✗	✗	✗	✗
Darken	✗	✗	✗	✗	✗	✗
Difference	✗	✗	✗	✗	✗	✗
Expansion	✗	✗	✗	✗	✓	✓
Feather	✗	✗	✗	✗	✗	✗

Figure 8.6 – Support for masks features

- Lottie support for layer effects in AE:

Layer Effects	Android	iOS	Windows	Web (SVG)	Web (Canvas)	Web (HTML)
Fill	✗	✗	✗	✓	✓	✓
Stroke	✗	✗	✗	✓	✓	✓
Tint	✗	✗	✗	✓	✓	✓
Tritone	✗	✗	✗	✓	✓	✓
Level Individual Controls	✗	✗	✗	?	✓	✓
Gaussian blur	✓ (4.1+)	✗	✗	?	?	?
Drop Shadows	✓ (4.1+)	✗	✗	?	?	?

Figure 8.7 – Support for layer effects features

- Lottie support for shapes and graphics-driven transparencies in AE:

Mattes	Android	iOS	Windows	Web (SVG)	Web (Canvas)	Web (HTML)
Alpha Matte	✓	✓	✓	✓	✗	✓
Alpha Inverted Matte	✓	✓	✗	✓	✓	✓
Luma Matte	✗	✗	✗	?	?	?
Luma Inverted Matte	✗	✗	✗	?	?	?

Figure 8.8 – Support for mattes features

- Lottie support for shape combination techniques in AE:

Merge Paths	Android	iOS	Windows	Web (SVG)	Web (Canvas)	Web (HTML)
Merge	✓ (KitKat+)	✗	✓	✗	✗	✗
Add	✓ (KitKat+)	✗	✓	✗	✗	✗
Subtract	✓ (KitKat+)	✗	✓	✗	✗	✗
Intersect	✓ (KitKat+)	✗	✓	✗	✗	✗
Exclude Intersection	✓ (KitKat+)	✗	✓	✗	✗	✗

Figure 8.9 – Support for merge paths features

- Lottie support for other effects in AE:

Other	Android	iOS	Windows	Web (SVG)	Web (Canvas)	Web (HTML)
Expressions	✗	✗	✗	✓	✓	✓
Images	✓	✓	✓	✓	✓	✓
Precomps	✓	✓	✓	✓	✓	✓
Time Stretch	✓	✓	✗	✓	✓	✓
Time remap	✓	✓	✗	✓	✓	✓
Markers	✓	✓	✓	✓	✓	✓

Figure 8.10 – Support for other features

Let's now learn how to deal with previous versions of `lottie-react-native` in cases when our version of React Native requires a version other than the latest.

Installing previous versions

Depending on which version of React Native we are building our project with, we will need to install a specific version or range of versions. The list of versions to be installed can be found in the previous chapter, so now we are going to learn how to install one of those specific versions:

1. Identify which React Native version our project is using. For this, we can check our `package.json` file at the root of our React Native app project. Inside this file, look for the `react-native` dependency and note down the version number:

```
"dependencies": {
  "@types/react-redux": "^7.1.18",
  "expo": "~42.0.1",
  "expo-device": "^3.3.0",
  "expo-status-bar": "~1.0.4",
  "lodash": "^4.17.21",
  "react": "16.13.1",
  "react-dom": "16.13.1",
  "react-native": "0.64.1",
  "react-redux": "^7.2.5",
  "redux": "^4.1.1"
},
```

Figure 8.11 – Finding out your project's React Native version

2. Look at the `lottie-react-native/react-native` compatibility list in the previous chapter and select the right `lottie-react-native` for your project.
3. Install the selected version of `lottie-react-native` using npm or Yarn by specifying that version number after an `@` sign, for example, `npm install -save lottie-react-native@4.1.3` or `yarn add lottie-react-native@4.1.3`.
4. As we saw in the previous section, we need to install `lottie-ios` as a dependency; the `lottie-react-native/lottie-ios` compatibility list can be also found in the previous chapter.
5. Install the selected version of `lottie-ios` using npm or Yarn by specifying that version number after an `@` sign, for example, `npm install -save lottie-ios@3.2.3` or `yarn add lottie-ios@3.2.3`.

Summary

We now have `lottie-react-native` and its dependencies properly installed and ready to be used to render Lottie animations within our React Native app.

Our project can now be successfully built on both iOS and Android devices, so let's start the magic and integrate our first Lottie animation. We will cover how to do this in the next chapter.

9
Let's Do Some Magic: Integrating Your First Lottie Animation

Our app is now ready to display Lottie animations on its screens. In this chapter, we will learn how to integrate a Lottie file, whether downloaded from `https://lottiefiles.com/` or generated by us in Adobe **After Effects** (**AE**). The requirements to perform this integration successfully are as follows:

- Have a JSON file with the Lottie animation exported from AE using the Bodymovin plugin or downloaded from LottieFiles.
- Have the React Native project ready after having followed the steps described in *Chapter 8, Installing lottie-react-native*.

The final result will be our app displaying the provided Lottie animation on the initial screen. The topics we will cover in this chapter are as follows:

- Understanding the Lottie file
- Using a Lottie file in a React Native app
- Using `lottie-react-native` in your TypeScript app
- Finding documentation for `lottie-react-native`
- Using remote Lottie files

Understanding the Lottie file elements

As we saw in previous chapters, Lottie files are JSON representations of our AE animations that have been transformed and exported using the Bodymovin plugin. As a JSON object, we can open it in a text editor and see that Lottie files are just a collection of keys and values storing the assets that need to be rendered and to which transformations should be applied on each frame of the animation.

Let's take a look at a sample Lottie file:

```
{
    "v":"4.8.0",
    "meta":{
        "g":"LottieFiles AE "
    },
    "fr":30,
    "w":500,
    "h":250,
    "nm":"Comp 1",
    "assets":[],
    "layers":[
        {
            "nm":"Ellipses 3",
            "ks":{
                ...
            },
            "shapes":[
                {
```

```
                "ty":"gr",
                "nm":"Ellipse 1",
                "mn":"ADBE Vector Group",
                "hd":false
                ...
            }
        ],
        ...
    }
  ],
  "markers":[]
}
```

Lottie files are usually much larger than this one, but we have summarized it for educational purposes. Let's now go through the most important values in this sample file:

- `"v"`: Specifies which version of the file this one is. It has no direct effect on the animation as it serves as mere information for developers and designers.
- `"meta"`: General information about the file such as name and license, for example.
- `"fr"`: Also known as **frame rate**, this represents the number of frames per second that the animation should be rendered in.
- `"w"`: The width of the animation.
- `"h"`: The height of the animation.
- `"assets"`: A list of external assets that will be shown within the animation.
- `"layers"`: Details for each of the AE layers used in our animation.
- `"layers/ks"`: Information about how to display a specific layer on a specific frame.
- `"layers/shapes"`: Shapes used on each layer, including their metadata and rendering options.

In general, it's best to modify our Lottie animations on AE, but changing values in the exported Lottie JSON file is possible and may affect the animation itself.

Using a Lottie file in a React Native app

Once we have our animation exported into a Lottie file, we can integrate it into any React Native app and start the animation on any iOS or Android device. In this section, we will show how this is done on the main screen of a sample blank React Native app, but the process can be extrapolated into any screen or component within any React Native app.

The first thing we have to do is store our Lottie file in a folder inside our app. We need to make sure we can import files from this folder in our React components and screens. For example, we could store our Lottie files in the `assets` folder, where all images used in our app are stored:

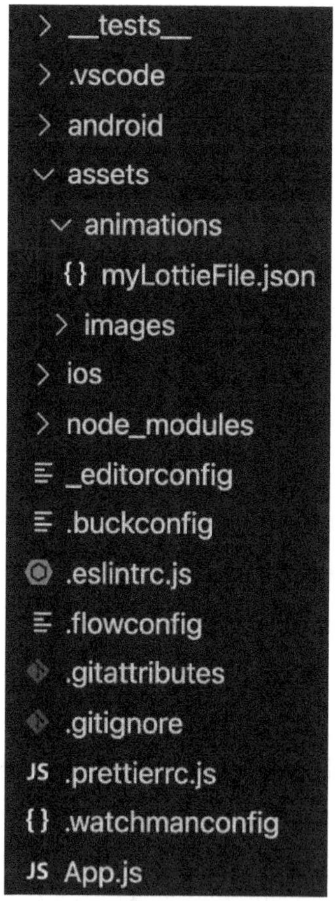

Figure 9.1 – Storing animation in the app folder structure

In this case, we stored a JSON file named `myLottieFile.json` inside the `assets/animations` folder so it's accessible through a simple `import` statement: `require('./assets/animations/myLottieFile.json')`.

Let's now see an example of how `App.js` would look using the integrated Lottie file in the proposed folder structure:

```
import React from 'react';
import LottieView from 'lottie-react-native';
import {SafeAreaView, View, StyleSheet} from 'react-native';

const App = () => {
  return (
    <SafeAreaView>
      <View style={styles.container}>
        <LottieView
          source={require('./assets/animations/myLottieFile.
          json')}
          autoPlay
          loop
        />
      </View>
    </SafeAreaView>
  );
};

const styles = StyleSheet.create({
  container: {
    width: '100%',
    height: '100%',
    justifyContent: 'center',
    alignItems: 'center',
  },
});

export default App;
```

In this file, we are displaying our Lottie animation on the main screen so users can see it just after opening the app. There are a number of things we should consider about this file:

- `SafeAreaView` is used to prevent the animation from going under the notch on notched-screen devices (for example, the iPhone 13).
- Having `LottieView` inside a sized container is important to prevent the animation from resizing or being cropped. That's why we use a `100%` width and height-sized view containing the `LottieView` component.
- `LottieView` is a React component that will render the Lottie animation. It requires a source prop to import the JSON file containing the animation. It also accepts a number of properties to control and configure the animation. We will take a deeper look into these properties in this chapter.

The props passed to the `LottieView` components are also worth noting:

- `source`: This needs to receive the imported JSON file for the animation. The path for importing the animation, as it works with the `require` statement in JavaScript, can be absolute or relative to the parent component/screen.
- `autoPlay`: When specified (or set to `true`), this makes the app start playing right after the component is mounted. This is normally used when the parent component makes sense only when the animation is running.
- `loop`: When specified (or set to `true`), this will repeat the animation until the component gets unmounted.

The former component example is the simplest representation of a Lottie animation being rendered inside a React Native app but it's a good example of how important it is to place the `LottieView` component in a sized container.

If your app uses classes instead of functional components, you should know that `lottie-react-native` can still be imported and used in a very similar fashion.

Let's see an example of a Lottie file being integrated in to a class-based React native app:

```
import React from 'react';
import LottieView from 'lottie-react-native';
import {SafeAreaView, View, StyleSheet} from 'react-native';
export default class App extends React.Component {  render() {
return (
      <SafeAreaView>
            <View style={styles.container}>
                  <LottieView source={require('./animation.
```

```
                    json')} autoPlay loop />;
                </View>
            </SafeAreaView>
        )  }}
const styles = StyleSheet.create({
  container: {
    width: '100%',
    height: '100%',
    justifyContent: 'center',
    alignItems: 'center',
  },
});
```

Similar to the previous example, the main difference in class-based apps is the need to return the rendering component inside the `render` method. One of the basic props (`colorFilters`) allows users to control and change the colors of the layers.

Let's take a look at how this prop can be used to do so:

```
import React from 'react';
import LottieView from 'lottie-react-native';
import {SafeAreaView, View, StyleSheet} from 'react-native';

const App = () => {
  return (
    <SafeAreaView>
      <View style={styles.container}>
        <LottieView
          source={require('./assets/animations/myLottieFile.
          json')}
          autoPlay
          loop
          colorFilters={[
            {
              keypath: 'button', color: '#F00000',
            },{
              keypath: 'Sending Loader',color: '#F00000',
    },
```

```
            ]}
          />
        </View>
      </SafeAreaView>
    );
};

const styles = StyleSheet.create({
  container: {
    width: '100%',
    height: '100%',
    justifyContent: 'center',
    alignItems: 'center',
  },
});

export default App;
```

In this case, the `colorFilters` prop in the `LottieView` component is modifying the colors of two layers (which should have been defined with the same name in AE) to render them as black, no matter which color they were defined as during the animation creation process.

TypeScript has become the de facto language for modern React Native apps. In the previous example, we used plain JavaScript, but the `LottieView` component is TypeScript-ready.

In the next section, we will show what caveats a user may find when using `lottie-react-native` in their TypeScript applications.

Using lottie-react-native in your TypeScript app

The `lottie-react-native` library includes types, so `LottieView` components can be easily integrated with TypeScript applications. These types are defined in the file found in the `lottie-react-native/src/js/index.d.ts` (type definition file) path inside the library's code. They are also accessible in the library's repository through `https://github.com/lottie-react-native/lottie-react-native/blob/master/src/js/index.d.ts`.

Besides the definition of the props and methods applicable to `LottieView`, this file includes types for the following objects:

- `AnimationObject`: Types for the Lottie JSON file when it gets translated to a JavaScript object
- `ColorFilter`: Types for the filters that can be applied to change colors in the animation
- `TextFilterIOS`: Types for the filters that can be applied to change fonts on iOS devices
- `TextFilterAndroid`: Types for the filters that can be applied to change fonts on Android devices

The main caveat when using `lottie-react-native` concerns the way we import the Lottie component (`LottieView`) in our app. Depending on how TypeScript is configured in our project, we would need to import it in a different way:

- If your `tsconfig.json` file defines `"esModuleInterop": false`, you will need to use `require` to import `LottieView` in the following way: `const LottieView = require("lottie-react-native");`.
- If your `tsconfig.json` file defines `"esModuleInterop": true` and `"allowSyntheticDefaultImports": true` (`true` is the default value), you will need to import `LottieView` in the standard ES6 way: `import LottieView from "lottie-react-native";`.

Let's see how both ways could be implemented in the sample code we developed previously:

```
import React from 'react';
import {SafeAreaView, View, StyleSheet} from 'react-native';
import LottieView from 'lottie-react-native'; // if you have
"esModuleInterop": true
// import LottieView = require('lottie-react-native'); //
otherwise you have "esModuleInterop": false

const App = () => {
  return (
    <SafeAreaView>
      <View style={styles.container}>
        <LottieView
```

```
            source={require('./assets/animations/myLottieFile.
            json')}
            autoPlay
            loop
          />
        </View>
      </SafeAreaView>
    );
};
```

In the next section, we will see where to find the best resources to work around other caveats when using the `lottie-react-native` library.

Finding documentation for lottie-react-native

Getting stuck when using a third-party library might be a frustrating experience but in the case of `lottie-react-native`, there is a large knowledge base accessible on the public repository of the library: `https://github.com/lottie-react-native/`.

This knowledge base includes the following elements:

- **README** (`https://github.com/lottie-react-native/lottie-react-native/blob/master/README.md`): This is the main source of truth for the library. It includes a *Getting Started* guide and code samples to integrate and use `lottie-react-native` (at a basic level). This file serves as a good introduction to the library and should be the first resource to check when looking for help related to library usage.
- **API** (`https://github.com/lottie-react-native/lottie-react-native/blob/master/docs/api.md`): This is a good explanation of all properties and methods that can be used in the `LottieView` component to control the animations in our apps.
- **TypeScript caveats** (`https://github.com/lottie-react-native/lottie-react-native/blob/master/docs/typescript.md`): As we saw in the *Using lottie-react-native in your TypeScript app* section, TypeScript can be difficult to integrate. This document explains what problems we might run into and how to work around them.
- **Glossary** (`https://github.com/lottie-react-native/lottie-react-native/blob/master/docs/GLOSSARY.md`): A list of specific terms and their definitions related to `lottie-react-native`.

- **CHANGELOG** (`https://github.com/lottie-react-native/lottie-react-native/blob/master/CHANGELOG.md`): A list of the versions released for the library. This document is very useful when having issues with a specific feature or platform so we can revert/update to versions where those issues don't exist.
- **Contributing guide** (`https://github.com/lottie-react-native/lottie-react-native/blob/master/CONTRIBUTING.md`): This document explains how to request help or contribute code updates to the open source repository.
- **Pull requests** (`https://github.com/lottie-react-native/lottie-react-native/pulls`): This is the list of contributions that are proposed to the library. Users can use this list to find out about upcoming fixes or discussions about bugs and features.
- **Issues** (`https://github.com/lottie-react-native/lottie-react-native/issues`): Here, library users share their problems, bugs, or questions about the library. This is a good resource to search through when getting problems with library usage or integration.
- **Lottie for iOS repository** (`https://github.com/airbnb/lottie-ios`): A source of information for the iOS-specific library for Lottie. This can be used to search for iOS-specific issues or features.
- **Lottie for Android repository** (`https://github.com/airbnb/lottie-android`): A source of information for the Android-specific library for Lottie. This can be used to search for Android-specific issues or features.

Now we have all the resources to get started, let's import and use our first Lottie file in our app.

Using remote Lottie files

For optimal performance, animations should be included locally within the app's folder structure but, in some cases, it could be useful to use a remote JSON file as a Lottie animation to be rendered in our React Native apps. For these cases, `lottie-react-native` allows us to transparently specify a remote URL as the source of the animation through the source prop passed to `LottieView`.

Let's see how our initial example would look if we used a remote animation instead of a local one:

```
import React from 'react';
import LottieView from 'lottie-react-native';
import {SafeAreaView, View, StyleSheet} from 'react-native';

const App = () => {
  return (
    <SafeAreaView>
      <View style={styles.container}>
        <LottieView
          source={'https://raw.githubusercontent.
          com/lottie-react-native/lottie-react-native/
          b96fd04c5d92d2acd55e6eb6cb8c3dd119d1a786/example/js/
          animations/LottieLogo1.json'}
          autoPlay
          loop
        />
      </View>
    </SafeAreaView>
  );
};

const styles = StyleSheet.create({
  container: {
    width: '100%',
    height: '100%',
    justifyContent: 'center',
    alignItems: 'center',
  },
});

export default App;
```

As this example shows, only the `source` property needs to change its value. In this case, we replaced the `require` statement with a simple URL that points to a JSON Lottie animation that is hosted on a public server. For external sources, users need to make sure that the app will always have access to the external file, as failing to reach the remote URL would show an empty space instead of showing the animation itself.

Assets (such as images) can also be used inside Lottie files and rendered with `lottie-react-native`. Let's take a look at how this behavior can be achieved through code.

Using Lottie files with assets

Lottie animations may contain external images displayed in them to make richer and more complex animations. When using AE and the Bodymovin plugin to create animations, the exported JSON may have various assets to rely on, such as the following:

```
...,
  "assets": [
    {
      "id": "image_name",
      "w": 200,
      "h": 100,
      "u": "images/",
      "p": "img_name.png"
    }
  ],
  ...
```

In these cases, our app needs to include the files inside its binary, so you will need to add the files to the project and re-build it from scratch running `yarn ios` or `yarn android` so the app is compiled together with the newly added assets being used in the animation. Adding the assets to the project differs depending on which platform we are targeting:

- **iOS**: Open **Xcode**, right-click on the `resources` folder you can find in the right-hand column, and click on **Add file to "LottieReactNative"...** to select the images required.

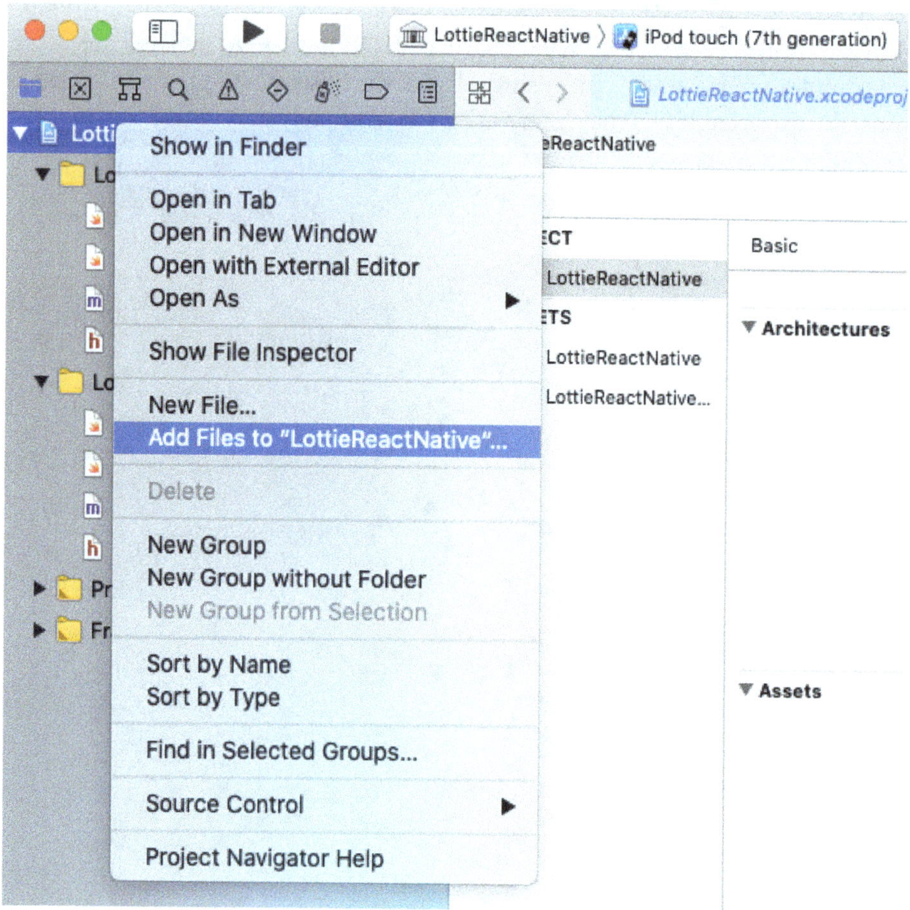

Figure 9.2 – Adding animation assets in Xcode

- **Android**: Your images should be copied to `[PROJECT FOLDER]/android/app/src/main/assets`. It is a good practice to establish a `lottie` subdirectory and then a folder for each animation. You'll need to refer to that folder in the `imageAssetsFolder` prop for the animation, using its relative path.

Let's take a look at an example of this:

```
<View style={styles.container}>
  <LottieView
    source={require('./assets/animations/myLottieFile.
    json')}
    autoPlay
    loop
    imageAssetsFolder='lottie/animation_name'
  />
</View>
```

It is possible to rename the assets once you have them in your project, but you will need to modify the JSON file containing the Lottie animation too in order to identify the asset file by its new name:

```
...,
  "assets": [
    {
      "id": "image_name",
      "w": 200,
      "h": 100,
      "u": "images/",
      "p": "new_image_name.png"
    }
  ],
  ...
```

With this, we will have our shiny assets loaded into our animations, making them fully capable of rendering external images.

Summary

In this chapter, we have learned about the way Lottie animations can be loaded into React Native, using basic integrations such as TypeScript types, and adding external assets into our animations. This gives us the ability to display complex animations inside our React Native apps, but what happens if we need to be in control of the playback (for example, tell the animation to start/stop based on events happening in the app)?

Let's move on to the next chapter to discover how controlling Lottie animations in `lottie-react-native` is done.

10
How To Nail It: Controlling Your Animation

At this point, we have a fully functional animation in our React Native app that starts playing as a loop when it is mounted and stops when unmounted. But what if we want to control the playback of the animation? Let's give an example: we need to display the animation of a loading bar while we sequentially download five different files into our app. The loading bar will show the progress of the downloading files by filling itself (20% more each time a file is downloaded), resulting in a fully filled bar once those five files have been downloaded.

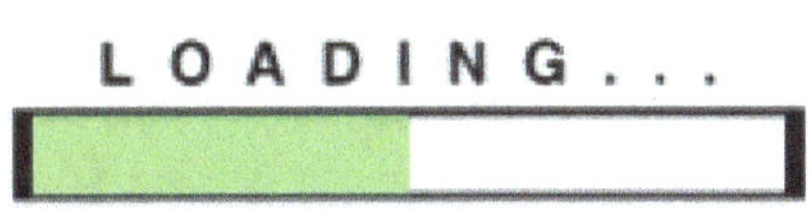

Figure 10.1 – Animated loading bar used as an example

In this case, we need to control the animation, updating it every time a file has been fully downloaded and stopping it while the next download is in progress.

To explain how this process works in `lottie-react-native`, we will review two different alternatives: the declarative and the imperative APIs. By the end of this chapter, we will know not only how to render Lottie animations in our React Native apps but we will be able to control their playback and layout.

To explain how this process works in `lottie-react-native`, we will review different alternatives:

- The declarative API
- The imperative API

Technical requirements

To complete this chapter, we have to have a functioning React Native app running on a simulator or device. We will modify this app to include a `LottieView` component as we learned in previous chapters so we can modify and control the animation through methods and properties.

The declarative API

The most frequent explanation for the distinction between imperative and declarative programming is that imperative code instructs the computer on how to perform tasks, whereas declarative code concentrates on what you want the computer to do.

Your code in imperative programming is made up of statements that affect the program's state by instructing the computer what to do. To put it another way, your code is built around defining variables and altering their values.

Your code in declarative programming is made up of expressions that evaluate their output based on their input by telling the machine what you want.

React was designed following the declarative paradigm, although it allows you to control some components the imperative way when needed. So does `lottie-react-native` as it provides different APIs for imperative or declarative control on the animations rendered within an app.

In this section, we will focus on how to control the example animated loading bar with the `lottie-react-native` library's declarative API.

Here's an example of how controlling a Lottie animation can be achieved with the declarative API:

```
const numFilesToDownload = 5;
const duration = 2000;
const App = ({downloadedFiles}) => {
  const progress = useMemo(() => new Animated.Value(0), []);
  useEffect(() => {
```

```
    Animated.timing(progress, {
      toVal4deue: downloadedFiles.length / numFilesToDownload,
      duration: duration,
      useNativeDriver: true,
      easing: Easing.linear,
    }).start();
  }, [downloadedFiles, progress]);
  return (
    <SafeAreaView>
      <View style={styles.container}>
        <LottieView
          source={require('./assets/animations/loadingBar.
          json')}
          progress={progress}
        />
      </View>
    </SafeAreaView>
  );
};
export default App;
```

In this example, our `App` component receives a prop named `downloadedFiles` including the information of the files downloaded by the app. This information can be provided by Redux, MobX, a component wrapping app, or any other way. What's important for the sake of this example is to know that `downloadedFiles` is an array that will increase its size from `0` until the maximum number of files to be downloaded (defined by `const numFilesToDownload = 5;` in the example).

We are using the Animated API from React Native to hold the progress of the animation: `const progress = useMemo(() => new Animated.Value(0), []);`. This is an `Animated.Value` that will start from `0` and progressively reach `1`, defining we want our animation to be complete. We are using `useMemo` here. As `progress` is a variable, we want to update it using React Native's Animated API:

```
  useEffect(() => {
    Animated.timing(progress, {
      toValue: downloadedFiles.length / numFilesToDownload,
      duration: duration,
      useNativeDriver: true,
```

```
      easing: Easing.linear,
    }).start();
  }, [downloadedFiles, progress]);
```

In this part, we are creating an effect that will update `progress` based on the number of files downloaded (`downloadedFiles.length`) and the number of files to be downloaded (`numFilesToDownload`). With this, we will be pushing the progress bar 20% toward its total every time a new file is downloaded. For example, if we've downloaded 2 of 5 files, `progress` will be set to 0.4, meaning the animation needs to smoothly play until 40% of its total play time.

We also define the duration for every push of the loading bar in the following line of code:

```
const duration = 2000;
```

The most important part in this example is the `LottieView` component:

```
<LottieView
  source={require('./assets/animations/loadingBar.
  json')}
  progress={progress}
/>
```

We use the `progress` prop here so we can declare the progress of the animation based on an Animated value (`progress`), which depends on the number of files being downloaded at a certain moment.

We can find all the declarative properties, their descriptions, and default values in the `lottie-react-native` library's README file (`https://github.com/lottie-react-native/lottie-react-native/blob/master/docs/api.md`).

All of them can be declaratively used on a `LottieView` component to control the rendering and behavior of our Lottie animations. In the next section, we will learn how to control our animations with the imperative API for those cases where we need to explicitly say what to do to our animation instead of reacting to state changes.

We have already learned how to use some of these properties in our `LottieView` objects. We will now show examples using other important props.

speed

The speed property is a number that sets the speed of the animation based on how many times the default speed should be played:

```
<LottieView
    source={require('./assets/animations/myLottieFile.json')}
    speed={2}
/>
```

The example above will play our animation twice as fast as the original animation speed.

```
<LottieView
    source={require('./assets/animations/myLottieFile.json')}
    speed={-1}
/>
```

The example above will play our animation in reverse at the original animation speed. With this in mind, we could create a loop that renders the animation back and forth every 2 seconds instead of repeating it over:

```
const App = ({}) => {
  const [speed, setSpeed] = useState(1);
  const reverseSpeed = useCallback(() => {
    if (speed === 1) {
      setSpeed(-1);
    } else {
      setSpeed(1);
    }
  }, [speed]);

  useEffect(() => {
    setTimeout(() => {
      reverseSpeed();
    }, 2000);
  }, [reverseSpeed]);

  return (
    <SafeAreaView>
```

```
      <View style={styles.container}>
        <LottieView
          source={require('./assets/animations/loadingBar.
          json')}
          autoPlay
          speed={speed}
        />
      </View>
    </SafeAreaView>
  );
};
```

onAnimationFinish

The `onAnimationFinish` property is a callback that will be triggered when the animation completes its playback. We can use it to navigate away to a new screen when the displaying animation finishes its playback:

```
const App = ({navigation}) => {
  const onAnimationFinish = useCallback(() => {
    navigation.navigate('NextScreen');
  }, []);

  return (
    <SafeAreaView>
      <View style={styles.container}>
        <LottieView
          source={require('./assets/animations/loadingBar.
          json')}
          autoPlay
          onAnimationFinish={onAnimationFinish}
          loop={false}
        />
      </View>
    </SafeAreaView>
  );
};
```

Note `loop={false}` is necessary for `onAnimationFinish` to work properly as a looped animation won't ever finish.

colorFilters

The `colorFilters` property is an array of objects containing the string-coded hex colors that enables developers to change the colors for specific layers programmatically. For this prop to work properly, the correct keypath (a property set when creating the app in After Effects and stored in the Lottie JSON file) needs to be provided along with the code:

```
<LottieView
    autoPlay
    source={require('./assets/animations/loadingBar.json')}
    colorFilters={[
      {
        keypath: 'button',
        color: '#FF0000',
      },
      {
        keypath: 'circle',
        color: '#00FF00',
      },
      {
        keypath: 'square',
        color: '#0000FF',
      },
    ]}
/>
```

This piece of code modifies three After Effect layers (`button`, `circle`, and `square`) to change their colors to red (`'#FF0000'`), green (`'#00FF00'`), and blue (`'#0000FF'`) respectively.

textFiltersAndroid and textFiltersIOS

`textFiltersAndroid` and `textFiltersIOS` contain an array of objects including texts to replace so we can programmatically modify a specific text in the animation. This property is useful when dealing with translations in our apps:

```
<LottieView
  autoPlay
  source={require('./assets/animations/loadingBar.json')}
  textFiltersAndroid={[
    {find: 'Hello!', replace: 'Hola!'},
    {find: 'Bye!', replace: 'Adios!'},
  ]}
    textFiltersIOS={[
    {find: 'Hello!', replace: 'Hola!'},
    {find: 'Bye!', replace: 'Adios!'},
  ]}
/>
```

In this example, we are replacing the text `'Hello!'` with `'Hola!'` and `'Bye!'` with `'Adios!'` in our animation for both iOS and Android devices.

Now that we have learned how to use the declarative API, let's move on to a different way of interacting with our Lottie animations: the imperative API.

The imperative API

Sometimes, it's just easier using imperative programming in our app, for example, sometimes we need to play/stop our animation based on user interactions inside the app. For these cases, we can use the `lottie-react-native` library's imperative API, which allows developers to control the animation playback in a very straightforward way.

React automatically provides the `ref` prop on all its components and the `useRef` hook to be used whenever we need to control the component in an imperative way.

The piece of code we wrote in the previous section is actually a good example of how imperative programming makes more sense when we need to directly trigger an action on a component, improving readability and making our code easier to reason about:

```
import React, {useEffect, useRef} from 'react';
import LottieView from 'lottie-react-native';
import {SafeAreaView, View, StyleSheet} from 'react-native';
```

```
const numFramesPerFile = 9;

const App = ({downloadedFiles}) => {
  const animation = useRef(null);

  useEffect(() => {
    if (downloadedFiles.length === 0) {
      animation.current.reset();
    } else {
      const startFrame = numFramesPerFile * (downloadedFiles.
      length - 1);
      animation.current.play(startFrame, startFrame +
      numFramesPerFile);
    }
  }, [downloadedFiles]);

  return (
    <SafeAreaView>
      <View style={styles.container}>
        <LottieView
          ref={animation}
          source={require('./assets/animations/loadingBar.
          json')}
          loop={false}
        />
      </View>
    </SafeAreaView>
  );
};

const styles = StyleSheet.create({
  container: {
    width: '100%',
    height: '100%',
    justifyContent: 'center',
    alignItems: 'center',
```

```
  },
});

export default App;
```

For this approach, we need to first identify how many frames our animation contains and how many frames we need to render once we download each of the files to be downloaded. In this example, we could calculate it in the following way:

1. Number of frames contained in the animation: `45`
2. Number of files to be downloaded: `5`
3. Number of frames to be played on every file download: `45 / 5 = 9`

Then, we define the calculated number of frames to be played on every file download as a constant in our code:

```
const numFramesPerFile = 9;
```

Next, we need to create a reference to our `LottieView` component that will enable us to call imperative methods on it. We do this using the `useRef` hook provided by React:

```
const animation = useRef(null);
```

This reference needs to be passed as the `ref` prop to our `LottieView` component:

```
<LottieView
  ref={animation}
  source={require('./assets/animations/loadingBar.
  json')}
  loop={false}
/>
```

We also see how we explicitly pass `loop={false}` so the animation doesn't repeat when we call any imperative playback methods on it.

Having all this setup ready, we can create an effect that will be triggered on every file download. This effect will use the imperative play method on the referenced component. This play method accepts the initial and the final frames we want to play in the animation.

We will use these parameters to reproduce just a part of the animation on every file download:

```
useEffect(() => {
  if (downloadedFiles.length === 0) {
    animation.current.reset();
  } else {
    const startFrame = numFramesPerFile * (downloadedFiles.
    length - 1);
    animation.current.play(startFrame, startFrame +
    numFramesPerFile);
  }
}, [downloadedFiles]);
```

When we know how many files the app has downloaded (`downloadedFiles.length`), we can easily calculate what the initial frame will be where the next animation part should start:

```
const startFrame = numFramesPerFile * (downloadedFiles.length -
1);
```

Then, we reach the most important part of this code: the part where we use the imperative API to reproduce the animation from the initial frame (`startFrame`) until the final frame (`startFrame + numFramesPerFile`):

```
animation.current.play(startFrame, startFrame +
numFramesPerFile);
```

Note how we reset the animation if the number of downloaded files is zero, so we make sure we always start from the initial frame:

```
  if (downloadedFiles.length === 0) {
    animation.current.reset();
  }
```

Besides `play` and `reset`, we can find other imperative methods in the `lottie-react-native` library's README file found at `https://github.com/lottie-react-native/lottie-react-native/blob/master/docs/api.md`.

Summary

In this chapter we reviewed the differences between the declarative and the imperative APIs for `lottie-react-native`, which can be used to control the looks and the playback of our animation. On top of that, we learned how to use React Native's Animated API to smoothly control the progress of a Lottie animation.

In the next chapter, we will go through some of the most common issues, pitfalls, and problems we may face when using `lottie-react-native` in our React Native apps.

11 Any Questions? lottie-react-native FAQs

Even with all the information contained in this book, some questions may arise when using Lottie-based animations in our React Native apps. In this chapter, we will go over some of the most commonly asked questions by developers when it comes to `lottie-react-native` usage. For convenience, the following is the list of questions and issues you will find in the following pages:

1. I added an effect in my animation, but it's not rendered in the app.
2. The animation is not rendered at all in my app.
3. The animation looks stretched.
4. How can I pause an animation?
5. How can I reverse an animation?
6. My animation is rendered on an iOS device but not on an Android device.
7. My animation is rendered on an Android device but not on an iOS device.
8. My app is not building after installing `lottie-react-native`.
9. Some frames are not showing in my animation.

10. My animation is showing the wrong colors or no colors at all.
11. How can I use my Lottie animation as a splash screen?
12. There are images missing in my animation.
13. How can I center my animation in the app?
14. How can I play my animation a set number of times?
15. My animation has a low playback performance.
16. How can I change the colors of my animation programmatically?
17. How can I use a remote Lottie animation file in my app?
18. My app is crashing on Android.
19. An error shows on my app – **Cycle dependencies between targets**.
20. An error shows on my app – **Gradle 7: unable to resolve class MavenDeployment**.

1. I added an effect to my animation but it's not rendered in the app

There are a number of effects in Adobe After Effects that are not supported on certain platforms. When this kind of error happens, it's best to go to the list of supported effects in Lottie's documentation at `https://github.com/airbnb/lottie/blob/master/supported-features.md`.

Take into account that this list may change over time, as Lottie is being constantly improved. As the list shows, the same effect may show on a specific platform but might be missing on a different one.

The most common approaches for these cases are to remake the animation, remove the selected effect, or create a different animation for the failing platform, as there is no programmatic solution for this problem.

2. The animation is not rendered at all in my app

Check that the JSON file containing the animation is placed within the React Native app project folder structure and is reachable through an `import/require` statement in the component in which the animation should be rendering. To test this, you can `console.log` the contents of the JSON file; if they log as `undefined`, it means that the file was not reachable by the component:

```
const animation = require('./assets/animations/loadingBar.
json')
console.log(animation)
```

In this case, you might want to move the JSON file to a different folder or try with a different JSON file, as it's possible the file was damaged or inconsistent. Using a JSON linter can help to identify and fix this kind of issue.

3. The animation looks stretched

`LottieView` inherits its size behavior from the standard React Native `View` component, and therefore, it can be changed through the style property on its containing parent. If the image size looks wrong, try first explicitly changing the parent's size:

```
<View style={{width: 300, height: 150}}>
      <LottieView
        ref={animation}
        source={require('./assets/animations/loadingBar.
        json')}
        loop={false}
      />
</View>
```

If that didn't work, try changing `width` or `height` explicitly in the `LottieView` component:

```
<LottieView
      ref={animation}
      source={require('./assets/animations/loadingBar.
      json')}
      loop={false}
```

```
        style={{width: 300, height: 150}}
    />
```

Parent-relative sizes (percentages) can also be used in both approaches. Always be aware of the parent size, as many issues can be fixed by making sure the parent size is correct. Also, take into consideration using the `flex` property if needed.

4. How can I pause an animation?

There are several approaches to this issue:

- If you are using the declarative approach in your code, you can use the `speed` prop on `LottieView`, as setting it to `0` will stop the animation.
- If you are using the imperative API, you can use the `pause()` method on the animation reference, which will immediately stop your animation playback. Conversely, the `play()` method will restart the playback whenever you need it.

5. How can I reverse an animation?

The simplest approach to achieve reverse playback is to use the `speed` prop on the `LottieView` component, as negative values will make the animation play backward. If you want to play the animation in reverse but at its original speed, you need to set the `speed` prop to `-1`, but you can also play it at double speed by setting it to `-2` or half-speed by changing it to `-0.5`:

```
<LottieView
  source={require('./assets/animations/loadingBar.json')}
  speed={-1}
/>
```

If you are using the animated API to control the progress of your animation, you can use methods such as `Animated.timing`, and make sure you are passing descending values:

```
  // start animation at frame 300 and go decrementally to frame
     0
  const progress = useMemo(() => new Animated.Value(300), []);
  useEffect(() => {
    Animated.timing(progress, {
      toValue: 0,
      duration: 500,
```

```
      useNativeDriver: true,
      easing: Easing.linear,
    }).start();
  }, [downloadedFiles, progress]);

  return (
    <SafeAreaView>
      <View style={styles.container}>
        <LottieView
          source={require('./assets/animations/loadingBar.
          json')}
          progress={progress}
        />
      </View>
    </SafeAreaView>
  );
```

6. My animation is rendered on an iOS device but not on an Android device

The newest versions of `lottie-react-native` can only be used on AndroidX projects. This means that if your app hasn't been migrated to AndroidX (`https://developer.android.com/jetpack/androidx`), it won't be able to display any Lottie animations.

In this case, you can try older versions of `lottie-react-native`. For example, try running the following:

```
yarn add lottie-react-native@3.0.2
yarn add lottie-ios@3.0.3
```

Take into account that for these cases, the API might be different or some extra installation steps might be required. Always check the version-specific documentation when using older versions of `lottie-react-native`.

7. My animation is rendered on an Android device but not on an iOS device

`lottie-react-native` requires some extra installation steps for it to work properly:

- Remember to install the `lottie-ios` peer dependency by running `yarn add lottie-ios`.
- Remember to run `pod install` in the `ios` folder from your React Native project.

8. My app won't build on iOS after installing lottie-react-native

The most common building issue for `lottie-react-native` in iOS has to do with the lack of support for React Native projects with Swift libraries. In this case, you need to create a Swift bridging header in order to get your app ready for Swift libraries:

1. Add a new file through the Xcode menu: **File** | **New** | **File**:

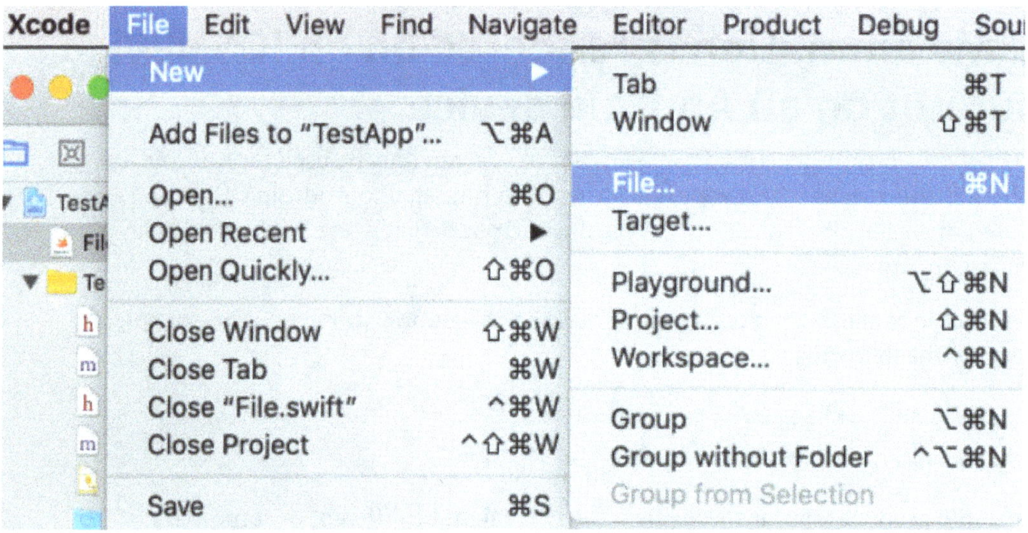

Figure 11.1 – Create a new file in your Xcode project

2. Select **Swift File**:

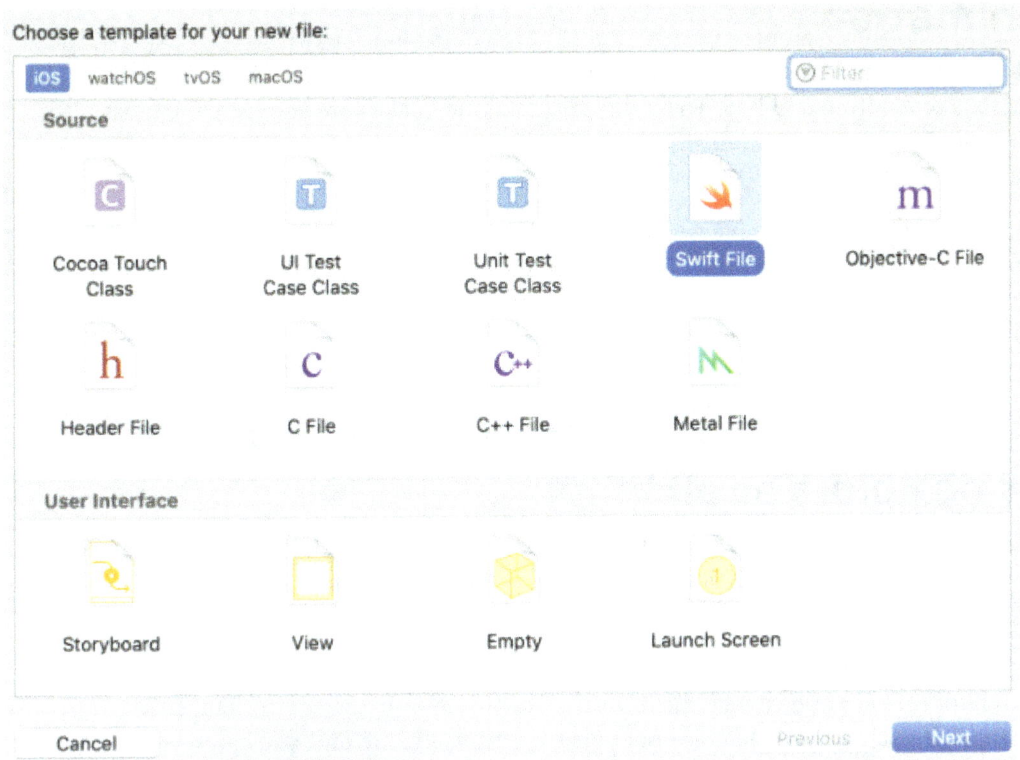

Figure 11.2 – Select Swift as the file type

3. Click on **Create Bridging Header**:

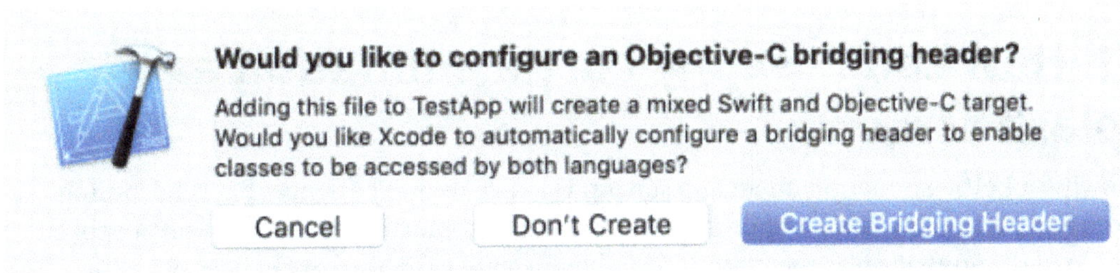

Figure 11.3 – Confirm the creation of the bridging header

You may need to rebuild your project for the changes to take effect. Once this is done, `lottie-react-native` should be ready to display your animation on iOS.

9. Some frames are not showing in my animation

Older versions of Lottie have rendering issues and won't work properly with newer versions of Android and iOS. To fix this kind of issue, make sure you have the most adequate `lottie-react-native` version for the platform version you are running your app in.

You can find a list of available versions for `lottie-react-native` in the `projects` repository (`https://github.com/lottie-react-native/lottie-react-native`) or the npm site (`https://www.npmjs.com/package/lottie-react-native`).

10. My animation is showing the wrong colors or no colors at all

This is often not a problem with `lottie-react-native` but with the way `Bodymovin` exports colors. You may still be able to fix this problem by manually going through your JSON file and manually modifying them.

Layer colors in the JSON file usually are defined by the key named `"sc"`, so you can search for that key and change the hex value for the color you want to change. For example, if you expect a red color but you are getting a white one, you can search for `"sc":"#ffffff"` and replace it with `"sc":"#ff0000"`.

Take into account that there might be more than one layer with that color defined, so you might need to do trial and error until you find the exact layer you need to change.

11. How can I use my Lottie animation as a splash screen?

Showing a Lottie animation on an app startup is a nice user experience that is becoming more and more popular as mobile apps become more sophisticated. A common approach is to load the animation as the main screen, have a state variable that changes once the animation is finished, and change to the real main screen immediately after most of the initial data has been loaded:

```
import React, { useState } from 'react';
const App = () => {
  const [animationFinished, setAnimationFinished] =
```

```
useState(false);
  useEffect(() => {
    loadAppData(); // load initial data
  }, []);

  if (animationFinished === false) {
    return(
      <View style={styles.splash}>
        <LottieView source={require('./assets/animations/
        splashAnimation.json')}
          autoPlay
          loop={false}
          onAnimationFinish={() => {
            setAnimationFinished(true);
          }}
        />
      </View>
    )
  } else {
    return(
      <MainScreen />
    )
  }
};
```

If we want to display a Lottie animation as a splash screen, we need to put this component as the initial one, so the first thing that the app does is to load this animation. Note how we call `loadAppData()` when the component is mounted to start loading the initial data, before the component shows that data to the user.

12. There are images missing in my animation

If you created your animation with external assets (images), you need to add those images into your app and let `lottie-react-native` know where those images can be found. This is done at a native level and requires some configuration, as explained in *Chapter 9, Let's Do Some Magic: Integrating Your First Lottie Animation*, in the section named *Using Lottie files with assets.*

Make sure that you do the following:

- Add those images into the project's folder structure.
- Configure your project in a way that makes those files accessible through code.
- Pass the `imageAssetsFolder` property to the `LottieView` component with the right relative route to the folder containing those assets.

13. How can I center my animation in the app?

`LottieView` component inherits its layout behavior from the standard `View` component in React Native, and therefore, centering should be done in the same way we would center `View` in React Native. This can be done by either using the `alignSelf: 'center'` key on the `style` property for the `LottieView` component or making sure that the parent component has the correct size and uses `alignItems: 'center'` in its `style` property.

If this approach didn't work, we should make sure the parent component has the right size, as most of the alignment problems derive from that issue.

14. How can I play my animation a set number of times?

The easiest approach would be to use the imperative API and adjust the `play()` method and the `onAnimationFinish` prop repeat that plays the animation when its playback is finished:

```
import React, {useState, useRef} from 'react';
const App = ({}) => {
  const animation = useRef(null);
  const [numPlaybacks, setNumPlaybacks] = useState(0);

  return (
    <SafeAreaView>
      <View style={styles.container}>
        <LottieView
          ref={animation}
          source={require('./assets/animations/loadingBar.
          json')}
```

```
            loop={false}
            autoPlay
            onAnimationFinish={() => {
              if (numPlaybacks + 1 < maxNumPlaybacks) {
                animation.current.play();
                setNumPlaybacks(numPlaybacks + 1);
              }
            }}
          />
        </View>
      </SafeAreaView>
    );
  };
```

The key in this piece of code is how `onAnimationFinish` is used to repeat the animation, controlling the number of times through a state variable (`numPlaybacks`) and a constant maximum number of repetitions (`maxNumPlaybacks`).

15. My animation has a low playback performance

As mobile operating systems evolve, they use different graphic rendering techniques. Lottie adapts to those changes by releasing new versions periodically that improve the performance of the animations rendered. It's important to always use the latest version of `lottie-react-native` because it may contain performance improvements based on the latest rendering engines for Android and iOS devices.

React Native also offers an out-of-the-box performance improvement for the animated API by accepting the `useNativeDriver` parameter, which leverages the native capabilities of some UI components. Using this parameter may help when using `Animated` combined with `lottie-react-native`.

If you want to ensure that you are using the latest version of `lottie-react-native`, make sure you check the README documentation in the `lottie-react-native` repository, following its installation guidelines.

16. How can I change the colors of my animation programmatically?

`lottie-react-native` allows developers to use the `colorFilters` property in any `LottieView` component with the intention of changing the colors for specific layers in an animation. The names for those layers are defined in After Effects and stored in the exported JSON Lottie file, such as in the following code block:

```
import React from 'react';
import LottieView from 'lottie-react-native';
import {SafeAreaView, View} from 'react-native';

const App = ({}) => {
  return (
    <SafeAreaView>
      <View style={{width: '100%', height: '100%'}}>
        <LottieView
          source={require('./assets/animations/loadingBar.
          json')}
          autoPlay
          colorFilters={[
            {
              keypath: 'border',
              color: '#FF0000',
            },
            {
              keypath: 'bar',
              color: '#FF0000',
            },
          ]}
        />
      </View>
    </SafeAreaView>
  );
};

export default App;
```

In this example, we are changing the colors for two layers named `border` and `bar` to be fully red.

17. How can I use a remote Lottie animation file in my app?

The simplest approach would be to use `fetch()` to download the JSON file, parse it, and set it in a state variable so that it can be used as a `source` prop in a `LottieView` container:

```
import React, {useState, useEffect} from 'react';
import LottieView from 'lottie-react-native';
import {SafeAreaView, View} from 'react-native';

const App = ({}) => {
  const [animation, setAnimation] = useState();
  useEffect(() => {
    fetch('https://myserver.com/animation.json', {
      method: 'GET',
    })
      .then(response => response.json())
      .then(responseJSON => {
        setAnimation(responseJSON);
      })
      .catch(e => console.error(e));
  }, []);
  return (
    <SafeAreaView>
      <View style={{width: '100%', height: '100%'}}>
        {animation && <LottieView source={animation} autoPlay
        loop />}
      </View>
    </SafeAreaView>
  );
};

export default App;
```

If this approach is followed, it's important to control the `LottieView` component until the animation is fully downloaded (`animation && <LottieView`).

18. My app is crashing on Android

Several users have reported crashes on Android due to errors. The latest versions of React Native have refined this process, and updating these should fix the issue, but if this is not a possibility, you can manually link the required libraries as follows:

1. On your `android/app/src/main/java/<YourAppName>/MainApplication.java`, add `import com.airbnb.android.react.lottie.LottiePackage;` at the top.
2. In the same file, add `packages.add(new LottiePackage());` under `List<ReactPackage> getPackages()`.
3. On your `android/app/build.gradle`, add `implementation project(':lottie-react-native')` inside the dependencies section.
4. On your `android/settings.gradle`, add `include ':lottie-react-native'`.
5. Right after the line you just added, add `project(':lottie-react-native').projectDir = new File(rootProject.projectDir, '../node_modules/lottie-react-native/src/android')`.

Now, you should rebuild your app and find it is not crashing anymore.

19. An error shows on my app – Cycle dependencies between targets

This is a common error among React Native developers when having to deal with native code in iOS. The problem is related to changes in the dependencies tree that ended up rearranging which library depends on another. Therefore, the easiest solution is to reset the dependencies tree in our iOS project, ensuring that we end up with a clean dependency chain.

To achieve this, we can clean our `builds` folder by pressing *Command* + *Shift* + *K* on Xcode and then rebuilding the app, by pressing the **play** button on Xcode or running `yarn ios` on the command line while being in the `project` folder.

20. An error shows on my app – Execution failed for task ':lottie-react-native:compileDebugJavaWithJavac'

This error may arise after updating to a newer version of React Native and running the app on an Android device for the first time. Sometimes, just cleaning the `builds` folder fixes this problem, but there are two other approaches that may fix it if cleaning didn't do the trick:

- Migrate your app to AndroidX by adding `android.useAndroidX=true` and `android.enableJetifier=true` to your `gradle.properties` file and running `npx jetifier` immediately afterward. This prepares your app to include the AndroidX-based libraries.
- Make sure you are using JDK v8 instead of a newer version (Android Studio may install newer versions). You can follow the environment setup instructions on the React Native website (`https://reactnative.dev/docs/environment-setup`) and configure that version of Java as your default one in your shell configuration file.

Summary

Thank you for reading through this final chapter, in which we presented the most common questions and issues reported when working with `lottie-react-native`. There are many other infrequently asked questions that can be found in the `lottie-react-native` repository issues (`https://github.com/lottie-react-native/lottie-react-native/issues`) and on Stack Overflow, so make sure that you turn to those resources if you find yourself in need of more specific answers.

Index

Symbols

A

I

J

K

L

Z

Packt.com

Subscribe to our online digital library for full access to over 7,000 books and videos, as well as industry leading tools to help you plan your personal development and advance your career. For more information, please visit our website.

Why subscribe?

- Spend less time learning and more time coding with practical eBooks and Videos from over 4,000 industry professionals
- Improve your learning with Skill Plans built especially for you
- Get a free eBook or video every month
- Fully searchable for easy access to vital information
- Copy and paste, print, and bookmark content

Did you know that Packt offers eBook versions of every book published, with PDF and ePub files available? You can upgrade to the eBook version at packt.com and as a print book customer, you are entitled to a discount on the eBook copy. Get in touch with us at customercare@packtpub.com for more details.

At www.packt.com, you can also read a collection of free technical articles, sign up for a range of free newsletters, and receive exclusive discounts and offers on Packt books and eBooks.

Other Books You May Enjoy

If you enjoyed this book, you may be interested in these other books by Packt:

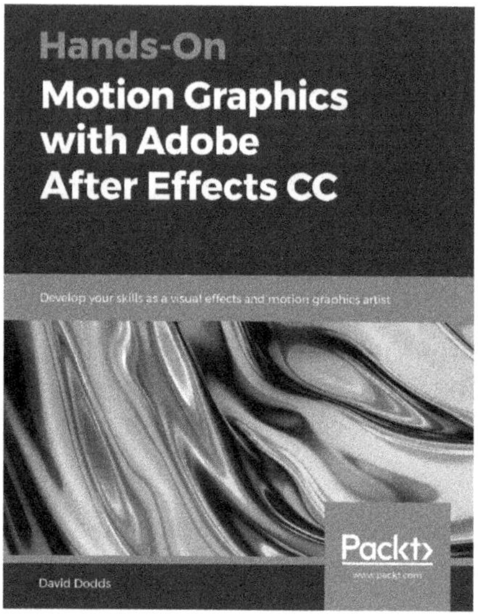

Hands-On Motion Graphics with Adobe After Effects CC

David Dodds

ISBN: 978-1-78934-515-5

- Create a lower third project for a TV show with complex layers
- Work with shape layer animation to create an animated lyrics video
- Explore different tools to animate characters
- Apply text animation to create a dynamic film-opening title
- Use professional visual effects to create a VFX project

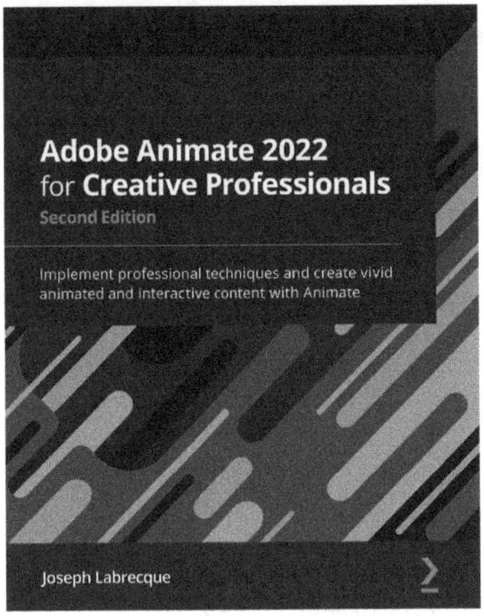

Adobe Animate 2022 for Creative Professionals - Second Edition

Joseph Labrecque

ISBN: 978-1-80323-279-9

- Gain a solid understanding of Adobe Animate foundations and new features
- Understand the nuances associated with publishing and exporting rich media content to various platforms
- Make use of advanced layering and rigging techniques to create engaging motion content
- Create dynamic motion using the camera and variable layer depth techniques
- Develop web-based games, virtual reality experiences, and multiplatform mobile applications

Packt is searching for authors like you

If you're interested in becoming an author for Packt, please visit `authors.packtpub.com` and apply today. We have worked with thousands of developers and tech professionals, just like you, to help them share their insight with the global tech community. You can make a general application, apply for a specific hot topic that we are recruiting an author for, or submit your own idea.

Share Your Thoughts

Now you've finished *UI Animations with Lottie and After Effects*, we'd love to hear your thoughts! Scan the QR code below to go straight to the Amazon review page for this book and share your feedback or leave a review on the site that you purchased it from.

`https://www.amazon.ae/review/create-review/error?asin=1803243805`

Your review is important to us and the tech community and will help us make sure we're delivering excellent quality content.

www.ingramcontent.com/pod-product-compliance
Lightning Source LLC
LaVergne TN
LVHW080526210926
848481LV00022B/3161